By William P. Baldwin, III
Photography By N. Jane Iseley

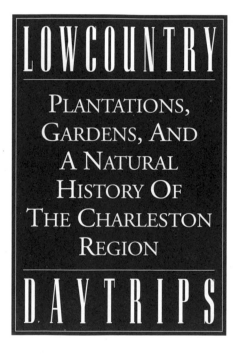

LOWCOUNTRY

Plantations, Gardens, And A Natural History Of The Charleston Region

DAYTRIPS

Legacy Publications
A Subsidiary of Pace Communications, Inc.
Greensboro, North Carolina

TEXT © BY WILLIAM P. BALDWIN, III
PHOTOGRAPHS © 1993
BY N. JANE ISELEY

ISBN 0–933101–07–4

LIBRARY OF CONGRESS
CATALOG CARD NUMBER 93–078032

EDITED BY DEBRA J. BOST

DESIGN: JAIMEY EASLER

MAPS: GREG HAUSLER

ILLUSTRATIONS: NANCY RODDEN

COVER: 1889 U.S. COAST AND
GEODETIC SURVEY MAP COURTESY OF
ANTIQUITIES GALLERY

PRINTED IN THE
UNITED STATES OF AMERICA

*This book is dedicated
to the memory of my father
William P. Baldwin*

ACKNOWLEDGMENTS

I'd like to thank all the friendly people I met along the way.
The staff members of the parks and other sites were always helpful, as were the
chamber of commerce employees I contacted. I tried to visit the library in
each community at least once, and now, more than ever, I'm certain that
librarians are the glue holding Western civilization together: a special thanks
to them. And a special thanks to the following: Clarice and Lang Foster, Bob
Barker, Janson Cox, Julie Finlayson, Genevieve Peterkin, Gurdon Tarbox,
Robin Salmon, Aurora Olivieri, George Rogers, Ben and Betsy Caldwell,
Anne Bridges, Pat Young, Dianne Belle, Cathy Townsend, Oliver Buckles,
Richard Fairey, Mary Belle, Brother Stephen, Bob Mitchell, Irvine Rutledge,
George Garris, Joe Anderson, Will Alston, Tommy Strange, Glen Stapleton,
Erin Bronk, James and Helen Maynard, Vanessa Thaxton, Rena Riddle,
Cindy Cole, Betty Cotton, Lucy Hall, June Berry, Bob Cuttino, my father's
friends at Four Hole Swamp, Bill Obrst, Peggy Harleston, Steve Hoffius,
Harlan Greene, Mary Giles, Margaretta Childs, Mark Wetherington and
everyone connected with SCHS, Mike McLaughlin, Agnes Baldwin (my
mom), David Blair, Jay Shuler, and D. J. Bost, my editor.
−William P. Baldwin, III

I'd like to thank the special people who helped with the fact-checking and who
graciously gave their time to help drive tours and check mileage, and to the
good friends who offered their support: Horry and Dorothy Kerrison,
Bob and Mary Dean Richards, Richard Coen, Elinor Euliss, Virginia Griggs,
Cornelia Barnwell, and Beau Iseley. Thanks especially to the following
people at Pace Communications, Inc.: Sarah Lindsay, Carol Medford,
Greg Hausler, Sheryl Miller, Jaimey Easler, Patricia McConnell,
Robert Hudson, and Bonnie McElveen-Hunter.   *−N. Jane Iseley*

CONTENTS

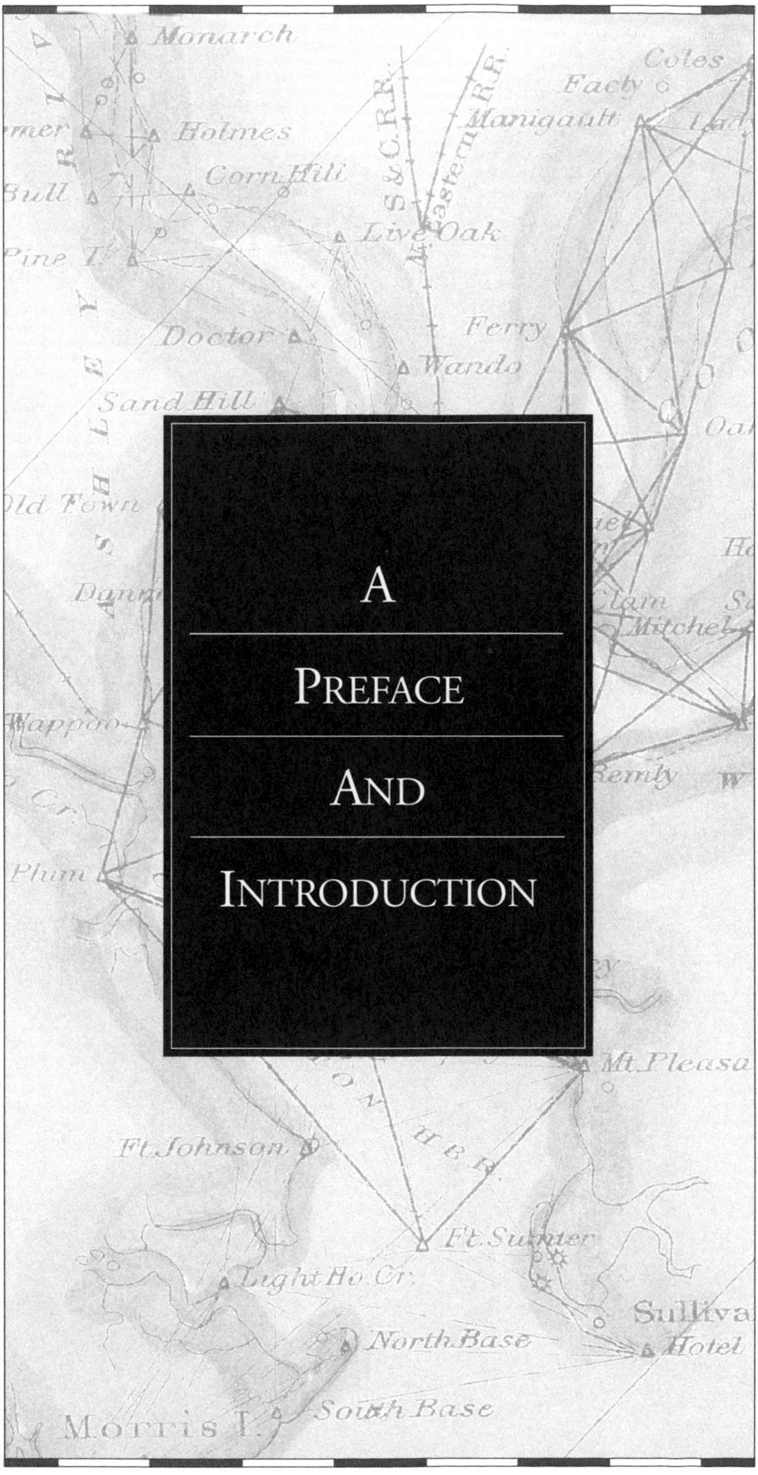

A Preface and Introduction

N

LOW-
COUNTRY
DAY
TRIPS

MYRTLE
BEACH

MURRELLS
INLET

PAWLEYS
ISLAND

GEORGETOWN

Santee Delta

McCLELLANVILLE

*Lake
Moultrie*

Bulls Bay

SUMMERVILLE

MT.
PLEASANT

CHARLESTON

WALTERBORO

JACKSONBORO

EDISTO ISLAND

St. Helena Sound

BEAUFORT

Port Royal Sound

*Atlantic
Ocean*

HILTON HEAD
ISLAND

SAVANNAH

PREFACE: From Murrells Inlet south to the Savannah River and inland forty miles, the Lowcountry is, in the words of historian W. J. Cash, "unique." He felt that there had been no time between the invention of Eli Whitney's cotton gin and the Civil War for a true aristocracy to form in most of the South. But the Lowcountry was an exception—one of the few places that had been settled early enough to have "something that could be called effective settlement and societal organization." Here, there was a true gentry of indigo and rice planters with wealth, leisure, and learning, educated abroad or well tutored at home. Their sons were our statesmen; their daughters danced at grand balls, and even married European royalty. Yet the plantation system rested on a "mud sill" of forced labor, and the very ground they farmed bred malaria.

Even before the Civil War, the bloom had faded. The white population was often outnumbered ten to one by its enslaved servants. Political power shifted away from the Lowcountry, and its residents demanded more loudly than ever to be separated from the Union. Romance, violence, death—the Civil War started here, and the aftermath of glory was not sweet. People were too poor to build new houses or even pay the taxes on the ones they owned. Rice, phosphate, cotton, half-wild cows and hogs—eventually they all played out and, in the end, there was only the wilderness. Nothing changed and, suddenly, that has become an asset: The old buildings are "authentic"; the wilderness is "wilderness." The Lowcountry has been discovered.

Some are alarmed by this sudden invasion of outsiders and wonder if the isolated and fragile culture can survive. I expect it can, for certain traditions of attitude and place and cultural and personal eccentricities are too firmly planted in this rich soil to be uprooted easily. So, if you're a newcomer, welcome to the Lowcountry; and if you're an old-timer, welcome anyway.

I was born here and have spent most of the last forty-eight years in the vicinity. Roots—I've got them. On my mother's side, one ancestor arrived from Barbados in 1670. He was a planter and deputy governor. His daughter had four husbands, and we're descended from the third. In 1694, another ancestor, a young Dutch soldier, indentured himself long enough to pay for his voyage; he became a carpenter. Others followed from France, England, Ireland, and Scotland. Among my ancestors there were at least one Indian trader, two lawyers, two doctors, two surveyors, one silversmith, one magistrate, three schoolteachers, two storekeepers, one boat captain, one minister, and one sheriff. They fought Indians and owned slaves. At least six had plantations, and yet, with the exception of the first, the deputy governor, there were none that you could  point to and call aristocrats—no true gentry. They were planters; they farmed the land and lost it. Their wives raised families and went to church. "Pioneer stock," historian Cash would have called them: "The dominant trait of this mind was an intense individualism. Everywhere and invariably, his fundamental attitude is purely personal and purely self-asserting." For better or worse, I suspect such traits are inherited and occasionally have found their way into this guide.

These are called "day trips," but it usually took me longer to make them, and I'd already seen most of the sights at least once or twice. But I tracked mileage, gathered information, and spoke with guides and naturalists. My father, William Sr., went with me about a third of the time. He came south in 1938 as a federal wildlife biologist and has worked here since as forester, land management consultant, and plantation broker. He was the naturalist on the trips we made together, and a source of much curious Lowcountry lore. My wife, Lillian, accompanied me on about a third of the trips as well. She, too, has lived her life here, and since she worked with Jane Iseley on *Plantations of the Low Country*, she could often remember the roads, places, and people better than I. Occasionally, my sister Becky would come along. She was good company and fearless on the nature trails.

To the three of them, my heartfelt thanks. When I went alone, I usually tried to pick up a local guide. Many are mentioned by name in the text, but to them, again, thank you very much.

A Note About Hurricane Hugo

On the night of September 21, 1989, Hurricane Hugo made landfall on the South Carolina coast. The eye crossed over Charleston, which meant the worst of the storm struck in the Bulls Bay area thirty miles north of the city. Here the winds were estimated at 140 miles per hour, and the water of the "hurricane surge" rose twenty feet above sea level. Elsewhere, the rage of the wind and sea did not quite reach these proportions, but nowhere in the Lowcountry, from the Ashley River up to Murrells Inlet, escaped.

Perhaps, for the purposes of this book, the less said about Hurricane Hugo, the better. All over the Lowcountry, individuals in both the private and the public sectors have worked hard to soften the scars left behind by the great storm. They have succeeded amazingly well, and in most cases the visitor taking these tours will have a hard time spotting the repaired damage. There are some exceptions, but they're noted in the text and are dramatic enough to be interesting.

There's been debate about whether this was the storm of the century, the storm of two centuries, or the worst storm ever to hit our coast. These are academic questions. Hopefully, it is the worst that any of us will have to go through. Twenty-nine people died. It's a miracle that thousands of others didn't. Property damage was extensive—record breaking, in fact. Hugo, because it was so large and held together for so long, left a path of destruction not only through the Lowcountry, but through half of South Carolina and across North Carolina and Virginia as well. At the time, it was the costliest storm in United States history.

In years past, when the reckoning of time was not the exact science it is today, the citizens in our part of the world measured time by such catastrophic events. The Civil War, the Great Earthquake of 1886, the Hurricane of 1893—all were landmarks on the calendar, for they dramatically interrupted the linear flow of everyday events. For better or worse, what we were before Hugo is not what we are today. Keep that in mind when you take the tours of the Ashley River and all those to the north of Charleston. But don't let it spoil the fun. It's all part of nature's way, and nature heals her own. And man, being nature's child, repairs his own, as well.

How to Use This Book

This book deals with the coastal section of South Carolina from Murrells Inlet south to the Savannah River and inland from the coast about forty miles. You can drive its length in five hours and its width in less than one. We chose Charleston as a central point because, geographically and historically, it is the center of the area. You don't have to use Charleston as the starting point, though, for the maps and directions can be followed beginning anywhere within these bounds. There are eleven trips altogether and they offer a wide variety of stops—plantations, towns, museums, nature walks, churches, boat rides, fish hatcheries, forts, beaches, houses, parks, and much, much more.

THE INTRODUCTION is a short essay on the entire Lowcountry region and discusses its geography, history, architecture, and natural history.

A BRIEF GENERAL DESCRIPTION begins each of the eleven day trips, listing what can be visited in that particular area. I've done my best to include as entries practically anything and everything to which the public has at least limited access. And here, you'll see listed the days and hours of operation, whether there is an admission charge, and phone numbers for information and reservations. This information was accurate at publication; we hope it won't have changed too much. There are so many entries, you should be able to make a day's trip out of only a portion of what's offered.

DRIVING INSTRUCTIONS from Charleston begin each tour, and between each entry, further directions are given. MAPS are provided not only for the highways you'll be traveling, but for some of the towns, villages, and nature walks as well.

The text for the *Day Trips* is a collection of entries about each site or point of interest. In each, we've tried to give a brief history, a physical description, and the entertainments offered—in short, what there is to see and do. Along the way, there's also an occasional comment on a particular spot or historical markers passed. Don't feel compelled to stop, though, especially if the battle was 200 years ago and it's a soybean field today.

If you are starting your trips from Charleston and want to return each evening, then it's suggested that you stick with the sites that interest you the most in each trip. Otherwise, if you try to see them all, your return may be very late, indeed! That's just a suggestion, though.

The idea for *Day Trips from Charleston* wasn't original. We borrowed it from Dr. William Johnson, an intrepid Charleston doctor who, in the late 1920s, would set out on the weekends and journey into the countryside for as long as possible and record what he saw. His day started before dawn and would sometimes end at 2 a.m. You may want to follow Johnson's example, but it would probably be more enjoyable just to ramble along at your own pace and take what comes.

A Few Last Reminders

1. Unless it's the dead of winter, CARRY INSECT REPELLANT ON ALL TRIPS.

2. Wherever you are, FOLLOW THE SAFETY INSTRUCTIONS. On the nature trails,

KEEP AN EYE OUT FOR POISONOUS SNAKES AND DEER HUNTERS, and DON'T FEED THE ALLIGATORS.

3. Remember that IN AND AROUND CHURCHES AND IN BURIAL GROUNDS, YOU ARE A FAVORED GUEST, not a wandering tourist.

A Last, Last Reminder

This is not a genealogy, history, architecture, zoology, or botany textbook. When a man's life, a battle, a three-story building, or a forest is reduced to one sentence, there's a good chance something will get left out. The mistakes are honest ones. The facts—well, there's a remote possibility that there really isn't a four-hundred-year-old French dwarf ghost living in the basement of that castle. And we'll never know for sure if Drunken Jack was, in fact, a "yard axe" preacher trying to slip away from his congregation for a weekend binge. Better to include a little bit of everything, though; better safe than sorry.

When to Use This Book

Deciding which way to go is easy; deciding when to go is a little trickier. It depends on how much you enjoy the company of other people. It's not likely you'll be waiting in line, but the gardens and towns like Summerville and Beaufort are particularly beautiful in the spring when the azaleas, dogwood, and wisteria are in bloom. They're also the busiest then. If you want a more solitary visit, content yourself with the architecture and off-season plantings. Autumn foliage can be just as nice—golds, browns, and purples; even the salt marsh changes.

The beaches and towns of Georgetown and Beaufort that depend on an influx of summer visitors are most crowded then, but that is also the time when the majority of the individual tours are available and the park staff is full time.

The same is true for weekends and holidays. These are usually the most crowded times, and you'll find a few places like the maritime culture centers closed.

Spring and autumn are usually the recommended seasons for the nature trails, but the middle of winter might be best for seeing ducks or combing the beach for fossils. Watch out for the mosquitoes and deerflies during the summer. Even with insect repellent they can be unbearable.

These are decisions you'll have to make, but there should be plenty to keep you busy, no matter what time of year, week, or day you travel.

INTRODUCTION: The Lowcountry is low. In fact, in many places, it barely rises above sea level. Protective barrier islands line this two-hundred-mile section of the South Carolina coast, and great expanses of salt marsh usually  lie between the islands and the mainland. Here, bays and tidal creeks meander about, then eventually join up with an equally bewildering alignment of freshwater rivers and streams flowing out of the upcountry.

In terms of geological time it is a new country, one only recently surrendered by an ocean that covered this area half a million years ago. Along the coast and well inland, ancient sand dunes form slightly higher sand ridges and hills. Our highways often follow their crests; the towns and villages we pass through are invariably built upon them. They, too, are islands in a sense, for vast swamplands surround them on all sides.

The European settlers were amazingly quick to understand the potential of this landscape and alter it to suit their needs. They cut, burned, diked, plowed, and built, turning whatever lay in their path into a moneymaking enterprise. In the beginning, it was wilderness, and much of it is wilderness once more. The imprint made on it is there, though faint in places, but still visible; and, of course, there are the buildings—of plantations and towns.

The Walled City

In the spring of 1670, the English settled on the west bank of the Ashley River. Their palisade and collection of cabins was called Charles Town in honor of their king, Charles II. Charles had given the great province of Carolina to the eight "Lords Proprietor" because they had helped him regain the throne. And it was the Proprietors who were financing the settling of what would become known as the Lowcountry. Ten years later, the settlers moved across the river to the present site of Charleston and built a walled city—a fortress to keep out Indians, Spanish, French, pirates, and, occasionally, each other. Gradually the city spilled beyond these confines into suburbs that at first went for blocks and now stretch for miles. From the first days of settlement, however, the adventurous and ambitious were pushing much farther into the unknown. They traveled first by river and Indian trail, then by road and even railroad, but all these routes eventually returned to Charleston.

The city's relationship with the surrounding Lowcountry would be symbiotic, a partnership, for it was from the harbor around the urban peninsula that the produce of the countryside was shipped to distant markets. In 1728, the Proprietors were ousted and, in 1782, so was the king. Much political power shifted inland then, but the city was hardly without influence. It remained the arbitrator of all matters of taste and refinement. After all, the fashions and concerns of Europe were only a ship's voyage away, and Charleston was one of the wealthiest cities in North America—its wealth earned in the indigo plots and cotton and rice fields of the surrounding plantations. Great pains were taken to make sure this produce continued to come through Charleston, often at the expense of Georgetown and Beaufort, and even the distant Savannah. The plan failed, of course; other harbors were deeper, or at least more convenient. Cotton was being planted far inland, to the Mississippi and beyond, but on the eve of the Civil War, the city was still prosperous and so was the countryside surrounding it. In five short years, both would lie in ruin. Now, a century later, both are rebounding—rebounding because they have remained unchanged for so long.

Islands

There are two kinds of barrier islands. Those to the north of Charleston are called "beach-ridge"; they are formed by the action of the ocean currents and winds. Winter storms wash them down, gentler summer waves build them up. Because of the predominant inshore flow, they erode on the northern end and build on the south (until jetties interfere). Narrow and low, they are often little more than deposits of sand held in place with the help of stubborn vegetation. (Look closely and you can usually see fine sand piled around the base of these plants, one of the stages of dune formation.)

The islands to the south of Charleston are called "erosion remnant" because they are sections of the mainland that have been cut off. The soil here is richer, but these, too, are usually fronted by the same beach-ridge formation and the plants and animals to be found there are the same. It's a young country, and one that is rapidly disappearing. Twelve thousand years ago, the ocean began to rise again, and the shoreline has moved several miles west since then. You may see shrimp trawlers working where there was dry land only a century ago.

Along the wide, gently sloping beaches you'll find a great variety of shells, flotsam, and even fossils of extinct animals and shards of pottery made by vanished Indians. Higher up, the beaches blend into the dunes where familiar sea oats grow, now protected by state law. Just beyond these, wax myrtles and the red-berried cassina begin. "Salt tolerance" is the key to understanding this maritime forest. Palmettos come next, along with cedars and live oaks draped with Spanish moss. Just inland are magnolias fighting for sunlight beneath giant loblolly pines. Deer browse on smilax here, raccoons ramble down sandy paths, and alligators rest on the banks of brackish ponds, but none of these are on constant display for visitors. The birds are more obliging; migratory and permanent, they are abundant. Especially during the winter and spring "off-season," the Sea Islands are a bird watcher's mecca.

Much of the vegetation characteristic of the area can grow and even thrive on the very edge of the ocean and creeks. But only one plant, Spartina, or marsh grass, can actually grow in the salt water, for its hollow stalk and ribbonlike leaves are a miniature desalinization processor. Only recently appreciated, the continual growth and decay of the marsh grass in conjunction with the tidal flow creates a priceless nursery ground for much seagoing life. More obvious to us are the oyster beds crowding the banks. Here fiddler crabs scurry, while in the creek itself mullet leap clear of the water as rolling porpoises pursue them. And there are more birds, of course—oyster catchers, skimmers, egrets, herons, terns, and pelicans—exotic to the visitor, a pleasure for all.

On the mainland the forest is at first much like that of the islands, but as we move up onto higher ground, the pines begin to dominate. Beneath them an occasional white splash of springtime dogwood shows. Squirrels chatter, birds call. The wildlife is as abundant, but even more elusive. Pockets of hickory and oak intrude. Then the ground drops away to swamps and river bottoms. Massive stands of cypress and tupelo gum once dominated here, and still do in a couple of the places we are fortunate enough to visit. Once more, alligators drift by, nostrils and eyes barely above water. Wood ducks whistle by overhead. The strange "knees" of the cypress rise from the coffee-brown water, and a wealth of natural wonder awaits the attentive viewer. This was the land before the white man came.

Aboriginal People

Ten thousand years ago, roving bands of hunters passed this way, but other than an occasional finely worked spearpoint, we have no evidence of their presence. About 2000 B.C., however, a revolution of sorts took place along these shores. The first pottery in North America suddenly appeared and, in association with strange ring-shaped deposits of oyster shells, suggests that the Indian population had taken the first step toward a semistationary, village-oriented lifestyle. A rudimentary agriculture would follow that made possible the great Mississippian culture.

By the time English settlers reached these shores, though, that culture had long since waned, and living here they found about a dozen small independent tribes. These aboriginal people generally summered in villages close to the salt marsh and rivers. They gathered shellfish and tended gardens of corn, squash, and beans. They hunted deer, gathered acorns and hickory nuts, and took from the forest practically anything that was edible. During the winter they abandoned the coast and, breaking up into family groups, moved well inland. They lived in balance with nature, but it was a precarious balance, especially when faced with the white man's weapons and the far more deadly smallpox that the Europeans brought. Within a generation of contact, these tribes had been decimated, and within a century, they had virtually disappeared from the Lowcountry landscape. Their campsites remain, however. The middens of shell, with broken pottery and other kitchen scraps, are still sheltered by the same oaks and hickories.

Plantations

The first settlers depended on the Indians for food and protection, and almost immediately they looked to them for commercial gain as well. Deerskins bought by often ruthless Indian traders were a major export of the colony; then, even the Indians themselves were sold. Hogs and cattle were let loose to roam freely. The forest was cut and tapped for "ship stores." Surveyors went to work setting out property boundaries, and a great variety of agricultural experiments began.

For the newcomers, land was wealth and the key to social order. That principle was written into the colony's charter. The eight Lords Proprietor intended to divide Carolina into vast 12,000-acre baronies that would be  sold or given to noble landgraves and cassiques, the colonial equivalents of earls and lords. The less fortunate would receive far less property. The plan failed, for though birth and breeding still mattered, the rigors of settlement seldom suited the lifestyle of a true country gentleman. Within a short time, though, an aristocracy of survivors had established itself, and property was still the basis of wealth and power. The land had become plantations and the settlers were now planters.

The concept of the plantation was hardly unique to the Lowcountry. On Barbadian estates, slaves were growing sugar cane, and in Virginia, tobacco. All Carolina needed was a crop. Olives, grapes, and silk were among the experimental crops, but rice proved to be the answer. Beginning in the early 1700s, inland swamps were cleared and diked—reservoirs provided the water for cultivation. Then, after the American Revolution, the rivers themselves, or at least the surrounding forest and marshes, came under cultivation—the ocean tide pushed fresh water into the fields through special water-control devices, or "trunks." We'll see remnants of the early fields and trunks as well.

In about 1745, indigo was introduced as an upland crop. Several planters were experimenting, but credit for the discovery usually goes to a sixteen-year-old Barbadian girl, Eliza Lucas. Indigo produced a dye so valuable that the English offered a bounty to keep it out of the hands of the French, but that incentive ended with the Revolution. We'll visit a vat where the dye was made.

Following the Revolution, Whitney's invention of a better cotton gin brought sudden prosperity to the inland planters, who had the land to grow short-staple cotton. At the same time, Sea Island cotton was being introduced along the coast. With a longer and finer fiber, this long-staple cotton was considerably more valuable. There was less land on which to grow it, but enough so that both cottons could make millionaires of still more Lowcountry planters. Even after the Civil War, its cultivation would continue until the boll weevils' final assault during the first part of this century. Some of the land once used to grow cotton is still planted in vegetables, but most is overgrown. If we look carefully, though, we can sometimes spot the rows in the floor of a forest.

The planters prospered. At least most did, and for the luckiest there were the finest wines, thoroughbred horses, and handsome furniture in handsome homes. The sons had the best educations that money could buy, and the daughters, the finest prospects of a good marriage. Coachmen drove liveried carriages. The libraries were grand; the conversation, sparkling. In these homes, an 1804 visitor wrote, "you meet the polish of society, and every charm of social life; an abundance of food, convenience, and luxury."

These plantations, at least the larger ones, were little worlds unto them-selves. There was a mansion for the owner, often some flanker buildings, and always a kitchen at some distance from the house. Close by were a smokehouse and creamery or icehouse, and somewhere, a privy. The over-seer had a house of his own, and the slaves, a "street" of small single- or dou-ble-room cabins. In addition, there were sometimes an infirmary and praise house for the workers, workshops for carpenters and blacksmiths, stables and pasture for livestock, a rice mill or cotton gin, a winnowing house, great storage barns, and a river dock or landing. Beyond that, there were fields. Today, no plantation exists completely intact, but we get some idea at Boone Hall and an even more complete picture at Middleton Place. Bear in mind that even in the world of planters there were greatly varying degrees of success. Some did quite well on what could more honestly be called farms, rather than plantations.

Gardens

Often, as much care went into the grounds surrounding a plantation man-sion as into the house itself. The live oak avenues are familiar—they are old, but seem older. The saying goes, "An oak grows for a hundred years, lives for a hundred, and dies for a hundred." The avenue was fashionable in England and easy to come by here. Often overlooked, however, are the cedars and magnolias that were equally popular. The gardens themselves were begun along Old World lines—formal, geometric, and trimmed—but by the 1840s, camellias and azaleas were becoming common, and a more romantic approach to plants and their arrangement began. (This was also a time of revival, and many of the oak avenues date from this fairly late date.) At Magnolia and Middleton, we'll see excellent examples of both kinds of gardens; in many other places, too, fine gardens were and still are kept.

Gullah

From its very beginning, Carolina (the Lowcountry in particular) was not viewed with kind eyes—most especially when slavery was the issue. Early Quakers were offended by it and finally settled elsewhere. Bishop Asbury, "the father of American Methodism," traveled here often after the Revolution and wrote, "How much worse are the rice plantations! If a man-of-war is a 'floating hell,' these are standing ones." Similar accusations would be made by early Baptists as well, and then loudly voiced by Northern aboli-tionists until war ended the institution.

If the plantations did succeed in becoming romantic little worlds unto themselves, theirs was not a romance or ease shared by all. They were popu-lated overwhelmingly by slaves—slaves who, to many masters' amazement, were not content with their station in life. The Reconstruction period fol-lowing the Civil War was one of chaos. Blacks, in most cases, would eventu-ally move away or isolate themselves by choice or command in their own communities—communities that kept alive a rich African-American-Creole culture well into this century.

The Gullah language (perhaps a local pronunciation of the word

"Angola") is still spoken by the oldest generation, and religious and secular music draws heavily on these roots. Times change, though. In recent years, small cabins with doors and window frames painted blue to keep out the "haints" have been replaced with trailers and brick veneer homes. Marsh tacky ponies and mules have long since given way to car payments. The black population, however, still takes pride in its unique heritage. We'll see basket makers selling their wares at the roadside and, if we're lucky, hear an occasional lapse back into the old music and speech.

The Malarial Coast

Slavery wasn't the only dark cloud over the Lowcountry. Malaria, then called "country fever," was certainly another. "Miasma," or night vapor, was thought to be its first cause—it was quickly associated with the swamps and, hence, with rotting vegetation. Today we know that the female Anopheles mosquito transmits the disease. During the first phase of its life, the malaria parasite develops in the stomach wall of the mosquito. Later in its life cycle, the parasite releases a threadlike spore that the mosquito transfers to a warm-blooded host—in this case human. Once in the host's bloodstream, the spore enters a blood cell where it grows, eventually causing the cell to rupture, leaving the spore to attack another cell. Another mosquito bites the host, extracting the parasite, and the cycle continues.

What this meant for the human carrier was a succession of chills and high fever, bouts of which could recur about every three days. At their very worst, they could be accompanied by delirium, coma, and sometimes death. A strong adult might escape and even build up an immunity, but for the very young and old, it was easily fatal. It was also a leading cause of aborted pregnancies. Many planters took their families and moved inland or even left the state. Those who remained here did so at considerable risk.

Summer Retreats

From its earliest days, the Lowcountry had earned a well-deserved reputation as a dangerous place to live. Yellow fever, also transmitted by mosquitoes, was even more deadly than malaria, but more urban. From 1700 on, warnings were sent out to prospective colonists that many settlers did not survive the first year's "seasoning." The problem reached epidemic proportions following the Revolution, however, when a particularly virulent form of the disease swept through the countryside, killing literally thousands. At that point, the planters began to abandon their plantations between May and November, and to abandon many of their earliest towns and villages altogether. New villages were formed, often only a few miles away. Inland, they were called pineland retreats; it was thought that the pines growing on the high sand ridges prevented the disease. Along the seashore, the credit went to the sea breeze.

Despite the grim purpose that brought these people together, the life of the summer villages was usually remembered as the happiest of times, for it gave the solitary planters a community life. Dances, picnics, and horse racing were favorite pastimes—and, of course, visiting. Following the Civil

War, these communities became year-round refuges for an entire displaced agrarian population. The passage of a railroad or, later, a new highway, might bend their boundaries, but many are surprisingly intact. You'll notice that, though malaria has long since been eradicated, the distribution of today's population is still dictated to an amazing degree by the flight range of the female Anopheles mosquito.

The two early towns of Beaufort and Georgetown remained safe enough from the fever to be continually occupied. Many other centers of commerce had been started, but the competition from Charleston was keen, and the self-sufficient plantations had little use for village-based artisans or merchants. The coming of the malaria epidemics meant their end. In these two towns, however, and in the little pineland and seashore retreats that still exist, we'll catch a glimpse of a quieter, gentler way of life and see some interesting architecture as well.

Architecture—Country and Home

About one hundred antebellum plantation houses still stand in the Lowcountry, and most can be visited at least once a year on tours sponsored by churches or historical societies. However, only seven are open to the public year-round, and five of these happen to be Georgian. There were three King Georges, and so practically all eighteenth-century architecture is Georgian. This architecture stressed symmetry: A typical dwelling was two-story with a low-pitch roof and a small central portico entry. That style would change here, for verandas were added quickly and the original portico, if small enough, was hidden away beneath later alterations. These aren't the traditional white-columned mansions most expect. Only Hampton Plantation fits that description, and may have the earliest such grand portico in the South.

Styles changed slowly here, and Georgian was never completely abandoned, especially its floor plans. In the earliest homes, there were central public rooms with drawing rooms to the side, as in Drayton Hall, but later Georgian houses were traditionally four rooms over four with a central-hall wall dividing each floor, an arrangement popular up to the Civil War and afterward.

Next in America came the Federalist period—the thirty years following the Revolution when the influence of England's Adam brothers was felt. The Georgian facade might remain, but now with delicate moldings inside and out; curved Palladian windows were seen, and trim double porticoes. We'll see these in Georgetown and Beaufort.

Then came the period of Classical Revival: Great Greek columns found their way onto the fronts of many buildings, and we'll see some beautiful ones in Beaufort. Charleston-born Robert Mills, famous as "America's first native-born architect" and the designer of the Washington Monument, built public buildings in this style, such as the Georgetown Court House and at least the portico of Walterboro's.

Following the Greek influence, but hardly replacing it, were the truly

Romantic revivals—a look back at past fashions and a rather loose interpretation of what was seen. Italianate-style homes, inspired by the villas of Italy, have survived in Beaufort. Gothic was the return to medieval England, and  such "cottages" are identified by heavily trimmed gables of steep roofs and arched windows. Of these, only Rose Hill survives, but we'll see plenty of the Episcopal churches built in this style. A couple of parapeted Gothic "castles" are around as well.

Victorian is the last style we'll look at. An extension of the three revivals that preceded, especially Gothic, the mood here was definitely away from the early balance and conventionality of Georgian architecture. The buildings are asymmetrical, with gingerbread trim and turrets and towers. The Victorian period lasted from 1860 to about 1900, and we'll see it best represented in Summerville, but also on Sullivan's Island and, to a much lesser extent, in many other communities.

Churches

When eighty-year-old Governor Sayles stepped ashore here in 1670, he had left Bermuda behind for good—a small, crowded island of dwindling resources racked by religious factionalism. The same description could have been used for England, the origin of most of his settlers. The same for Barbados, too, but those settlers were all Anglican and learned the factionalism when they arrived. Sayles saw this wilderness as a place to settle "millions" of Presbyterians. After the revocation in 1685 of the Edict of Nantes, which had guaranteed the Huguenots the right to private worship, French Protestants lost religious freedom, their rights to private property, their protection under the laws, and sometimes even their lives. And so, they came. Sometime around 1690, William Screven led a party of Baptists down from Kittery, Maine, and his Charleston-based church established at least five rural churches. Reverend Archibald Strobo, returning from the failed Scotch colony near Panama, was "ship wrecked on these shores," and he established five rural Presbyterian churches in the early 1700s. In 1706, however, the French Huguenots allied with the Barbadian Anglicans. The resulting "Church Act" established the Church of England as the official state church and divided the colony into ten parishes.

Others were free to continue to worship as they wished, but the Anglicans would have their churches built at the colony's expense and many of these sturdy little brick buildings still can be visited today. The Presbyterians contented themselves with simple frame meeting houses, most lost by now. Because of their opposition to slavery, the Baptists almost disappeared during the eighteenth century and then revived in the nineteenth century. This also was the time of the Methodist Revival. Their Bishop Asbury entered the state following the Revolution, mocked the Presbyterians and Anglicans for fighting over who had the highest church steeple in Charleston, and rode out into the countryside to save souls. Other "circuit riders" followed: Wherever eight or ten would listen, the preacher erected a "brush arbor," which would be replaced with a pole cabin, and eventually with a meeting house; the Baptists did much the same. By the 1830s, the rural meeting houses of Presbyterians, Baptists, and Methodists were taking on a few of the trimmings of Greek Revival monuments. The early Anglican churches, renamed Episcopalian, were sometimes abandoned, often to be replaced by more conveniently located Gothic buildings. For the most part, all churches remained fairly small and simple. The thrust of the Protestant movement had been to return God's word, the Bible, to the people. And these small buildings, often equipped with high pulpit and sounding board, suited that purpose well. The bell towers and spires, you'll notice, often came as much later additions and sometimes not at all.

Quakers had given up on the Lowcountry early, and several other denominations had been unable to get started in the countryside. The Catholics persisted, though, and so did the Jews, and we'll visit a monastery of the first and a cemetery of the latter. All these places of God are there for us reverently to see and appreciate.

Battle Lines

In a sense, for much of the time, the Lowcountry was a large and ever-shifting battlefield. The early Charlestonians did well to wall their city, for the grounds beyond were uncertainly held. The Spanish in Florida were a continuing threat and were always allied with the Indians and sometimes, the French. The Yemassee Indians, whom the English had won away from the Spanish to start with, attacked the colony in 1715, and if the Cherokee had joined in, they might well have annihilated it. The Cherokee waited instead until the late 1750s to make one last passing raid through this area.

Along the coast, pirates and privateers careened their ships on the beaches, took on fresh water, and hunted wild cattle. To the planters inside Charles Town and out they traded their ill-gotten goods. They did so until Blackbeard blockaded the harbor and it was decided that things had gotten out of hand. The pirates were successfully discouraged, but Charlestonians didn't get around to building real coastal defenses until the British attacked in 1775; we'll visit Fort Moultrie.

In 1780, Charles Town was flanked from the south and fell. From then on it was British troops and Loyalists in the countryside pitted against guerrilla leaders like General Francis Marion. If it appears that Marion fought at every bridge and crossroads, it's because he did. These were usually not grand battles, just skirmishes, but they were the only American victories at the time. Cornwallis surrendered Yorktown in 1782, but the fighting here would continue for another year. More coastal defenses came with the War of 1812.

It was the Civil War, however, that was to have the greatest impact. Though the majority of heavy fighting in the area took place around Charleston Harbor, Beaufort and the Sea Islands to the south fell the first year. And all along the coast there was continuing contact with Union army and naval forces. General William T. Sherman entered the state at the war's end and, with associated forces, burned a large path across the southern corner of our area. In isolated spots throughout, there was wholesale destruction.

With the exception of Virginia, no other state has taken such a continuous pounding, so don't be surprised by the numerous references to battles won and lost, or to the many ancient forts and battle-scarred ruins that dot the countryside.

Internal Improvements

The independent nature of the planters did not lend itself to cooperative efforts, at least not constructive ones. Rivers were the earliest roads for the colonists, who traveled them by canoe, then by flats and rice schooners, and finally by steamboats. The latter, along with gasoline-powered freight boats, supplied many of these rural communities into the mid-1930s. Public commissions depended on private cooperation. Roads were usually Indian paths that had followed the high ridges of the land, but along the coast it was necessary to supplement these with additional highways, bridges, ferries, and causeways. These and short "cuts" between convenient streams were usually a combination of both public and private effort and were poorly maintained.

In 1800, a private canal company managed to connect the Santee and Cooper rivers and thus gave Charleston a direct link with the inland producers. In 1818, a state commission was established that initiated the digging of new waterways and the building of a toll road to Columbia; all soon fell into disrepair. In 1832, the first real railroad in the United States was built to connect Charleston with the Georgia frontier. Then, Columbia, Camden, and eventually Savannah and Charlotte lines were added. In the years following the Civil War, "railroad mania" swept through and completely joined at least the inland portions of the Lowcountry.

Roads came last. If anything, they deteriorated badly after the Civil War. (It has been successfully argued that the South reverted to "a frontier state" during that time.) And Dr. William Johnson could report in 1926 that the only section of the coastal highway paved was the twenty-nine miles between Charleston and Adams Run. The Savannah, Cooper, and Waccamaw rivers were still being crossed by ferry. The work to change this had already begun, but the infusion of federal money during the Depression made it a reality.

The Lowcountry canal was finally finished then as well. We call it the

Intracoastal Waterway today, but in the beginning it was the "Inland Passage," a seemingly endless twisting of poorly connected saltwater creeks. The Army Corps of Engineers claims John C. Calhoun as its unlikely patron: In his earliest years as secretary of war he had empowered the Corps to make such improvements, and it has pursued them with a vengeance. The waterway got most of its straight, man-made sections during the mid-1930s when rushed to completion by the threat of submarine warfare off the Lowcountry coast. Today, however, the main traffic is yachts.

Nature Trails

Several early naturalists passed through the Lowcountry and gave accounts of what they saw: John Lawson, Mark Catesby, and William Bartrum came before the Revolution; in the next century, John James Audubon and his good friend Reverend Bachman collected specimens for the former's masterpiece portfolio. It is strange to read their accounts of endless and purposeless shooting of the birds Audubon so skillfully depicted.

Most wildlife, including birds, had been a source of revenue and food from the beginning, but following the Civil War, an impoverished people put extra strain on this natural resource. Carpetbaggers reportedly wiped out most of the shore birds in Bulls Bay. It was not just outsiders who massacred, however. At a later date, shore birds perched at high tide on a tiny bank are described as being shot by cannon in the middle of the night. Egrets and herons were hunted until World War I, when fashions changed and their feathers were no longer necessary for women's hats. Ducks, too, were shot for food and sport in ever-increasing numbers and, well into this century, it was still possible to have an illegal hundred-duck day. Such shooting finally took its toll, but the majority of the blame was put on the destruction of summer breeding grounds in the northern plains. Today the decline of other migratory bird populations is blamed on a similar destruction of winter grounds—the rain forests of South America.

In 1928, the Savannah Wildlife Refuge was established, joined three years later by Cape Romain and soon after that by the Francis Marion National Forest. Since then, the federal and state governments have increased their holdings and have been joined by a variety of other organizations like the Audubon Society and the Nature Conservancy.

Comparatively, then, the Lowcountry is doing well, for there is a concerted effort to conserve what wilderness remains and to preserve the wildlife in it. We find hundreds of thousands of acres held in trust for wildlife habitat and literally thousands of miles of paths, roads, and beaches that can be explored by those wishing to enjoy this natural heritage.

Modern Times

Some will argue that modern times have never come to the Lowcountry. Others think that "modern" means just this side of the antebellum period. They say "The War" when they mean the Civil War, forgetting that there have been five wars since. In 1886, an earthquake flattened much construction and sent a small tidal wave that destroyed the crops on the Sea Islands. In 1893, the great hurricane that drowned thousands and left tens of thousands homeless marked the beginning of the end for rice planters. Phosphate mining began just after the Civil War; by hand or dredge, it was stripped from the earth south of Charleston to be pounded into fertilizer. Populist governor Ben Tillman is accused of taxing this industry out of existence in 1890, but there was already growing competition from elsewhere. By 1920, the boll weevil had finished off the cotton, and "truck crops" took its place. These vegetables, along with soybeans, are still being grown in ever-decreasing fields. For 250 years, the Lowcountry had been open range: Cattle were sometimes branded, and hogs sometimes had their ears notched, but both ran wild until the 1930s. At the beginning of the century, a new system of mechanized logging reached the Lowcountry forests, and today lumber and pulpwood are harvested even more systematically. Much of the land that was once cultivated has reverted to forest. At least most of the small areas of virgin timber are designated as wilderness and will remain untouched.

Following the Civil War the population quickly turned to the "creek" for food and a livelihood. Oysters and terrapin were two of the earliest exports. Surprisingly, Charleston was the chief producer of shrimp in the nation in 1880, but that would have been seining and casting; a real shrimp boat wouldn't show up for another forty-five years. They still harvest oysters and shrimp today, but it's possible these previously maritime occupations will soon move inland to the abandoned rice fields and even into scooped-out cotton fields.

Modern times. When do they really begin? When does an essentially rural community become urbanized? When people commute to work? Get electric lights? Or buy a television? When no one nearby remembers your grandparents? With the Lowcountry the process probably began with the New Deal. The Army Corps of Engineers moved a lot of dirt around, and the "Gov'ment" bought up a lot of land. You'll see that. And now it's more fashionable than ever in this conservative section to grumble about the wastefulness of the federal government up there in Washington, D.C., but Franklin Roosevelt poured millions of dollars into this area during the 1930s. He educated people, gave them health care, and gave some of them their first real jobs. His success was marginal. In 1940, South Carolina was still the most illiterate state in the Union. Even today, we rank dismally in any contest that ranks practically anything—unless it's toxic waste or voter apathy. That's the downside of a basically unchanging culture.

Our day is coming. Maybe it's already arrived. Drive around and take a look at the treasure of architecture and landscape that has been preserved. That's the upside of an unchanging culture. And keep an eye out for what our Lowcountry poet laureate, Archibald Rutledge, called "life's little extras": sunsets, wildflowers, summer breezes, birds' songs, and those intangibles that don't get ranked in national surveys. These little extras are included here at no extra charge. On the house. Be my guest. And begin.

A Note from the Publisher

1. DRIVE CAREFULLY. Remember, only you are on a leisurely sightseeing tour, and the rest of the world is involved in its daily rat race.
2. The number before each entry corresponds with the numbered location on each tour map.
3. Each tour begins and ends at one of three places:

   a. The south side (the side away from downtown Charleston) of the Ashley River Bridge on U.S. 17.

   b. The north side (the side away from downtown Charleston) of the Cooper River Bridge on U.S. 17.

   c. At the intersection of Interstate 26 (Exit 221) and U.S. 17.

4. Before each driving instruction, there are two numbers. The first, or left-hand, number is the cumulative mileage for the tour. The second, or right-hand, number is the mileage since the last driving instruction. Example:

45.6	**1.5**	**A**t the stop sign, turn . . . .
46.5	**0.9**	**T**urn left at the corner of . . . . .

5. All the tours in this publication were driven with the same car, but since odometers vary in accuracy, accept the mileages as approximations.

6. Because the mileages are approximations, use mileages in combination with road numbers and road and street names to arrive at your destination.

7. A digital odometer was used to clock the mileages, so no fractions smaller than tenths were available. Therefore, be aware that, as a rule, the mileages may be short.

8. The cumulative mileages were recorded by adding the mileages from each instruction. As a whole, mileages may be short because all distances shorter than a tenth of a mile were lost.

9. In South Carolina, as a rule, the county highway numbers, such as S-18-345, are printed in white on black rectangular signs at the top of stop signs.

10. South Carolina intercounty highway numbers, such as S.C. 48, are

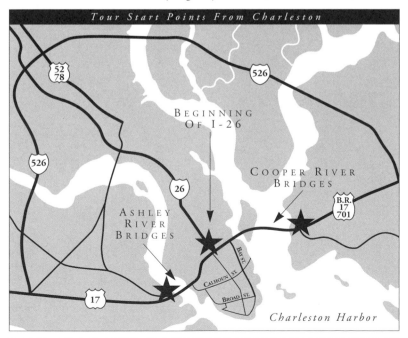

posted along highways on white signs with black lettering.

11. United States highway numbers, such as U.S. 78, are posted along highways on white signs with black lettering inside a black outline of a shield.

Highway Numbers

12. Interstate 26, or I-26, signs are marked by a shield-shaped sign with a blue background and red-and-white lettering.

13. The mileages for this guidebook were driven three times, with the last tours driven in early 1993. But because of road construction in the Charleston area, be aware that there may be detours or new roads that may change your route.

14. This is a driving-tour guide. It contains directions for reaching the sites, but you must use your own good judgment for safe driving. Sightsee *only* after you have safely stopped the car.

15. The tour information presented was correct when this book went to press; every effort was made to confirm that sites were indeed open to the public and that boat and walking tours were scheduled as listed here. The publisher cannot be responsible for changes in schedules or status.

Additional Reading

A good place to start general reading about South Carolina is David Duncan Wallace's *South Carolina: A Short History*. Stoney, Simons, and Lapham did the first definitive book on plantations: *Plantations of the Carolina Low Country*. I did the text for the second definitive book, *Plantations of the Low Country*. My mother, Agnes Baldwin, did the research, and Jane Iseley did the wonderful color photography. It is a good buy. Sam Stoney's book is back in print, but Harriette Leiding's excellent *Historic Houses of South Carolina* is harder to find. You can still buy Mills Lane's *South Carolina: Architecture of the Old South*. Look for E. T. H. Shaffer's *Carolina Gardens* and James Henry Rice's *Glories of the Carolina Coast* in the library. For naturalists, there are at least a dozen early books to enjoy—Lawson, Catesby, Bartrum, and Audubon are all in print in one form or another. Arthur Wayne's *Birds of South Carolina* and Edward Burnham Chamberlain's and Alexander Sprunt's *South Carolina Bird Life* are thorough studies. As for field guides, there are many on the market. Audubon and Peterson both worked here, and the books bearing their names are, of course, excellent for birders. In addition, you can find guides covering everything from seashells to wildflowers—on a local, regional, or national level. Bert Bierer's *Indians and Artifacts in the Southeast* is the best handbook on Indian artifacts. Gene Waddell's *Indians of the South Carolina Low Country* contains every colonial word ever written on the Lowcountry's original tribes. Frederick Dalco's 1820 history of the Episcopal church can be read for more than church history, but the same can be said for the many other excellent church histories. *South Carolina: A Guide to the Palmetto State* was published in 1941 by the workers of the Federal Writers Program. It was one of my inspirations, and you'll see it referred to as the "WPA guide." My other inspiration was Dr. William Johnson, whose three bulging scrapbooks are in the South Carolina Historical Society. He's usually referred to here as "Dr. Johnson." *The South Carolina Historical Magazine* is a wonderful source of information, and *South Carolina Wildlife Magazine* was an invaluable aid.

Look at the end of each day-trip tour for suggested reading about that particular area.

NOTES

TOUR 1:

ASHLEY RIVER

FROM CHARLES

TOWNE LANDING

TO MAGNOLIA

GARDENS

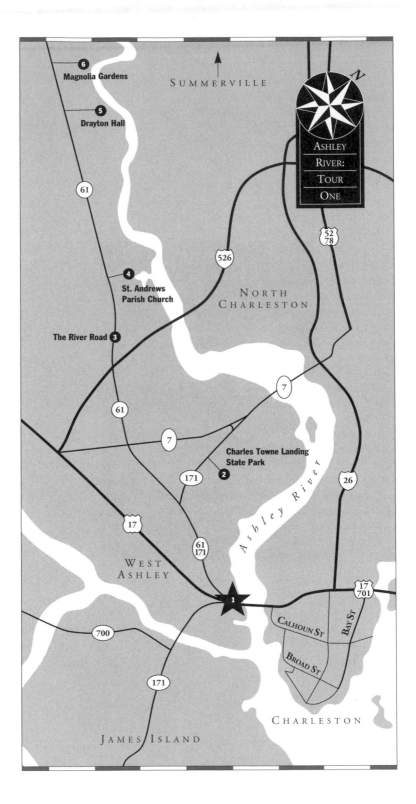

ASHLEY RIVER: CHARLES TOWNE LANDING TO MAGNOLIA GARDENS

We start this tour on the far side of the Ashley River Bridge and follow scenic highway S.C. 61 along its south bank for about twelve miles. Our first stop is CHARLES TOWNE LANDING STATE PARK. Site of the first English settlement in 1670, this park allows the visitor to see the "New World" as the first arrivals might have. Close by is ST. ANDREW'S PARISH CHURCH. Built in 1706, it's the oldest church in the state, and one of the prettiest, encircled by ancient oaks and graves. A few minutes farther along S.C. 61 is DRAYTON HALL. Here on the banks of the Ashley we tour a grand Georgian mansion—the first in America to use the distinctive Palladian portico. Just next door is MAGNOLIA GARDENS. Developed in the 1840s, this was one of the earliest of America's Romantic or informal gardens. A world-famous tourist attraction at the beginning of this century, the plantation and garden offer the modern visitor even more, including the AUDUBON SWAMP GARDEN.

Charles Towne Landing State Park, c. 1670/1970

This state park offers a museum, introductory movie, tram tour, replica of a sailing ship, settlers' area, animal forest, snack bar, gift shop, and restrooms.

Open 9:30 a.m. to 5 p.m. (6 p.m. in summer), seven days a week.
"Carolina" (thirty-minute film): Every half hour, beginning at 9:30 a.m.
Tram ride to the ketch Adventure: *Begins at 9:15 a.m., then 5 minutes past the hour until 5:05 p.m. in summer, 4:05 p.m. in winter.*
Admission charged. Telephone: (803) 556-4450

St. Andrew's Parish Church, c. 1706

Grounds open daily.

Drayton Hall, c. 1738

A Palladian mansion. Extensive guided house tour, riverside grounds to walk, gift shop, restrooms, picnic benches.

Open 9 a.m. to 4 p.m., seven days a week. Guided tours on the hour: November through February, 10 a.m. to 3 p.m.; March through October, 10 a.m. to 4 p.m.
Admission charged. Telephone: (803) 766-0188

Magnolia Plantation and Its Gardens / Audubon Swamp Garden

Extensive plantation garden, house tour, petting zoo, canoeing, birding, Audubon Swamp Garden and boardwalk, sandwich shop, restaurant, slave street, and graveyard.

Open 8 a.m. to 5:30 p.m. daily.
Magnolia Gardens: Admission charged. House: Admission charged.
Audubon Swamp Garden: Admission charged.

---- ❖ ----

0.0	**0.0**	**T**ake U.S. 17 South out of Charleston. Begin clocking mileage at the south side of the Ashley River Bridge.

1. ASHLEY RIVER BRIDGE, c. 1926

Travelers crossed the Ashley River here by ferry until 1803. The original bridge was burned by General P. G. T. Beauregard when he learned that Sherman had entered the state. Ferry service resumed until 1885 when a toll bridge was built: five cents for walkers and ten cents for horse-drawn vehicles. The current structure opened in 1926 as a memorial to those soldiers killed in the Great War. (After the next war, it was a memorial for both.) Brand new, the bridge was billed as "the handsomest and widest in the South," and an important link in the new Atlantic Coast Highway, the "all paved road from Quebec to Florida."

How the Ashley River Got Its Name

The Ashley and Cooper rivers were both named for one of the Lords Proprietor, the Earl of Shaftesbury, otherwise known as Anthony Ashley Cooper. Described as short and ugly and having a surgical drainage tube permanently implanted in his side, His Lordship still had a reputation as a notorious rake. His patron, King Charles II, once referred to him as "the biggest whoremonger in England." More noteworthy was the almost Machiavellian political career of this early defender of English democracy and "father of the Habeas Corpus Act." Though he'd been given his share of Carolina as a royal gift, for a time he ran the colony from a cell in the Tower of London.

200 ft.	**200 ft.**	**V**eer right onto S.C. 61 North / St. Andrews Blvd.
2.0	**2.0**	**V**eer right onto S.C. 171 / Old Towne Road.
2.9	**0.9**	**T**urn right into entrance gate of Charles Towne Landing State Park.

History of Charles Towne Landing

The ocean voyage of the first permanent English settlers was a stormy one. Of the three ships setting out, two had to be replaced in mid-passage—only the *Carolina* survived. They were fortunate accidents, though, for along the way the settlers chanced upon their "marooned" Indian interpreter and negotiator, young Dr. Henry Woodward. They also picked up a new governor, the eighty-year-old Bermuda administrator William Sayles. The choice of a town site was equally fortunate, for their Proprietor sponsors had planned to settle them at Port Royal. Wanting protection for his tribe, the chief of the Kiawah Indians warned that this area was open to attack from both the warring Westoes and the Spanish. Governor Sayles listened to the Kiawah recommendation and chose this peninsula well up the Ashley River. About 150 settlers came ashore here in April 1670. They called their town Albemarle Point in honor of the Proprietors, who renamed it Charles Towne in honor of the king.

A fair number of letters and documents have survived from this period, so we know something of the hopes and needs of the settlers, their political squabbles, and even their personalities. Surprisingly, we know very little about the actual town and adjoining settlements. Apparently, the first project undertaken was to erect a palisade across the ten-acre tip of the point; this was soon supplemented with trenches, moats, embankments, and "seaven great Gunns." "Settled in the very chaps of the Spaniard," one colonist wrote. In September of that same year, the enemy and his Indian allies attacked, but were repelled at some distance by the colonists and their Indian allies.

In the summer of 1672, an eighty-acre tract just beyond the palisade was divided into sixty-two building lots, each with a ten-acre garden plot nearby. From the beginning, the houses here were no doubt crude. Governor Sayles was allotted "a mansion," but later, subsequent Governor West described the ones he built only as "convenient." Experiments in agriculture came quickly, as we'll see, and craftsmen were encouraged by the Proprietors to immigrate. Cattle, hogs, sheep, and horses arrived soon after humans, and the cattle soon provided a good source of income. Rosin, timber, and deerskins traded from the Indians, however, were the first exports. Barbados was a chief trading partner, and Barbadians looking for new land were eager immigrants.

But even as Charles Towne was being divided into lots, another settlement was being planned. Governor Sayles was ill and would live less than a year, but he had the foresight to set aside six hundred acres of Oyster Point (now Charleston) for a future town and fort. Plans for this new port town continued, and in 1680, the government officially moved across the river to a new Charles Towne. The spot between the Ashley and Cooper rivers was an immediate success—it grew from four houses to one hundred by 1682. The original settlement was quickly deserted and ended as Old Towne Plantation—owned by the Waring family in this century.

3.6   0.7   State park parking lot.

2. CHARLES TOWNE LANDING STATE PARK, c. 1670/1970

Open to public.

Opened as part of the state's tricentennial celebration, this park gives the visitor some idea of what the first arrivals would have seen and felt in 1670. We receive a map-brochure at the entrance and are free to choose our own route from there. I've visited here in the winter when there weren't a dozen people in sight, but on a midsummer tour the park was filled with visitors—mostly families. My wife and I soon met an old friend with two children in tow, and she assured us that this was "a great place for kids. They see something new each time." Of all the sites in this book, this park and Palmetto Island Park on the opposite side of Charleston seemed to make children the happiest.

It should be mentioned that Hurricane Hugo caused some problems here, but the staff has worked hard to get the park back into shape quickly.

"Carolina": The Movie

You might want to begin with the thirty-minute film "Carolina." Nature photography at its lyrical best shows the wilderness as the first European settlers saw it. Great flocks of ibis take flight, deer browse, rivers cloak themselves in early morning mist, and tremendous cypress and tupelo trees rise up out of the still, black water. All so natural and wild you forget that it was filmed only twenty years ago, and there's nothing in the movie that you can't see for yourself today.

Tram Ride to the Ketch Adventure

Weaving beneath moss-draped oaks and beside spring-fed lagoons, this thirty-minute tram ride goes the length of the park. As you travel, the driver points out places you will want to return to on foot or bicycle to investigate further. We go through the reconstructed palisade of the first defense to where a dozen cannons today guard a seventeenth-century trading ketch, the *Adventure*. A short inspection stop is made. The vessel is fifty-three feet long and would have only been used for coastal trading, but the replica is a favorite attraction, especially for children. And since the vessels of passage were hardly bigger than this one, it does give us some idea of the hardships of ocean crossing. An easy tram passage takes us back to our starting point.

Interpretive Center

(Currently closed because of Hurricane Hugo; repairs under way.)
This was a controversial piece of architecture twenty years ago and time has done nothing to mellow it. A supposedly space-age combination of concrete, steel, aluminum siding, and thin air, it's hard to imagine any building more alien to the history it was meant to celebrate and conserve. Below ground, however, the museum offers an excellent picture of the colony's first one hundred years.

This site was an Indian ceremonial center long before the Kiawah invited the English, and a collection of artifacts made of bone, shell, and pottery greet the visitor. Next is a sample of the large variety of seashells that can be found on the beaches nearby. The displays that follow—artifacts, dioramas, recordings, maps, and pictures—offer a history of the area and portray the lives of all three races involved. Seven thousand years of Indian occupation is ended by "war, pestilence, . . . whiskey, and systematic slave hunts." African slaves and their life and work under the plantation system are not romanticized either, but the incredible music that resulted in part from that experience can be heard. The white man is here as Indian trader, pioneer, slave owner and planter, and sophisticated town dweller.

Settlers' Life Area

Here we find replicas of the first homes, shops, and gardens to be on this site. Before leaving England, Joseph West (the second governor) had been instructed to carry along "cotton seed, Indigo seed, Ginger roots . . . Canes . . . Ollive setts . . . and upon arrival build a right house for self and servants and then plant corn, beans, peacse, turnips, carretts, and Potatoes." He was also instructed to build a fence for the cattle that would soon be sent down from Virginia. A selection from this first experimental farm is grown today, but ironically both indigo and cotton were crops of the future, and the colonists were soon relying on Indian corn to keep from starving. Although cattle thrived, horses came early as well, and so they are shown here.

The house to the right would have been for a single man who slept above and had a shop below. Called "wattle and daub," this combination of sticks and clay was well known to the Old World, but would stand up poorly in the Lowcountry's warm, damp climate. The slightly larger house to the left is for a family; it too is of Old World design, half-timber construction. Architectural historian Mills Lane writes that here they would have filled in between the timbers with straw, clay, brick, and marsh grass, but more substantial half-timber houses were to be built in the new Charles Towne—the last one in 1818. There are no definite records, but historian H. A. M. Smith suggests that the first settlers built cabins with poles or axe-hewn beams. The park staff, pointing to the presence of a trestle saw and carpenters among the settlers, suggest otherwise: Construction from the beginning was at least as advanced as we see in this display. And it's true that timbers and sawn planks were an early export.

On the site, several craftsmen ply their trades—candle making, woodworking, and even printing. From the beginning, all sorts of artisans were encouraged to come, and some did. Still, a 1682 instruction advises newcomers to bring along clothing, shoes, ammunition, hardware, nails, and sails. Since the records are so scanty, the stocks we see are probably a guess, but a good one.

Though there was no outright religious persecution, crimes were committed that would have required punishment, and we often forget the number of indentured servants who would have needed reprimanding. (As soon as there was someplace to run to, many appear to have done just that.)

Animal Forest

These are some of the animals that the settlers would have seen. (The buffalo, wolf, and puma may have been smaller varieties.) The park encourages us to see the animals as the settlers first did, but we can't really because we've seen them all before, at least in pictures. For someone arriving from a wilderness-free England, the experience would be quite different. And for the Indians, the animals were sacred: brothers that they shared the wilderness with and that they depended on for a harmonious survival.

I've gone back to the early records for accounts of the animals: John Henry Logan's *History of the Upper Country of South Carolina* (1700), Mark Catesby's *The Natural History of Carolina, Florida and the Bahama Islands* (1731), and *Carolina* (1862) by Thomas Ashe, for whom fireflies and hummingbirds were the true marvels. You can also read the modern information inside the park.

The animal forest covers twenty acres of Lowcountry wilderness. Hurricane Hugo struck this area hard. No animals were lost but, at this writing, only about two-thirds of the inhabitants are on exhibit. The trail is a figure eight that often brushes against the marsh so that much of the viewing is done from bridges. (Some of the animals can be seen from several places, but I've listed them as they appear on the trail.) On this summer afternoon the wildlife is hot and listless and so are the humans. We enter through a snake house.

RATTLESNAKES—According to Logan, the Indians venerated these reptiles that often grew to seven or even ten feet in length. Lawson writes that he knew of no one actually killed by them, and adds that the Indians treated the bite with "snake roots" and used the cast-off skin as medicine, and that "the Rattles are reckon'd good to expedite the Birth."

FOXES—Of the gray fox, Lawson writes in 1700, "They make a sorry Chace, because they run up trees when pursued," which is why pioneer sportsmen quickly brought over the red fox from England. Logan claims that most of the grays ran right out of the colony.

RACCOONS—Their name comes from an Indian word thought to mean "he scratches with his feet." Lawson describes how they catch fiddler crabs and feed on oysters (still "coon oysters"), and adds a bit of misinformation—they dangle their tails in the water to bait up crabs.

SHORE BIRD AVIARY *(Hurricane Hugo repairs under way)*—The pelican, Lawson writes, has a pouch to hold its prey. "Web-footed, like a Goose, and shap'd  like a Duck. The food is never eaten but they make Tobacco pouches of his maw." Of herons, he writes: "They were the same as in England. Plentiful . . . White Herns . . . are as white as Milk, and fly very slowly." Aptly put.

WOLVES—Lawson writes that they run in packs and are not as large or as fierce as the European wolf. "They are not Man-slayers; neither is any creature in Carolina, unless wounded. . . None more troublesome or destructive than the wolf," says Logan. He identifies two species (so does Catesby): gray and the smaller black. Logan adds that the Indian dogs are like the black wolf, but they bark.

BLACK BEARS—Logan says that for the Indians the black bear was an "essential of their domestic and religious life," providing them with perfume, oil for skin and hair, insect repellant, and a preferred food. The only carnivore eaten by the Indians, Lawson says, "equalizes, if not excells any Meat I ever eat in Europe." Bears would sometimes eat the half-wild hogs that roamed the area, and today the few remaining in the Lowcountry are often referred to as "Hog Bears."

DEER—This was the most sacred of animals for the Indians and, next to combat, the number of deer slain by a brave was the best measure of his success. Millions were soon to be killed for their skins alone, and Logan complains that the carcass was often left to rot. Lawson points out several differences between the English deer and our "Fallow-Deer," and calls them "one of the best commodities Carolina affords."

ELK—Logan says that the elk was valued by the Indians for horn and skin; it was one of the first animals to disappear from the colony. The antlers of the last elk shot in South Carolina ended up in the British Museum.

BISON—For the Indians, the buffalo was "the Bull of the Gods." Even in Carolina, Logan says, they were stalked and stampeded as on the western plains. "A bunch on his back" is how Lawson describes the bison, and he says few remained in 1700.

ALLIGATOR—In Spanish, *aligarto*: "The lizard of the Indies." The name "alligator" wasn't but eighty years old when the colonists arrived. Logan incorrectly claims that the animal is the same as the crocodile. A threat to hogs and dogs in Carolina but not to men, he adds, but Lawson still tells a tale of being greatly frightened by the bellowing, and so does Catesby. The tail is eaten and the fat is used by the Indians to treat aches and pains (rheumatism). They "grow to a great length," writes Ashe in 1682, "from 16 to 20 foot, having a Mouth, beset with sharp keen Teeth." THERE ARE STILL PLENTY OF ALLIGATORS AROUND AND THEY CAN BE DANGEROUS.

WILD TURKEYS *(Hurricane Hugo repair under way)*—Wild turkeys were baited with maize into pens by the Indians or decoyed with tame turkeys. Lawson claims to have seen five hundred in one flock, and notes that eight hungry men get two meals from one bird. He correctly points out that the head of the wild variety was of one color.

BOBCATS *(Hurricane Hugo repair under way)*—These bobcats are quite different from those of Europe, notes Lawson. They are large, fierce, and nimble, with a "Tail that does not exceed four Inches," and can overpower swine and occasionally deer by leaping onto their backs from trees. "That he can conquer, he destroys," says Lawson.

BIRDS OF PREY AVIARY—The hawks are the same as England's, according to Lawson, but Carolina has an owl that is "as big as a middling Goose, and has a prodigious head. They make a fearful Hollowing in the Night time."

BOX TURTLES *(Hurricane Hugo repair under way)*—Lawson mistook the box turtle for the land "Terebin," which he declares can kill a rattlesnake.

PUMA—The panther was the "Cat of God" for the Indians. Children of the first Americans were made to sleep on its skin, says Logan. There were only a few left in the state in 1859, and there are only a few (smaller than this fellow) left today. "Greatest enemy of the planter," writes Lawson of the puma. In 1695, the colonial government demanded that every Indian bowman bring in yearly one wolf, one tiger, one bearskin, or two wild cat skins. The Indian was to be whipped if he failed, but soon this was replaced by a bounty, and these predators were on the way out.

OTTERS—This animal didn't surprise; the same as in Europe, Lawson says. "I shall insist no farther on that Creature. Their Furs, if black, are valuable."

And we'll insist no more on Charles Towne Park. It is a nice place to spend much of the day and fun for children especially.

───────────── ◈ ─────────────

3.6	0.0	Retrace to main gate of Charles Towne Landing.
4.3	0.7	Turn right onto S.C. 171 / Olde Towne Road and move into left lane.
4.6	0.3	Turn left onto Sumar Street.
4.6	1 block	Turn left onto S.C. 7 South / Sam Rittenburg Blvd.

| 6.1 | 1.5 | Turn right onto S.C. 61 North / Ashley River Road. |
| 6.5 | 0.4 | Veer right, continue on S.C. 61 North / Ashley River Road. |

3. THE RIVER ROAD

Highway 61 was once the "River Road." Most of these river systems had river roads—Indian trails and wagon paths that were widened to link plantations that were first reached by water. This road has been a matter of controversy because the giant oaks crowding its edges were a danger to the ever-increasing traffic. It appears that in this section, at least, the trees have lost the battle. It's not such a new problem, though, for E. T. H. Shaffer quotes a 1721 statute stating that the road commission would deliberately leave "such trees standing on or near the line of such road or path." Anyone cutting within ten feet of the path paid a fine of twenty shillings per tree. The pound is up. Somebody owes about seventy-five cents an oak.

| 9.0 | 2.5 | Turn right into parking lot of St. Andrew's Parish Church. |

4. ST. ANDREW'S PARISH CHURCH, c. 1706

Open to public.

St. Andrew's Parish was one of the ten created by the Church Act of 1706, and this building constructed in that same year is the oldest in the state. Over the west door is the inscription "Superv. 1706 J.F.-T.R.," probably left by Johnathan Fitch and Thomas Rose, early brick masons and wardens here.

Cruciform churches are not found in the Lowcountry very often. The nave to our left is the original building; the transepts (wings) and the chancel (for priest and altar) are a 1723 addition. The church is usually kept locked now, but if you're lucky enough to get in, note the reredos above the altar. These printings of the Ten Commandments and the Lord's Prayer date from 1723 as well. Also notice the marble baptismal font; its base is of three carved pelicans, the symbol of the Anglican Society for the Propagation of the Gospel.

A 1764 fire partly destroyed the building, and with the repairs, the window behind the altar was closed in. To cover the cost, the pews were sold and those too poor to pay went into the balcony. Like most other Anglican churches, this one fell on hard times after the Revolution, but vestryman William Bull repaired it in 1855, and Reverend Grimke-Drayton of nearby Magnolia Plantation kept the little congregation together until his death in 1891. The Colonial Dames repaired the building in 1933, but services didn't resume until 1948.

The ancient graveyard is a pretty one, with many stones crowding close to the structure to increase the chances of a heavenly reward. Off to the left, one stone bears the account of Thomas Nairn, "brutally murdered by the Indians." Nairn was the boldest of our Indian traders. Traveling out to the Mississippi, he sent back thoughtful reports—sprinkled with Biblical and classical allu-sions—to his supporters. His plan was to use Indian allies to take the Mississippi Valley from the French by force. The United States purchased the valley over a century later. Nairn was captured in the first moments of the Yemassee uprising, stuck full of lightwood splinters, and slowly burned to death for two days. Contrary to tradition, this is not his grave. His son is buried here, and the account of his murder is on his wife's stone.

Following Hurricane Hugo, this churchyard was a grand confusion of fall-en trees and broken stones. You can see for yourself that it's been straightened out as good as new. The same can be said for the other entries on this tour, so for today, this is the final word on the hurricane.

9.0   **0.0**   From church parking lot, turn
                                            right onto S.C. 61 North /
                                            Ashley River Road.

Scenic Highway 61

This section of S.C. 61 is designated a scenic highway, and though the oaks aren't quite so large as those just passed, this part is pretty well canopied. When the leaves fall, you can see that some of the low places are still marked by the eroded ridges of rice-field dikes. In other spots, there's the mounded earth left behind when phosphate was mined here after the Civil War.

From the very earliest days of settlement, this was plantation country. At first, any crop attempted by a planter was considered a plantation—ten acres or a thousand—but the meaning changed quickly, especially in this area. Runneymede, Ashley Wood, Soldiers Retreat, Archdale, MacBeth, and Millbrook: Shaffer says thirty-five mansions graced these banks before 1800—most surrounded by great groves and avenues, gardens and terraces, and the fields planted in rice. These were probably the finest estates in the Lowcountry, but it's sometimes debated whether after the years of settlement they continued as working plantations. Much of the money was being made in rice fields else-where and these were largely baronial estates. The debate goes on, but in 1865, Union troops moved up the river and burned almost all the houses.

———————— ◈ ————————

11.6   **2.6**   Turn right into Drayton Hall
                                            entrance.

5. DRAYTON HALL, c. 1738

Open to public.

Drayton Hall is considered by most to be the finest example of Georgian Palladian architecture in America. "Georgian" refers roughly to most eigh-teenth-century English design. "Palladian" refers to the sixteenth-century Italian architect Andrea Palladio, who, influenced by early Roman buildings, used columned porticoes to front domestic architecture. This, then, was the current style of the English country house at the time, but here the mansion is set down on what only a generation before had been the American frontier.

The gift shop sells an excellent paperback guide to the architecture you're about to see, but it's not absolutely necessary to have one. The National Trust for Historic Preservation owns this property jointly with the state, and every hour

Drayton Hall

one of their guides provides an extensive and thorough tour of the museum house. (You can't go in on your own.)

John Drayton began his house in 1738 and finished it four years later. "Mr. Drayton's Palace on the Ashley" was a description of that time. There is no known architect, but one of the massive Georgian overmantels has been

linked to a pattern book. Master builders worked from these books, and a really good one sometimes allowed the owner to bypass the architect. Drayton must have given either or both a pretty rough time, for there's clear evidence he widened his front entry room with no regard to the load-bearing foundation beneath.

Much of the tour guide's time is spent dispelling illusions about how life was lived in the house over the years—*Gone With the Wind* illusions as well as more justified ones. The entry was a public room that housed the stairwell, and on the second story was the main ballroom. Guests were entertained here, and the residents withdrew to the side rooms for privacy—withdrawing rooms, hence "drawing rooms." Over the years, the uses of the rooms would change. In early days dining was rather haphazard: no great long tables, but instead many small ones. Furniture was sparse and pushed against the wall when not in use, which is where we get the phrase "straightening the room."

The ceilings were reported at the time to be unfashionably low: The first floor is only twelve feet high and the second, a mere fourteen. One drawing-room ceiling sports a wet-plaster carving—the only one surviving in America. The interior decoration, in general, can be described as massive, balanced, and elaborate. Intricate carvings of mahogany and poplar are particularly distinctive. Drayton Hall has had only one coat of paint since it was built, so there are no thick layers of paint to disguise the details. In fact, relatively few changes have been made. Federalist windows went in when the originals blew out in a hurricane. Some Adamesque mantels, Victorian wood ceilings on the second floor, and shingles on the roof pediment were added later. The freed slaves burned the newel post for firewood, and perhaps removed the false doors, thinking they held secrets. Miss Charlotte Drayton lived here through much of the twentieth century without electricity or plumbing, so there was none of that to remove in a search for authenticity.

Drayton Hall was once as famous for its garden as for its mansion, but not many of the plantings remain. Once thirty support buildings stood here—one, an "orangery," or greenhouse where citrus trees grew. All are gone now except a solid little brick building that was once a seven-seat privy. And in the front, we see the brick foundations of the two flankers, one a kitchen, the other perhaps a laundry or bachelor's quarters. The walk to the river is short and pleasant, but we're left to imagine the past splendor of the owner's procession here.

It was said of the builder, "Such was his character, he lived in riches—but without public esteem. He died in a tavern, but without public commiseration." The guide adds that upon Drayton's death, his fourth wife, a sixteen-year-old bride, Rebecca, used the estate to provide well for six of her slaves. She retired to Charles Town, lived to be over eighty, and left what remained to her grandchildren. The Draytons were an interesting and illustrious family then and in later years. The house survives now, it's said, because the resident Drayton convinced Union troops that it was a smallpox hospital. In the years following the Civil War, phosphate mining allowed it to remain in the family's hands.

Perseverance and a great deal of luck have kept Drayton Hall standing over the years. The mansion is far more fragile than its stately appearance suggests, and the National Trust is simply trying to maintain an authentic treasure, to preserve the status quo. That alone is expensive business and it depends on our support.

| 11.6 | 0.0 | Retrace driveway and turn right onto S.C. 61 North / Ashley River Road. |
| 12.1 | 0.5 | Turn right into entrance of Magnolia Plantation and Its Gardens. |

6. MAGNOLIA PLANTATION AND ITS GARDENS / AUDUBON SWAMP GARDEN
Open to public.
We're given a map-brochure upon entering. To tour the original garden, we follow the numbered path signs; the miles of nature trail can be traveled by foot or bicycle. There are canoes for the waterfowl refuge impoundment. The unusual house is open to the public. A film introduces you to all this, and you can sit in a rocker on the porch and listen to a tape-recorded history of the house and family.

The House
The Drayton family started out on this site, not next door at Drayton Hall. Thomas, the father of Drayton Hall builder John, arrived from Barbados in 1679. He built a mansion that accidentally burned, and its replacement was burned by the Union. The current house, parts of which are pre-Revolutionary, was the family's hunting lodge that originally stood on another site. Dismantled and floated here in 1873, it was placed on the foundation of the previous structure. The Victorian details were added then and the curious square water tower as well. The stucco finish made from phosphate lime went on after the earthquake in 1886. Tours of the interior are given for a small extra charge.

The Garden
Today the plantation's garden spreads out informally about the house and meanders along the river for some distance, and being an "informal garden" is

what makes Magnolia famous. Originally, this was all the dream of Reverend
John Grimke-Drayton. A hunting accident killed his brother and unexpected-
ly left the young theology student heir to the family fortune. He completed his
degree, married a Philadelphian bride, and settled here. His church was St.
Andrew's, visited earlier.

Reverend Grimke-Drayton laid out the garden in the Romantic or informal pattern then popular in England. Before this, geometry and strict pattern
had been the rule, but now a more personal expression was allowed and a
greater value placed on the already existing forest. It was a happy choice for
man and land. In 1843, he imported Camellia japonicas, and five years later,
Azalea indica. In 1851, tuberculosis caused him to retire for a while and he
gave this project his full attention. "Dig in the soil" was the prescription—
what we might call therapy today, as well.

The Civil War brought ruin. Grimke-Drayton sold much of his property
and leased the rest for a time to a phosphate company. (He hated what they
did so much that he forbade a reoccurrence in his will.) But he managed to
save his garden, and in 1870 he opened it to the public. Visitors came up the
river by paddle-wheel steamboat, and the reviews were unanimous. Baedeker's
travel guide listed it with only two other American attractions—the Grand
Canyon and Niagara Falls.

Today we can enjoy the same. Arrows direct us down the paths that twist
and turn through a variety of botanical wonders. Ornate little white bridges
arch across narrow black-water lagoons. Two hundred and fifty varieties of
azaleas bloom in the spring. This was the traditional time for visiting and still
is the most dazzling. A great variety of camellias and the extensive plantings of
other shrubs, however, are gradually shifting the emphasis at Magnolia to a
more year-round display of color. In addition, small specialized areas within
the larger garden add interest as well as beauty.

The biblical garden near the path's beginning should delight both gardeners and biblical scholars. What really grew in the Holy Lands in ancient
times? Was Eve's apple really an apricot? Or a quince? Were the lilies of the
field narcissus? Did Judas hang himself from a Judas tree? Some of these
questions can't be answered, but in this unique little spot, they're growing
almonds, roses, papyrus, pomegranate, oleander, date palm, and even cedars
of Lebanon. Farther along, we come upon a maze copied from the time of
Henry VIII. In the movies, it seems as though the gout-ridden king is
always chasing Anne Boleyn around one of these. And there's an herb garden from the days of colonial Carolina. Most plantations had one, and in
fact, it's now thought there was no prejudice against having vegetables,
herbs, and flowers all together in the earliest gardens. Ashe says that in
1682, Carolina gardens already contained vegetables and herbs as well as
"Rose, Tulip, Carnation, and Lily." At the center of Magnolia, at the heart
of Drayton's larger creation, is a small patch of cultivation called
"Flowerdale" that may well date back to the 1680s and be the inspiration
for the rest of the garden.

Other Attractions

The entire 500 acres is a wildlife refuge, but 125 acres of that is rice fields, which we only walked a short way around and didn't canoe at all. Magnolia is well known to birders, but at the time of our tour, the ducks wouldn't be arriving for another four or five months. I visited the petting zoo alone, talked to the goats, and petted the ponies. No law against that, but a sign warns, "Not responsible for articles nibbled." Together my wife and I took the Audubon nature walk and stopped off at the slave cemetery. Influenced by his abolitionist aunts, the famous Grimke sisters, Drayton referred to his slaves as his "black roses" and broke the law by teaching them to read and write. We finished up the walk, which, though newly constructed, is already a pretty stretch of pathway—leading about and then through a reserve where islands of thick vegetation float. Unaided even by a Peterson's guide, my wife identified four bantam chickens that had wandered down from a nearby cabin. I was proud of the several bitterns I spotted until I read the Audubon notice on the way out declaring something to the effect that bitterns at that time of year were "as thick as pigeons."

We had a good time. We'll let Owen Wister have the last word. In his novel *Lady Baltimore* he wrote: "I have seen gardens, many gardens, in England, in France, in Italy . . . but no horticulture that I have seen devised by mortal man approaches the unearthly enchantment of the azaleas at Magnolia."

———————— ◈ ————————

12.1	**0.0**	**R**eturn to S.C. 61 / Ashley River Road and turn left.
21.7	**9.6**	**A**rrive at junction of S.C. 61 South and U.S. 17 North.
21.7	**0.0**	**C**ontinue straight on U.S. 17 North.
22.1	**0.4**	**A**rrive at south side of Ashley River Bridge.

ADDITIONAL READING

A great deal has been written about this section. I've already mentioned some works by name in the text, but look for Alexander Salley's *Narratives of Early Papers*, and Agnes Baldwin's *First Settlers of South Carolina*. Drayton Hall, Magnolia Gardens, and Middleton Place all have book selections in their gift shops.

NOTES

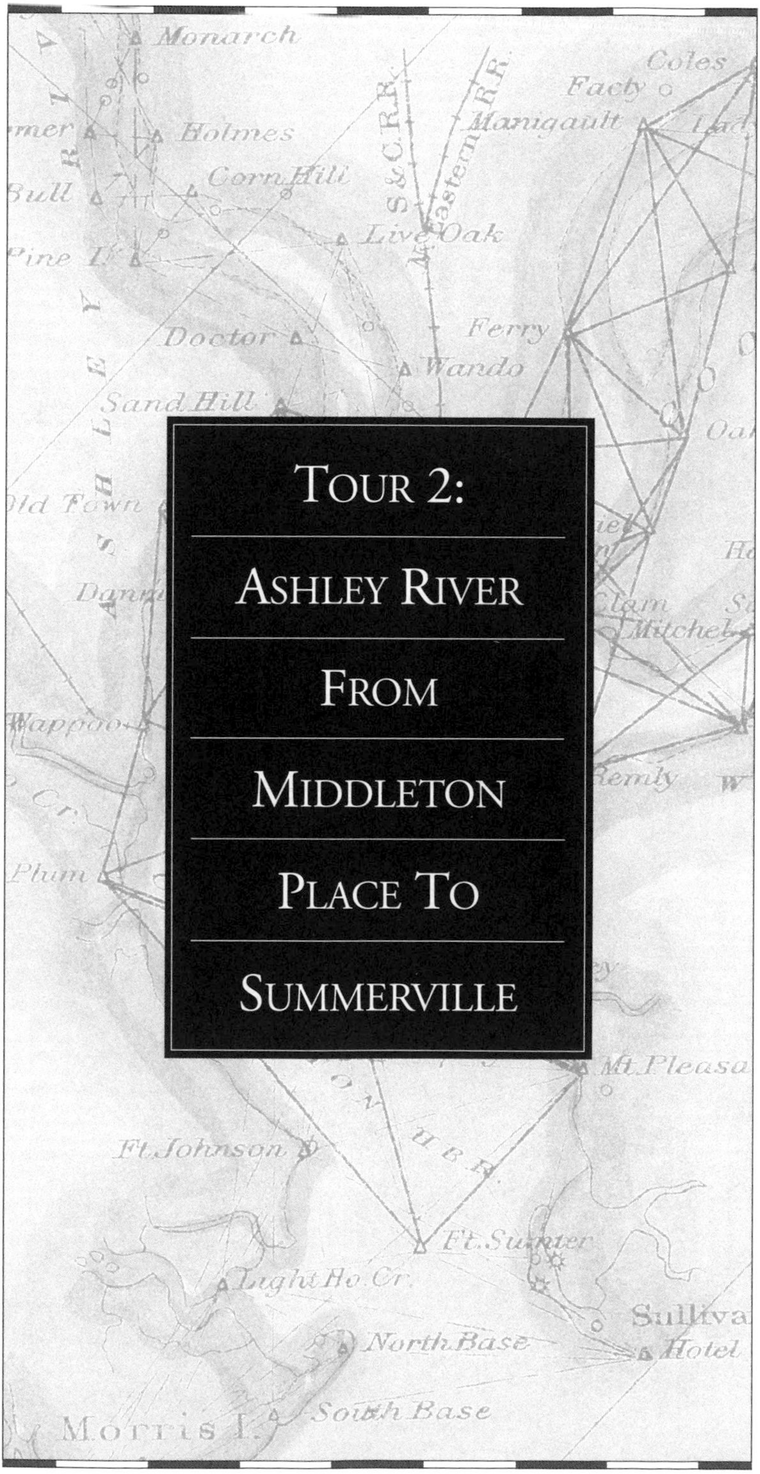

Tour 2: Ashley River From Middleton Place To Summerville

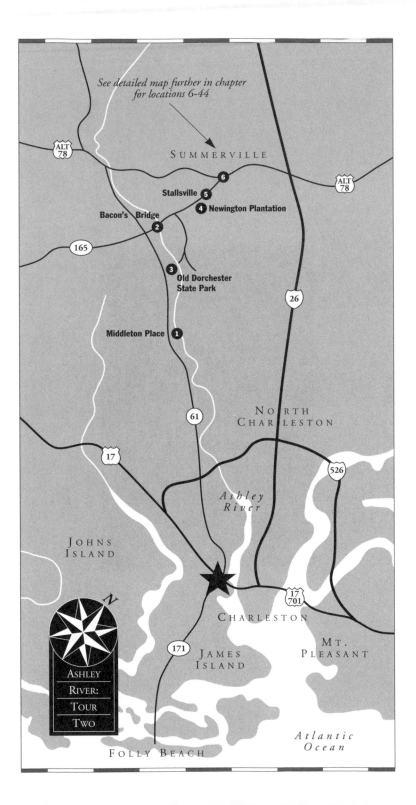

See detailed map further in chapter for locations 6-44

SUMMERVILLE

ALT 78

ALT 78

6

Stallsville 5

4 Newington Plantation

Bacon's Bridge 2

165

3 Old Dorchester State Park

Middleton Place 1

26

NORTH CHARLESTON

61

17

526

Ashley River

JOHNS ISLAND

N

ASHLEY RIVER: TOUR TWO

CHARLESTON

17 701

MT. PLEASANT

171 JAMES ISLAND

Atlantic Ocean

FOLLY BEACH

ASHLEY RIVER: MIDDLETON PLACE TO SUMMERVILLE

We begin this day on the Ashley River by driving up scenic S.C. 61 to MIDDLETON PLACE. The tremendous garden here is a century older than that of Magnolia and is laid out along more formal lines. There's a house tour and there are plantation craftsmen at work. A few miles ahead, we leave S.C. 61, cross the Ashley River, and arrive at OLD DORCHESTER STATE PARK. This is the site of a 1696 town, and we can walk through the fort and church ruins that remain. A right turn ahead and we've reached SUMMERVILLE. This "Flower Town in the Pines" is well known for springtime azaleas, but we'll be taking a look at its distinctive architecture as well.

Middleton Place, c. 1741

Extensive formal plantation garden, tour of finely furnished house, barnyard and crafts area, sandwich shop, and much more.

> *Open 9 a.m. to 5 p.m.*
> *House: 1:30 p.m. to 4:30 p.m. on Monday, 10 a.m. to 4:30 p.m. Tuesday through Sunday. House tour: Admission charged.*
> *Gardens and stableyard: Admission charged.*
> *Telephone: (803) 556-6020*

Old Dorchester State Park, c. 1696

Site of a 1696 village now vanished except for the bell tower of its church and the walls of its fort. Picnic tables, restrooms, and a nice shaded view of the Ashley River.

> *Open 9 a.m. to 6 p.m. Closed Tuesday and Wednesday.*
> *Admission: Free.*

Summerville

Active chamber of commerce. "Flower Town in the Pines." Beautiful old buildings surrounded by towering pines and flowering shrubs.

> *Chamber of Commerce / Visitor Center:*
> *Open 8:30 a.m. to 12:30 p.m. and 1:30 p.m. to 5 p.m.,*
> *Monday through Friday.*

◈

0.0	**0.0**	From Charleston, take U.S. 17 South and begin clocking mileage at south side of Ashley River Bridge.
200 ft.	**200 ft.**	Veer right onto S.C. 61 North / Ashley River Road.
2.0	**2.0**	Veer left, continue on S.C. 61 North / Ashley River Road.
3.8	**1.8**	Stay in right lane and follow 61-N.
13.4	**9.6**	Turn right into entrance gate of Middleton Place.

1. MIDDLETON PLACE, c. 1741

Open to public.

A leisurely day can be spent touring the house and grounds. Middleton is no longer just the world-famous formal garden. The house is on tour to offer an overall picture of both family and plantation history, as well as a lesson in interior design of the time. In a barnyard setting that offers a detailed look at plantation crafts and craftsmen, rice planting is explained, and black culture is emphasized. Middleton is as complete a look at plantation life as you're going to find anywhere in the Lowcountry.

The Garden

At the entrance, we're given a brochure-map; small arrows on the ground guide us through the mazelike tour, which begins in the parking lot. Just beyond, we come upon a long, rectangular lake. Eight hundred to a thousand visitors might pass this way on spring days or winter holidays, but on this November afternoon we have it pretty much to ourselves. Turtles sun on the far shore and to our left, white swans float on the black water. Middleton's garden was begun in 1741, so it's laid out in the formal geometrical design popular in Europe at that time. (Coming a century later, neighboring Magnolia would be more informal, or Romantic.) This lake marks the back leg of a gigantic triangle; soon, we're walking up another leg, through a forest of great camellias and grand magnolias. To the right, sheep graze and there's a distant view of the house or at least what remains of it. A couple of sharp turns and we're standing on the rubble of the pre-1741 original that was burned by the Union. "The Quake" brought down all the walls except those of the right flanker, a 1755 bachelors' quarters, which was rebuilt in a more Jacobean style than the original. Standing in what was once the center of the house, we get an excellent view of the river and the tremendous butterfly lakes in front. Notice that the axis of the landscaping from the River Road to the river ran

Middleton Place

straight through the center of the house. A right turn brings us to the remaining wing.

The House Tour

The house is actually the renovated 1755 flanker. When this became a house-museum, family members donated heirlooms of true museum quality, so it was possible to re-create in this small section of the mansion a portion of the vanished whole. On the ground floor are portraits of various family members by Benjamin West and Thomas Sully. A dining room and music room are fitted out with fine furnishings, and on display in the hall are such oddities as silver "marrow spoons" and piles of worthless Confederate money. (It's now appreciating faster than any currency in the world.)

The second floor is of equal interest. It contains a winter bedroom, which is opposite a summer bedroom: For summer, the headboard was taken off, the bed was moved to the center of the room, and the mosquito net was dropped. The original library had about ten thousand books stolen by a Union doctor, but in this upstairs library is assembled a nice collection of first editions. Especially interesting are the natural histories; they have a 1721 Catesby and original Audubon prints. One of the Middletons, John Izard, is called "the first American Archeologist," and his book Grecian Remains is on display. A children's room has fine furnishings and antiquated toys.

A Very Short History of the Middleton Family

The first Henry Middleton acquired this property in 1741 as part of his wife's dowry. He added the flankers to the existing house and began the formal garden. It took one hundred slaves almost a decade just to complete the terraces and walks, artificial lakes, and vistas we see today. Henry was president of the First Continental Congress and his son Arthur signed the Declaration of Independence. His son Henry (who would be governor and minister to Russia) was an avid botanist. Assisted by friend André Michaux, who was botanizing on the opposite side of the river for the French government, this second Henry experimented with thousands of exotic and domestic plants and added much to the garden. His son William may have made the single most important contribution to the garden—the azalea—but he's remembered instead as the signer of the Ordinance of Secession and the custodian of ruin. The family held on until 1975, when Middleton became a foundation and public trust.

Stableyard

A right turn brings us to the stableyard. Five carriages of varying models are housed in the first structure, but the rest are occupied by shops and stables. The early plantations were soon self-sufficient and slave craftsmen supplied the essentials. In the Middleton stableyard there are usually at least three craftspeople on hand. Spinning and weaving demonstrations are set up to the right. Just beyond, a guinea hen pecks about and a squirrel eats corn directly from the center of a grindstone. There's a cooper and carpenter's shop where everything from barrels to fine furniture is made, as well as a candle shop, laundry, and tannery. We see planking and shingle splitting, and food grown with the aid of hoe, plow, and scythe. Even a potter is at work.

The blacksmith, who happens to be a young woman, explains that it's "black" for the color of iron and "smithing" for smiting: "blacksmithing." But actually she's "whitesmithing" at the moment—filing a silver or white finish onto a kitchen utensil. On the plantation the smith would have been a jack-of-all-trades, but contrary to the popular view, he wouldn't have shoed horses. These horses went unshod because they traveled in the woods or on dirt roads, and they wore boots of leather and wood in the boggy fields. By the time of the Civil War, the self-sufficiency we see around us had passed. Goods were imported and the only craftsmen left at Middleton were three carpenters.

You can get a very good lunch here. Then head toward the river and the spring house; jars are stored here in cool water. On the second floor is an exhibit detailing a history of family and place and of the archaeological finds uncovered. One gigantic wing of the butterfly lake is to the right and ahead is a small rice mill with a display on rice culture. Shaffer has an interesting comment on them both—this is the only water-wheel rice mill that he knows of being driven by water from a decorative pond. And he has another comment even more curious. An ancient ex-slave told him of the "watuh-cow" that would sleep away its summer days almost completely submerged in this lake and others. It was one of the water buffalo that an antebellum Middleton had brought over from India to work in the rice fields. The experiment failed, however, and the rascal Yankees carried them off to a Northern zoo as the spoils of war.

There are more paths to wander and ponds and terraces to admire, but you can easily find your way. We'll let Shaffer, the author of Carolina Gardens, have the final words on Middleton: "Camellias of winter and the azaleas of spring, the roses of summer, and the magnolias blossoming are the major notes. Blending with these are the minor-heatherbell, hawthorn, lotus, iris, and a thousand more. The formal terraces and lakes at varied levels may recall better-known European gardens but the live oaks and Spanish moss weave a spell that is of a New World and an Old South."

———— ◈ ————

13.4	0.0	From Middleton Place parking lot return to S.C. 61 North / Ashley River Road and turn right.
17.9	4.5	Veer right onto S.C. 165.
18.7	0.8	Cross second bridge, which is location of the old Bacon's Bridge.

2. BACON'S BRIDGE

Dorchester settler Michael Bacon was keeping a bridge here across the Ashley River not long after 1700, and the crossing would remain important, as many were, during the Revolution. Marion kept a guard posted here and skirmished with the British. Dr. William Johnson points out "Marion's oak" that the men camped beneath, and a little farther along the "Tory oak" where one of the opposition was hanged. A road widening may have claimed those, or they may be part of the grove high and to our left. Summerville's waterworks is up there. Bacon's Bridge was a favorite swimming hole for Summerville youngsters at the beginning of this century and a favorite spot for church and community picnics.

———— ◈ ————

18.7	0.0	Continue on S.C. 165.
19.3	0.6	At stoplight, turn right onto S.C. 642 East / Old Dorchester Road.

| 21.1 | 1.8 | Turn right on Dorchester State Park Road / S-18-373. |
| 21.3 | 0.2 | Entrance gates into Old Dorchester State Park. |

3. OLD DORCHESTER STATE PARK, c. 1696

Open to public.

The state park service provides us with a map and brochure, and then we're free to wander the grounds. The town of Dorchester was founded at the end of the seventeenth century by Congregationalists moving south from Dorchester, Massachusetts. They came to "settell the gospell" here; not such an easy task, for their ship was "neer run under water ye stormy wind being so boistrous." This intrepid band of Puritans divided the surrounding four thousand acres into forty- to fifty-acre farm plots, but here at Dorchester, following New England patterns, they laid a common, a mill site, and a "place of trade." The spot was a good one, considered very healthy in those early days. (Several proposals were made to move the government here from Charles Town during the summer months.) Its location at the headwaters of the Ashley River made it ideal for Indian trading and transport of forest and farm produce to the port. A church was built nearby. Several stores were here along the bluff (the wharf of one still shows at low tide). There was a free school; there were weekly market days, fairs, and militia drills. The town prospered, but in the 1750s, the Congregationalists who felt that the spot was too crowded and unhealthy moved on to Georgia. Enough citizens remained for the town to be still the third-largest in the colony at the time of the Revolution.

In 1737, an Anglican church was built and the remaining tower added in 1753. (It once boasted four bells.) The British burned the building. Notice the gravestone of James Postell, for they sharpened their sabers on it. The church was partly restored after the Revolution, but was abandoned. Soon after, it was to house not a Christian fold, but an actual one: A local shepherd sheltered his flock here.

Overlooking the Ashley are the thick gray walls of Fort Dorchester. Built in 1757 as a result of the French and Indian War, it wouldn't actually see action for another twenty years. Francis Marion was the commander here early in the Revolution. The British occupied the fort in 1780, but were driven out by Colonel Wade Hampton and General Nathanael Greene the following year. This was an exceptional victory, for the Americans were outnumbered two to one and their attack was expected. The oyster-shell tabby is a familiar building material, especially for forts, but this pinwheel-shaped enclosure is unique to North America. At the fort's center are the remnants of a brick-and-earth-covered powder magazine.

Archaeologists have worked at this site for some time, and a display case exhibiting a small portion of their finds is close by. You won't see more evidence of a town than this, though. Bishop Asbury reported in 1788, "I passed Dorchester where there are remains of what appears to have been once a considerable town." A shift in trade routes and the abandonment by the

Congregationalists are sometimes given as reasons for this decline, but it seems most likely that the flight to nearby Summerville was for reasons of health.

Noted historian Judge H. A. M. Smith called Summerville home as well and wrote with some indignation about the early Congregationalists' claims that, here at Dorchester, they were settling an Indian frontier. The 1696 founders had spent their nights in neighboring plantations. Bacon bought his bridge from an earlier arrival. The Congregationalists built their church not by the river, but beside a well-established public road—"the Broad Path."

21.3	**0.0**	**R**eturn to park gates and continue straight on Dorchester State Park Road / S-18-373.
21.5	**0.2**	**A**t stop sign, turn left onto S.C. 642 West / Bacon Bridge Road.
23.3	**1.8**	**A**t second stoplight, turn right onto S.C. 165 West / Bacon Bridge Road.

The Road to Summerville

We're getting close to home now. Thirty years ago this bottom land we're driving into was a wilderness dissected not by streets, but by ancient rice-field dikes and ditches. They've canalled the area since then and planted houses.

24.5	**1.2**	**O**n right, pass by Newington Road.

4. NEWINGTON PLANTATION

At the top of the hill on the right is a small sign for Newington Road—one of the earliest of Summerville's now many, many subdivisions. I moved to the end of that lane when I was twelve in 1955 and stayed through high school.

Newington Plantation, for which our road was named, occupied most of the land beginning at Bacon's Bridge and extending into the edge of Old Summerville. The three-thousand-acre land grant was given in 1680 to Daniel Axtell, whose wife passed it on to her daughter, the wife of landgrave Joseph Blake. Blake's father had been a celebrated admiral under Cromwell's rule, but when the Restoration came, Charles II disinterred the seaman's body from Westminster Abbey. This sacrilege, so the story goes, sent Joseph off to Carolina. His son Joseph (Axtell's grandson) was one of the wealthiest men in the colony and built a tremendous mansion here. The "House of a Hundred Windows" it was called, and Eliza Lucas said of the house and oak avenue in 1742, it "seems designed by Nature for pious Meditation and Friendly Converse." Naturalist Catesby wrote at about the same time of the largest rattlesnake he had ever seen, "about eight feet in length, weighing between eight and nine pounds. This monster was gliding into the house of Colonel Blake of Carolina." Some ruins remain, but they're off to our left. Judging by Judge Smith's maps, our Newington Road was a little off the mark, and I may have been living on the less promising and less poetic Barren Heath Plantation.

24.5	**0.0**	Continue on S.C. 165 West / Bacon Bridge Road.
24.9	**0.4**	Pass through Stallsville.

5. STALLSVILLE

Next is the small pineland village of Stallsville. The area's first post office was here, and several antebellum dwellings still stand hidden away. Old Trolley Road joins on the right. It's a pretty straight shot out to the old Dorchester area—originally, this was to have been a trolley connection for commuters to Charleston, but it was abandoned and finally paved.

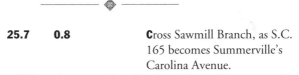

25.7	**0.8**	Cross Sawmill Branch, as S.C. 165 becomes Summerville's Carolina Avenue.

Next we cross Sawmill Branch, now widened and straightened into a canal, and this is where Summerville's history really begins.

25.7	**0.0**	Continue on S.C. 165 / Carolina Avenue.
26.0	**0.3**	At second stoplight, known as "Five Points" intersection, turn right onto U.S. 17A North / South Main Street.
27.1	**1.1**	Turn right onto East Doty Avenue, which runs parallel to railroad tracks.
27.2	**1 block**	Turn right into chamber of commerce parking lot.

Summerville's History

In 1707, this area was sawmill land, and the old dam that held the water that powered this mill wasn't obliterated until the area's drainage was improved in the 1880s. We know that planters were moving in this direction, but neither they nor the mill seemed to have interfered with the pines growing on these high sandy ridges. The occupants of Dorchester, searching for fever-free summer homes, deserted that town and started another here.

As in many other pineland communities formed during years of epidemic, the first houses were simple log cabins daubed with clay. All lived alike in this "democratic" atmosphere, until some returned to Dorchester for brick to make foundations and real chimneys. By 1800, clapboard-sided houses had introduced questions of status into the pioneer village. Built high above the ground, these were called "mosquito houses" (the malaria-bearing Anopheles and the other Lowcountry mosquitoes usually fly close to the ground). Judging by what has survived, they were traditional summer cottages with broad front porches and dormered attic bedrooms. It was only another step up to the larger "raised cottages" sometimes being built on plantations, and here these would become handsome enough and numerous enough to earn the name "Summerville style."

This is Old Summerville we're discussing. Its streets wind about following the paths of cows and wagons. The pleasures in those early days were picnics with dancing, visiting, and whist instead of poker. Church services were in homes or in the Lecture Hall until around 1830, when Episcopalians and Presbyterians got buildings. In 1832, the train "The Best Friend of Charleston" puffed in, and the new railroad company laid out New Summerville. There was not much growth there at first, but the plan was  eventually implemented just as drawn. The old village got a town hall in 1838, which was replaced twenty years later by the one we see today. Year-round residents, businesses, and a post office came by the mid-1840s.

From the beginning, the pines here were sacred, for, as elsewhere, it was thought that the trees somehow kept out malaria. In 1847, however, the railroad company cut trees in New Summerville for fuel and ties. The outraged citizens incorporated the town as a legal way of halting further cutting. Yellow fever epidemics beginning in 1852 brought an influx of visitors from Charleston, and six years later a regular commuter train to the city brought a real estate boom to the already prospering little town. The Civil War ended that, but the Union Army allowed the citizens to remain armed and, led by the Episcopal rector, they protected their property from marauders.

As was often the case, planters chose not to return to their plantations or lost them to bankruptcy, and they and their children took refuge here. Still basically rural and family oriented, the little town with its railroad depot began to transform into a commercial center for the surviving agriculture and new lumber industry. Commuting to Charleston and summer visiting resumed. After much disagreement, the town was adequately ditched and drained. Most residents enjoyed a modest prosperity.

Then, in August 1886, a great earthquake occurred. Large fissures opened up nearby. Geysers shot water fifteen feet into the air. The train derailed, the tracks twisted. Every chimney in the town toppled. Porches collapsed and some houses fell from their foundations. Estimated at 7.2 on the Richter scale, the force of "The Quake" was enough to ring church bells in New York, and leave a demoralized citizenry camping in their yards.

Yet Summerville was about to be discovered. In 1889, the Congress of Physicians meeting in Paris named it one of the two best places in the world for victims of lung diseases. Suddenly, wealthy visitors rushed to Summerville. In 1891, the new Pine Forest Inn opened its doors—a village unto itself, with the world's finest chefs, a sixty-horse stable, an eighteen-hole golf course, organized activities, and a rocking chair room with one hundred rockers. Theodore Roosevelt and William Howard Taft both stayed there, and dozens of other noteworthies. In 1915, however, the new Carolina Inn began to rival the success of the Pine Forest Inn—sixty-seven rooms, one of which was reserved for the use of J. P. Morgan's sister. There were other inns, too, dozens of smaller ones, and boardinghouses and rooms to let. And there were many new permanent residents who, once they visited the place, couldn't bear to leave. New houses and churches went up everywhere. A new business district and town hall were built on the spot laid out fifty years earlier by the railroad's civil engineer. Soon after, electricity and telephones went into service. Dr. Charles Shepherd was experimenting with tea farming, but that proved more successful as a charity. In the mid-twenties, they drilled for oil: "Spent $10,000 and found a pint." For those not dependent on visitors or commuting, or keeping shop, the well-established lumber and brickmaking businesses provided employment. (You'll notice no brick homes built in the years immediately after the quake, though.)

The Crash of 1929 hurt the inn business, but the town survived the Depression, and the war that followed changed people's ideas about how money was made. In the 1950s, industries found homes to the north of town. And the inns closed just as Summerville was being discovered by suburbanites, who would live not in the community but in an ever-widening circle around it. The original town is still there and it's relatively quiet once you're off the main street. The residential area, at least on this side of the tracks, has changed little during this century.

Before We Start

Somewhere along the line Summerville picked up the name "The Flower Town in the Pines," and it still lives up to that name. Hurricane Hugo, however, was particularly hard on great pines like these. The damage was extensive enough to warrant a firsthand inspection by President Bush—but many, many trees remain and "The Flower Town in the Pines" is well recovered. Incidentally, the pines aren't exactly original. They may have come only about ten thousand years ago when nomadic Indians moved through, burning the indigenous hardwood forest as they hunted. The azaleas were brought here, starting in the 1840s. In the spring, especially on Sunday afternoons, outside visitors have traditionally driven through, and now there's a week-long Azalea Festival celebrating the blooms. Dogwoods and wisteria should ask for equal billing, but so should the houses.

Victorian Houses

We've already mentioned the "mosquito houses" and raised cottages, but Summerville is unique in the Lowcountry in that it alone experienced a genuine post–Civil War prosperity. Elsewhere, we find communities where a handful of large Victorian houses were built by a few well-to-do citizens. On Sullivan's Island we see a holiday version of this style, but here alone was there a steady influx of money and newcomers (mostly Northern). Old houses were repaired unless completely destroyed by the quake, and new ones were built in the latest style.

Victorian architecture in this country generally dates from about 1860 to 1900. Its character depends heavily on the Gothic (a romanticized English cottage or castle) and Italianate (a romanticized Italian villa) styles that were introduced here in the 1840s. Victorian, however, carried these already highly romanticized interpretations to new extremes and borrowed from Greek Revival as well. In short, it was an experiment in beautiful excess that was foreign to most of the South in those still beleaguered times. Most often, these buildings have an asymmetrical facade, with steep-pitched and multigabled roofs. Siding is a collaboration of shingle and board, interrupted by large-paned windows, and decorated with much delicate and ornate trim. Depending on the combination of these characteristics, Victorian can be divided roughly into half a dozen styles, but we'll be seeing only Queen Anne, the Second Empire or Mansard, and Folk Victorian. This last style can technically cover many of the dwellings, but it's usually applied to traditional styles that have been given a spindle-trimmed porch and gingerbread roof trim. That definition doesn't quite do justice to these unique, elaborate, raised cottages, so even as we move into the Victorian era, we'll stay with the catchall "Summerville style" in some cases.

6. 106 EAST DOTY AVENUE
Greater Summerville Chamber of Commerce, c. 1890
Open to public.
The house occupied by the chamber of commerce was first owned by the railroad. The chamber has maps and tour brochures, but is closed for lunch from 12:30 p.m. to 1:30 p.m. and on the weekends.

The chamber of commerce sells *Beth's Pineland Village*, which is also available at nearby Guerins Drugstore and Dorchester Jewelers. On Richardson

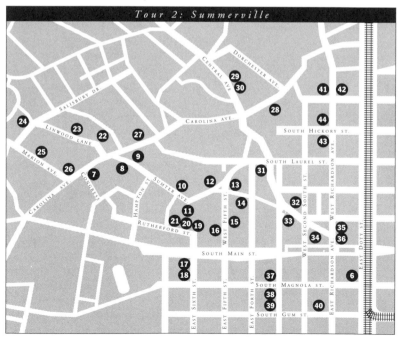

Tour 2: Summerville

Avenue is a bookstore selling Margaret Kwist's *Porch Rocker Recollections*. Between these two books, the town is well covered, but for the following tour, I also depended on my high school English teacher Clarice Foster, who edited *Beth's Pineland Village*. By all means, buy it; it's a far more detailed account than the following suggested tour. I've resisted the impulse to keep calling her "Miss Foster." She's Clarice from now on. She lives with her husband, Lang, in an 1861 cottage—but it's one hidden by shrubbery.

27.2	0.0	From chamber of commerce parking lot, turn right onto East Doty Avenue.
27.2	50 ft.	Turn right onto South Magnolia Street.
27.3	1 block	At stop sign, turn right onto East Richardson Avenue.
27.4	1 block	At stoplight, turn left onto South Main Street.
28.4	1	At stoplight, turn right onto West Carolina Avenue.

Carolina Avenue was once called the Great Thoroughfare, and later Main Street, for it went through the center of "Old Summerville." It's fairly narrow and well traveled, so watch the traffic. And I should say from the beginning that if you're interested in fine old houses surrounded by pines and azaleas, it's impossible to make a wrong turn in this area. The path we're following is just a suggestion.

28.6	2 blocks	First house on right just beyond Congress Avenue is 201 West Carolina Avenue.

7. 201 WEST CAROLINA AVENUE
Town Hall, c. 1858
Not open to public.
This Town Hall, a simple Greek Revival structure with four square "country columns," replaced an 1838 "Village Hall." The business center was here. A market stood behind this building on a street that has now disappeared. This building once more belongs to the town of Summerville.

28.7	1 block	Take first right onto Sumter Avenue (no sign).
28.8	Same block	Second house on right, 423 Sumter Avenue.

8. 423 SUMTER AVENUE, c. 1820
Not open to public.
The Summerville Preservation Society includes this street on its walking tour, and you might enjoy parking here and walking at least the next ten entries. There are many fine old residences on it. Two Gelzer brothers built three houses in a row here. We're looking at the rear of this one because it originally faced the market street. That roadway was obliterated when the railroad came in 1832, and business—and eventually the Town Hall—went elsewhere.

| 28.8 | 0.0 | Across street, on left, is site of Carolina Inn. |

9. CAROLINA INN SITE

Not open to public.

The tremendous Carolina Inn was still here thirty years ago. The 1915 building had been turned into apartments and a swimming pool was added, but it was finally replaced by a couple of new residences. In 1855, this was the site of an earlier inn, the Summerville House—a lodging that boasted a ten-pin alley and billiards room, wide piazzas, spacious parlors, and airy chambers. The clientele in that day usually rode the train from Charleston.

| 29.0 | 1 block | On left is 302 Sumter Avenue. |

10. 302 SUMTER AVENUE, c. 1896

Not open to public.

We used to call this "the House of Seven Gables." This type of Victorian architecture is often given the name "Queen Anne." Note the turret, pagoda, rounded porch, widow's walk, several steep-roofed gables, ornamentation, and finely turned porch supports. Well-known Charleston architect Albert Simons said it was one of the finest houses in town.

| 29.0 | 1 block | On right in curve is 223 Sumter Avenue. |

11. 223 SUMTER AVENUE, c. 1850s

Not open to public.

This was probably built sometime just before the Civil War. Classical Revival details embellish this "Summerville style" story-and-a-half home of the time. Because of the high ceilings, wide halls, and good ventilation, the influence of West Indies architecture has been suggested, but by this late date those were standard features of most Lowcountry homes. By the end of the nineteenth century, Victorian gingerbread had been added to the porches and roof trim of many well-ventilated houses, including those of the Caribbean, Summerville, and many other places. Three trees in the backyard are called "faith, hope, and charity."

| 29.1 | Same block | On left with iron fence is 208 Sumter Avenue. |

12. 208 SUMTER AVENUE

The Elizabeth Arden House, c. 1891

Not open to public.

Ahead on the left is a large Victorian home first used as a boarding school for "Northern Young Ladies," and tucked away beside it is one of the oldest of the early summer cottages. The handsome Victorian structure at 208 Sumter Avenue was built in 1891 by Barbadian arrival Samuel Lord, so it actually could show Caribbean influence. It's sometimes called "the Pirate House," but it was a little late for Lord to be pirating. Anyway, it's more often referred to as "The Elizabeth Arden House" after the cosmetics executive who bought it for a winter home in 1938.

29.1	**1/4 block**	**A**rrive at stop sign at corner of Sumter Avenue, Pressley, and West 5th South streets. It looks as if Sumter Avenue will run into First Baptist Church.
29.1	**0.0**	**T**urn into parking lot / street on right side of First Baptist Church onto Pressley Street / S-18-171. Drive through the Baptist church parking lot— parking lot and street are one and the same.

13. FIRST BAPTIST CHURCH, post–Civil War

Not open to public.

The First Baptist Church has a modern brick facade, but the structure is probably well over a century old. Black Baptist pastor Anthony Alston came up from Charleston and started preaching beneath a bush arbor down the street where the large new Catholic church is today. Alston served for forty-three years.

29.2	**1/2 block**	**O**n right is Wesley United Methodist Church.

14. PRESSLEY STREET / S-18-171
Wesley United Methodist Church, post–Civil War

Not open to public.

Wesley United Methodist Church is on Pressley Street, the little lane running beside the Baptist Church. (The pathway is also called Pike Hole Path, perhaps because there was good fishing in the stream at the bottom.) Another black congregation built a beautiful little Victorian church hidden away in here. The walls of the 1870s building have since been bricked in, but the ornate gable and steeple still attest to the skill of these churchgoing artisans. These little buildings are sometimes lumped together as Gothic, but this one is distinctly late Victorian.

29.2	**0.0**	**M**ake a U-turn onto other side of Pressley Street / S-18-171.
29.3	**1/2 block**	**A**t stop sign, turn left onto West 5th South Street.
29.4	**1/2 block**	**S**econd house on left is 127 West 5th South Street.

15. 127 WEST 5TH SOUTH STREET
Teacherage, c. 1882

Not open to public.

Note the cupola at the top. The center of the house has an octagonal room lit by an eighteen-foot skylight that also helped ventilation. In 1944, the school board housed teachers here, but sold the residence to author Paul Hyde Bonner ten years later. (He's probably best known for *Aged in the Woods*.)

Since Queen Victoria was around for the last two-thirds of the nineteenth century, it can be called Victorian architecture, but judging by the distinctive small gable on the piazza roof and bracketed eaves, this is a late Italianate building.

29.4	0.0	Across street on right is The Squirrel Inn.

16. 116 WEST 5TH SOUTH STREET
The Squirrel Inn, c. 1913
Not open to public.
Miss Raven Lewis built this inn, and it was operated for many years by the Sutter sisters. Ironically, real success didn't come until the 1940s when the larger inns were failing. Author Paul Hyde Bonner stayed here, used the inn in one of his novels, and moved in across the street. Today, it's condominiums and the front porch is closed, so you'll have to imagine the rockers, guests, and original facade. Across the street is the community center and the azalea-filled town park where the Azalea Festival is held each spring. Sad to say, Hurricane Hugo did its worst here in this bottomland park.

29.5	1/2 block	At stop sign, turn right onto South Main Street / U.S. 17A.
29.6	1 block	Turn left onto East 6th South Street / S-18-224. On right, facing South Main Street, is 705 South Main Street.

17. 705 SOUTH MAIN STREET, early 1900s
Not open to public.
The ballroom of this residence contained three thousand square feet. Note the "broken" pediment above the door and the substantial columns. We've moved out of the Victorian era and into the Colonial Revival period, but the surrounding veranda of an even earlier architecture remains. For years, this was the Pinewood School; it is now a seminary for the Reformed Episcopal Church.

29.6	1/2 block	On right is the Bishop Pengelley Memorial Chapel.

18. BISHOP PENGELLEY MEMORIAL CHAPEL, c. 1883
Not open to public.
In back of 705 South Main Street is the Bishop Pengelley Memorial Chapel that the seminary moved with it from its previous quarters. The distinctive little Gothic chapel was built in 1883 to serve "underprivileged whites" and is now used as an office and library.

29.6	0.0	Make a U-turn and return to South Main Street / U.S. 17A.
29.7	1/2 block	At stop sign, cross South Main Street continuing on West 6th South Street.

| 29.8 | 1 block | Turn left onto Rutherford Street. |
| 29.8 | Same block | First house on right is 102 Rutherford Street. |

19. 102 RUTHERFORD STREET, c. 1886

Not open to public.

The next three houses are strikingly different examples of post–Civil War construction, all of which could technically be called Victorian. The first, 102 Rutherford Street, is high off the ground, with an almost classical trim and dormer windows. It is closest to what we've been calling the Summerville style—cottage architecture refined, decorated, and expanded.

| 29.8 | Same block | Next house on right is 108 Rutherford Street. |

20. 108 RUTHERFORD STREET, c. 1871

Not open to public.

The next house is a design we see here a little less often. It was built about 1871 by a Charleston merchant, and it's clear the concern at that early date was still summer residency. (My parents lived in this one for years.) The veranda surrounded the house completely at one time and the ceilings are fourteen feet high. That's all ceiling—no second story. The only concessions to style are the small scalloped vergeboards (end rafters) and the double chamfered porch columns.

| 29.8 | Same block | Next house on right is 114 Rutherford Street. |

21. 114 RUTHERFORD STREET, c. 1888

Not open to public.

This house is distinctly and typically Second Empire Victorian. It is symmetrical with a mansard roof, bay windows, and French doors and windows, but porches still surround it on three sides and the ceilings are fourteen feet high as well. The Gothic style looked to medieval England, the Italianate to old Italy, but this romantic vision was French-inspired. François Mansard of mansard roof fame was a seventeenth-century architect whose style was revived during the reign of Emperor Napoleon III—the Second Empire. This was the "modern architecture" of the day.

29.9	1 block	At stop sign, turn right onto Hampton Street / S-18-74.
30.2	2 blocks	At stop sign, turn left onto Sumter Avenue.
30.3	1 block	At stop sign, cross West Carolina Avenue by veering left onto Linwood Lane / S-18-522.
30.4	First block	First house on right is 112 Linwood Lane.

22. 112 LINWOOD LANE
The Rectory, c. 1860
Not open to public.

Clarice writes that houses sometimes went by names instead of street numbers, but that's not so unusual in this case because it's "The Rectory." The church sold some of its silver and with the proceeds bought this little summer cottage around 1870.

30.5	**Same block**	**F**ifth house on right is 126 Linwood Lane.

23. 126 LINWOOD LANE
Out of Plumb, pre-1838
Not open to public.

This cottage is called "Out of Plumb" with good reason: It can claim not a single square or level corner. No exact date for construction is known, but it's listed in Hutchinson's 1838 history, so both old age and the Great Quake could be responsible for the name. My cousin Effie Wilder and her husband Frank lived in this house for years. (She co-authored *Pawleys Island—A Living Legend.*)

30.6	**1/2 block**	**A**t stop sign, look across Salisbury Drive to left for Pine Forest Inn gates.

24. PINE FOREST INN SITE
Not open to public.

This was the entrance to the old inn. Presidents Circle occupies much of the inn site today, but I can remember at least a substantial portion of the old building. Gradually collapsing, it was still filled with molding furnishings from that bygone era.

30.6	**0.0**	**T**urn left onto Salisbury Drive.
30.7	**1 block**	**A**t stop sign, turn left onto Marion Avenue / S-18-172.
30.8	**1/2 block**	**O**n left is 128 Marion Avenue.

25. 128 MARION AVENUE
Cuthbert House, c. 1825
Not open to public.

Look to your left for the old, square, two-story house surrounded by a veranda. The Cuthbert family lived here for over a century. When the house was built in 1825, cottages with second-story bedrooms under the eaves were the predominant summer-house style, so this was a cut above its neighbors. Still, the house is plain and simple, especially when compared to its finely spindled Victorian neighbor at 116 Marion Avenue. (It's a little symmetrical, but this comes close to being Queen Anne—the spindlewood variety.)

30.9	**1/2 block**	**O**n left is 100 Marion Avenue.

26. 100 MARION AVENUE, c. 1890s
Not open to public.

"Moved back, turned around, and set down," says Clarice of this villa, and so

it was. Once five and one-half feet off the ground and right on the street corner, it was relocated and handsomely restored in the 1950s. Kwist says the
house saw service as a gambling casino and as a retreat for nuns.

31.0	**End of block**	At stop sign, turn left onto West Carolina Avenue.
31.2	**2 1/2 blocks**	Turn left into St. Paul's Church parking lot.

27. ST. PAUL'S CHURCH, c. 1858
Not open to public.

The Dorchester congregation migrated here and built the first church on this
site in 1828. That building was outgrown and replaced thirty years later by
this similar one—a little larger and better finished. Weathered gravestones and
azaleas crowd in on every side. It's a handsome village church with simple portico and pediment, great arched windows, and bell tower, but Clarice points
out that the portico is Greek Revival, the windows Federal, and the bell tower
Gothic. "Eclectic" is what we call that in the tour-book business. A monument
to the Confederate dead is beside the steps. Inside, heavy columns were said to
have once supported a balcony, but now they only hold up a barreled ceiling. I
was confirmed in this church.

31.2	**0.0**	From St. Paul's Church parking lot, continue around St. Paul's white clapboard Sunday-school building on one-way drive.
31.3	**1 block**	At end of drive, turn left onto S-18-209.
31.4	**1/2 block**	At stop sign, turn left onto West Carolina Avenue.
31.8	**4 blocks**	Go straight through the light and cross Central Avenue.
31.9	**1/2 block**	On right is 517 West Carolina Avenue. HEAVY TRAFFIC—BE CAREFUL.

28. 517 WEST CAROLINA AVENUE, c. 1808
Not open to public.

Built in 1808 by Joseph Waring, this is probably the second-oldest house in
town, but summer cottages like this one would be built in pineland villages for
at least another century.

31.9	**1/2 block**	Turn left onto Dorchester Avenue / S-18-766.
32.2	**1 block**	At stop sign, turn left onto Old Postern Road.
32.3	**1 block**	At stop sign, turn left onto Central Avenue.
32.4	**First block**	Fourth house on left is 516 Central Avenue.

29. 516 CENTRAL AVENUE
The Allen House, c. 1849
Not open to public.

Once upon a time, "Miss Maria" Allen taught school here and had her students present skits on the lawn. Her son Glennie Allen wrote popular fiction in the servants' quarters. Art gallery curator Agnes Jacobs lived here, and her brother Samuel Gaillard, well known for his watercolors and silk-screens of Lowcountry scenes, still lives here.

32.4	**Same block**	On left, next door, is 510 Central Avenue.

30. 510 CENTRAL AVENUE, c. 1880s
Not open to public.

We've seen that mansard roof before on Rutherford Street, but here's a more symmetrical Victorian beauty. To make it livable, recent owners have made some major changes, but they're all on the inside and upstairs where they don't show.

32.7	**2 blocks**	At intersection of Central Avenue and South Laurel Street on right is the Summerville Presbyterian Church.

31. CORNER OF CENTRAL AVENUE AND SOUTH LAUREL STREET
Summerville Presbyterian Church, c. 1895
Not open to public.

This Summerville Presbyterian Church replaced the 1831 structure that replaced the Old White Church at Dorchester. It was built by A. J. Braid, the same contractor who did the Pine Forest Inn and the Elizabeth Arden House. Asymmetrical facade, contiguous windows, and some minor trim work—a sedate and pleasing adaptation of Victorian motifs transforms a large white meeting house.

32.8	**1 block**	On left is Epiphany Episcopal Church.

32. 212 CENTRAL AVENUE
Epiphany Episcopal Church, c. 1894
Not open to public.

This handsomely built little Victorian church was started sometime before 1894. The memorial in the churchyard is to Miss Catherine Springs, a well-educated black seamstress, who was instrumental in founding it. She also helped found a school.

32.8	**0.0**	Across street is Timrod Library.

33. 217 CENTRAL AVENUE
Timrod Library, c. 1915
Open to public.

The town of Dorchester had a lending library that was divided between those colonists heading for Georgia and those remaining behind. The last of this collection was reported being carried about in a cowhide bag by mule, before being finally divided up after the Revolution. Heir apparent but a century later was Summerville's Chautauqua Reading Circle that evolved into Timrod Literary and Library Association. It took possession of this brand-new building in 1915. Today, forty thousand volumes are here. Just looking at it makes me think of Sir Walter Scott and Robert Louis Stevenson, but maybe I was reading Classic Comics and I'm just confusing it with one of the drugstores up the street.

32.9	**1 block**	**B**ear straight onto narrow Central Avenue / S-18-523.
32.9	**0.0**	**O**n right are 143–145 Central Avenue.

34. 143–145 CENTRAL AVENUE
Tupper's Drug Store, early 1900s
Business District.
Tupper's Drug Store was built here about seven years after a fire swept this block in 1895, and most of the other buildings were built at about the same time. The drugstore was already closed in 1955, but the mortars and pestles were still in the window. Today the section is well revitalized with restaurants, boutiques, and gift shops. The Gaillard studio is here, also.

33.0	**1/2 block**	**A**t stop sign, look across Richardson Avenue to auto parts store which is 127 West Richardson Avenue.

35. 127 WEST RICHARDSON AVENUE
Mr. Cauthen's Mercantile, c. 1890s
Open to public.
Just to the left as you turn is an auto parts store that was once Mr. Cauthen's Mercantile. In 1915, it handled hardware, coffins, and groceries. It was another generation, but you could still "ask Mr. Cauthen" for hardware up until a few years ago.

33.0	**0.0**	**A**t stop sign, turn right onto West Richardson Avenue.

Business District
The business district was pretty well established as you see it by 1900. Beyond Guerin's, facing the town square, is a line of 1890s stores. If you read the metal decoration at the top of the Sires Building, you'll see that the post office was once here. A good friend of the town, philanthropist Saul Alexander, owned it for some time, and then Barshays Department Store was the main occupant. Soon it will be a shopping plaza. To our right, a new town hall overlooks the square just as the railroad's engineer predicted it would in 1832.

33.0	**50 ft.**	**O**n left, at corner of Old Main Street and West Richardson Avenue, is 140 Old Main Street.

36. 140 OLD MAIN STREET ON CORNER OF WEST RICHARDSON AVENUE
Guerin's Pharmacy, c. 1871
Open to public.
On the left is Guerin's Pharmacy. It was built in 1871, and today is run by the
nephew of Guerin's assistant.

33.1	**100 ft.**	Cross Main Street. (You're now on East Richardson Street.)

New Summerville
We've crossed over into "New Summerville." The streets are straight, and
though there are sometimes fewer trees, people made up for that by nam-
ing the roads after them. Those streets on this side of the tracks are
"South," the opposite, "North," and we can't leave town without a drive
down South Magnolia.

33.2	**1 block**	Turn right onto South Magnolia Street / S-18-208.
33.5	**2 blocks**	On right is 400 South Magnolia Street.

37. 400 SOUTH MAGNOLIA STREET, c. 1899
Not open to public.
The house at 400 South Magnolia Street is built in the Queen Anne style.
Beth McIntosh called this one "a valentine picture."

33.5	**0.0**	Across street on left is 401 South Magnolia Street.

38. 401 SOUTH MAGNOLIA STREET, c. 1860–1870
Not open to public.
The house at 401 South Magnolia Street is perhaps twenty years older than
the house at 400 South Magnolia Street and more in the Summerville style, so
they are a good comparison.

33.5	**Same block**	On left is 405 South Magnolia Street.

39. 405 SOUTH MAGNOLIA STREET, late nineteenth century
Not open to public.
This Queen Anne beauty was moved from South Main Street.

33.6	**End of block**	Turn left onto East 4th Street / S-18-354.
33.7	**1 block**	At stop sign, turn left onto South Gum Street.
33.9	**2 1/2 blocks**	On left is 210 South Gum Street.

40. 210 SOUTH GUM STREET, c. 1910
Not open to public.
This house is in the very late Victorian style, but it's impressive. We have one
last area to visit.

33.9	**1/2 block**	At stop sign, turn left onto East Richardson Avenue.

The West End

My guide says that this was the West End in the 1890s when Summerville was in its commuter heyday. A railroad executive, not wanting to walk from the nearby public station, had his own personal stop built here where he lived—"the West End."

34.6	**7 blocks**	At corner of West Richardson Avenue and South Palmetto Street, on left far corner facing South Palmetto Street, is 200 South Palmetto Street.

41. 200 SOUTH PALMETTO STREET
Linwood, c. 1883
Not open to public.

On the corner of West Richardson Avenue and South Palmetto Street is Linwood. It, too, is a gingerbread-trimmed version of the Summerville style. Julia Drayton Hastie built it as a summer home in about 1883. She was the daughter of Magnolia Gardens founder Reverend John Grimke-Drayton. Clarice says that Drayton spent much time here, and he died in this house.

34.6	**0.0**	Across street on right is 603 West Richardson Avenue.

42. 603 WEST RICHARDSON AVENUE
White Gables, c. 1890s
Not open to public.

White Gables was one of the smaller of the 1890s inns, and now, like the others, is a private residence.

34.7	**1 block**	Turn left onto West Carolina Avenue.
34.9	**1 block**	Turn left onto West 2nd Street / S-18-122.
35.0	**2 blocks**	Turn left onto South Hickory Street.
35.1	**3/4 block**	On right is 201 South Hickory Street.

43. 201 SOUTH HICKORY STREET
Judge Smith House, c. late 1880s
Not open to public.

This large Victorian home belonged to Judge H. A. M. Smith. Genealogists and historians are familiar with the judge's work, but he also designed this house—very up-to-date for the time—and was the botanist responsible for the exotic shrubbery surrounding it.

35.1	**0.0**	Across street on left is 202 South Hickory Street.

44. 201 SOUTH HICKORY STREET, c. 1880s
Not open to public.

Directly across Hickory Street is another nice Victorian—high off the ground with a front porch and dormer windows of the Summerville style.

Plenty of equally fine houses and beautiful gardens are on the opposite side of the tracks, and many more on this side, too, but I'm calling it a day, or at least a day trip. When I was twelve, the whole world lined up at that Main Street movie theater on Saturday morning to watch the weekly serial and see John Wayne shoot more Indians. The interior walls were lined with the mounted heads of numerous big game animals—the lions and the hippo were particular favorites to be harassed with popcorn. All that for a dime. Just ahead we cross the tracks. The second station has been torn down, so I guess this isn't even a whistle stop now, just a pretty suburban town. That's what they're claiming—the "Flower Town in the Pines."

————— ◈ —————

35.1	**0.0**	**T**o return to Charleston, continue on South Hickory Street.
35.2	**1 block**	**C**ross railroad tracks and turn right onto West Luke Avenue / S-18-183.
35.6	**4 blocks**	**A**t second stop sign, turn left onto North Main Street / U.S. 17A North.
37.4	**1.8**	**T**urn right onto I-26 East.
59.0	**21.6**	**E**nd of I-26 East at intersection of U.S. 17 at Exit 221 in downtown Charleston.

ADDITIONAL READING

As with the first Ashley River tour, you might enjoy Shaffer's *Carolina Gardens* and H. A. M. Smith's *Cities and Towns of Early Carolina*. A fair amount has been written about this area. For Summerville, don't forget *Porch Rocker Recollections*, with text by Margaret Kwist, photographs by Eleanor Randall, and research by Virginia Wilder; and, of course, *Beth's Pineland Village*—the articles of Beth McIntosh introduced, organized, and edited by Clarice and Lang Foster.

NOTES

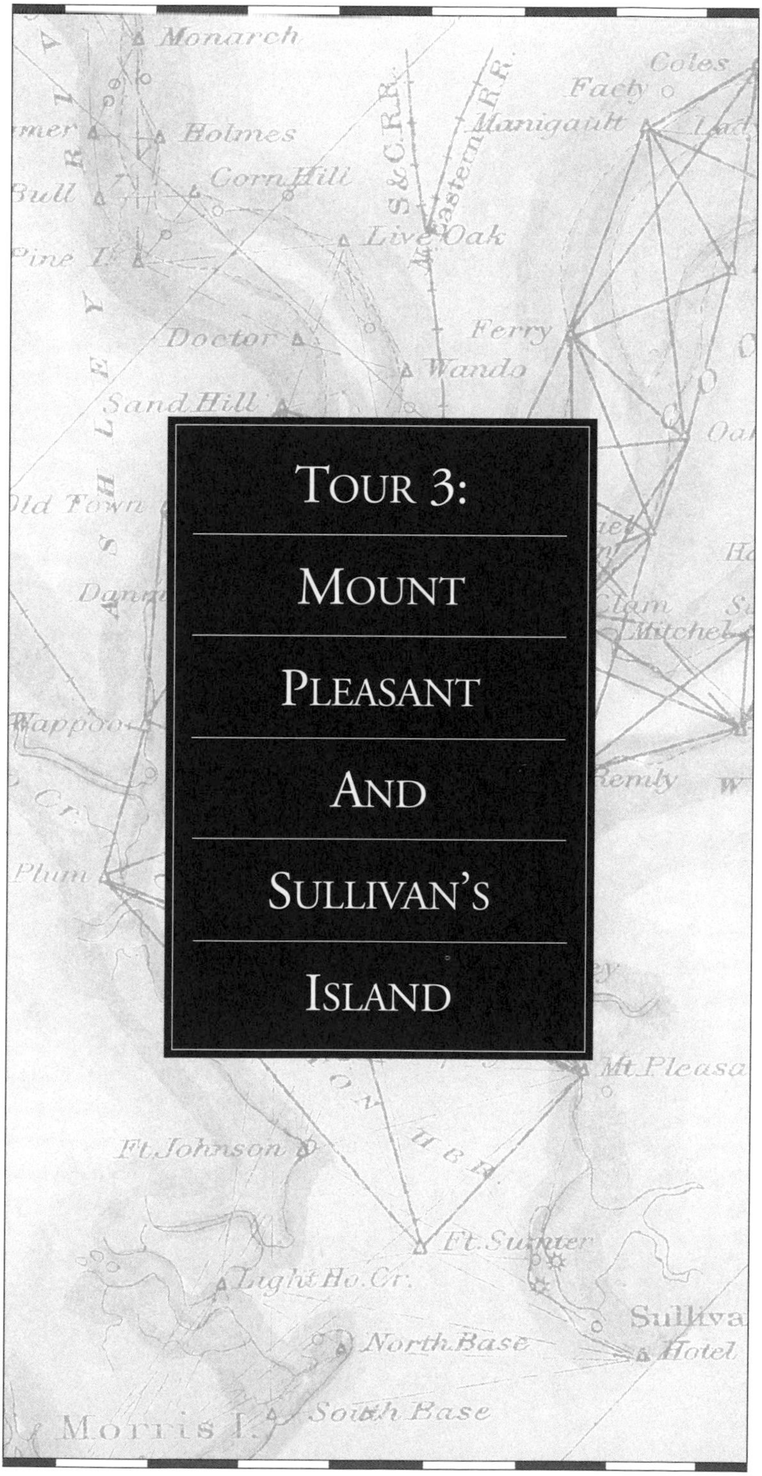

TOUR 3: MOUNT PLEASANT AND SULLIVAN'S ISLAND

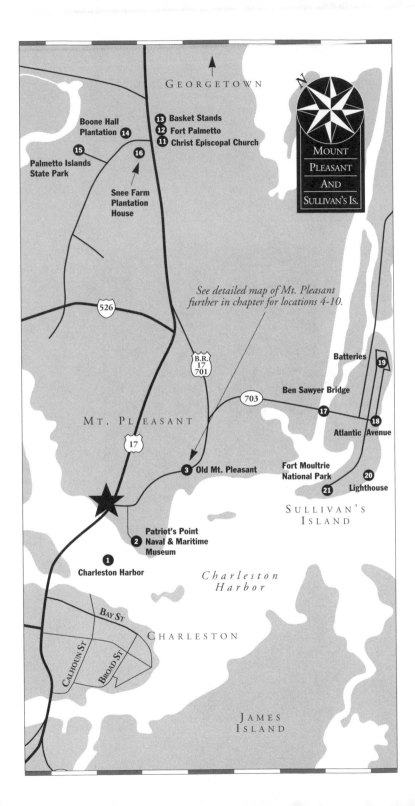

MOUNT PLEASANT

We stay fairly close to Charleston for this trip. Just across the Cooper River is
PATRIOT'S POINT, the world's largest naval and maritime museum. Close by,
we can stroll through an almost unchanged portion of the old village of
MOUNT PLEASANT. Heading north, a short drive brings us to CHRIST
CHURCH, one of the oldest churches in the state, and while in the neighbor-
hood, we can shop for sweet-grass baskets. Just off U.S. 17 is the entrance to
BOONE HALL, an antebellum plantation where house, grounds, and outbuildings are open for touring. Across the creek is PALMETTO ISLANDS COUNTY
PARK, offering a wonderful spot for your picnic lunch and an exceptional
nature walk. Another short drive brings us to SULLIVAN'S ISLAND to look at
some Victorian beach houses. We end the day on the island with a visit to
FORT MOULTRIE, a colonial fort that was in use until World War II, and is
now a national park.

Patriot's Point Naval and Maritime Museum, c. 1975

Open daily, 9 a.m. to 5 p.m. in winter, 9 a.m. to 6 p.m. in summer.
Tours self-guided.
Admission charged.

Mount Pleasant

No organized tours allowed. Walking advised.

Mount Pleasant Presbyterian Church, c. 1847

Churchyard open daily.

Christ Episcopal Church, c. 1725

Building closed except Sunday. Churchyard open daily.

Basket Stands

Open daily.

Boone Hall Plantation, c. 1681

House tour, antebellum slave cabins, extensive well-maintained gardens and
grounds, restaurant, and gift shop.

Open daily 9 a.m. to 5 p.m., 1 p.m. to 4 p.m. on Sunday; longer
hours in spring and summer. Grounds close at 6:30 p.m.
House tours every 20 minutes.
Admission charged.
Telephone: (803) 884-4371

Palmetto Islands County Park

Offers a wide variety of family-oriented entertainment, including a nature
trail. Crowded on summer weekends.

Open daily 10 a.m. to 5 p.m. (until 7 p.m. in summer). Closed New
Year's Day, Thanksgiving Day, Christmas Eve, and Christmas Day.
Admission charged.
Telephone: (803) 884-0832

Snee Farm Plantation House, c. 1754

Opening not yet scheduled.

Sullivan's Island

Beach community. Crowded on summer weekends.

Fort Moultrie National Monument, c. 1809, with later additions.
Guided and self-guided tours. Two introductory films. Observation platform
and gift shop.
Open daily 9 a.m. to 5 p.m.
Tours at 11 a.m., 2:30 p.m., and 3:30 p.m.
Free admission.

0.0   0.0

From Charleston, take U.S. 17
North across Cooper River
Bridge. Begin clocking mileage
at the north (away from downtown Charleston) side of bridge.

1. CHARLESTON HARBOR

You start the morning by crossing Charleston Harbor over the new COOPER
RIVER BRIDGE. Completed in 1966, its three lanes came just in time to supplement the 1929 bridge on our left, which in turn had replaced the ferries that
had crossed the harbor for a couple of centuries. The old bridge, named for
John P. Grace, was a wonder for its time, costing $5.7 million and fourteen
lives to complete. In 1946, a freighter dragged anchor and punched a hole in
the second span and one family perished. Otherwise, despite its narrow, twisting, camel-hump appearance, it's a safe way to travel. Crossing the old bridge
is slow in the morning, but so is crossing the new one in the afternoon.
Fortunately, we'll probably be traveling each during its light traffic hours, but
do avoid returning to Charleston between 5 and 6 p.m.

It's difficult for the driver to appreciate, but on the left is HOBCAW POINT.
It served as the colonial ferry landing and shipyard. Beyond are the white
cranes of the WANDO TERMINAL, where containerships unload the shipping
containers that convert immediately into truck trailers. The long white arch
beyond that is the MARK CLARK EXPRESSWAY that connects Mount Pleasant
with North Charleston and the rest of the state. To the right is the carrier
Yorktown and other ships of the MARITIME MUSEUM. That entire area is sometimes called Hog Island, but the actual Hog Island was a little piece of land at
the far end of this area. In the early 1700s, a substantial house and orange
orchard were advertised for sale there. The small island near the carrier is
Castle Pinckney. It started out as Shute's Folly: It's said that Shute tried to
duplicate the garden on Hog Island only to have it wash away. In the War of
1812, a fort (the second on the site) was built and named for the commander
of that war's Southern forces, Thomas Pinckney.

That is the Cooper River below, but it's also CHARLESTON HARBOR. In
colonial days it was filled with sailing ships because Charles Town was a major
port—a rival to New York and Boston. By the early 1800s, however, ships of
the day were too large to enter and there was a serious slump in commerce
that will probably never be completely overcome. There's plenty of traffic,

though—banana boats, tour ships, tugs, Coast Guard patrols, dredges, sailboats, crabbers, tourboats, containerships, and the many vessels passing to and from the naval base upriver. Most of the harbor's famous naval battles were fought around the distant Fort Sumter and Sullivan's Island. We'll get a closer look at these by the end of the day. It's said that the little 60-foot hull buried in the mud just as you exit is an early World War II experiment in cement construction. During the fall, this spot is a favorite for cast netters.

❖

0.0	**0.0**	**C**ross bridge in right lane. As bridge ends, veer right onto U.S. 17 North Business. Move into right lane marked "Mount Pleasant."
0.5	**0.5**	**T**urn right at first stoplight onto Patriot's Point Blvd. / L. O. "Bud" Darby Blvd.
1.1	**0.6**	**T**urn right into Patriot's Point parking lot.

2. PATRIOT'S POINT NAVAL AND MARITIME MUSEUM, c. 1975.
Open to public.

The centerpiece here is the aircraft carrier *Yorktown*, but there are also a destroyer, a submarine, a Coast Guard cutter, and the only U.S. nuclear-powered merchant ship. You can see the award-winning movie showing the *Yorktown* in action, take the self-guided tours, visit the aircraft exhibit, and more.

Obviously, a tour of the world's largest naval and maritime museum can easily take up a whole day. You can get a good glimpse of the complex as you cross the Cooper River, but it's not until you're here that you appreciate the size of the ships, and the carrier in particular. The 888-foot *Yorktown* was once a small town and airfield combined: During World War II she carried ninety aircraft and almost thirty-five hundred men. Today there are planes aboard for display only, and she's crewed for the most part by fellow visitors. A small printed guide and map come with your ticket, including a list of safety precautions that should be read and followed. Signs direct you up the ramp to the hangar deck. In this broad expanse, planes were once stored or repaired until the time came for them to be lifted above by one of three gigantic elevators. A gift shop sells the helpful book *The Ships of Patriot's Point*, as well as other souvenirs, and close by is a snack bar. And by all means, see the Academy Award–winning documentary, *The Fighting Lady*, being shown twice a day in the theater at your far right. The hour-long film, with its actual battle scenes shot on this carrier, helps the visitor populate the ship in his or her imagination and fully appreciate its contribution to our Pacific war effort.

The first carrier *Yorktown* was sunk by Japanese submarines in 1942, but the keel for this one had already been laid by then, and in the spring of 1943, she went to sea under the command of Captain "Jocko" Clark. She carried thirty-six fighter planes for long-range defense, and thirty-six dive bombers and eighteen torpedo bombers for attack, all of which would be put to good use. The *Yorktown* would spearhead the Fast Carrier Task Force that eventually defeated the Japanese Navy. On September 16, 1945, with the war over, she entered Tokyo Bay. In 1950 she was modified to carry jets, but reached Korea just after the war ended. Converted next to an antisubmarine carrier, she served off the coast of Vietnam. Coming home in time to recover the *Apollo 8* astronauts, she was decommissioned in 1970 and came to Charleston in 1975. You'll see evidence of this long, distinguished, and varied career as you walk the many decks, but there's still plenty to see in this hangar entry.

The most obvious attraction, of course, is the collection of planes. That's a B-52 on the far left, like the planes that Colonel Doolittle led on a successful bombing run of Tokyo in 1942. Amidships are four Navy trainers, and the small red-and-white-checked biplane hanging above them belonged to Bevo Howard, Charleston's world-famous stunt pilot. Next in line are the Corsair and the Hell Cat—the two most successful World War II carrier planes.

The remainder of the ship can be explored by following the six self-guided tours that are marked by different colored arrows. Keep your map handy, follow the arrows closely, and watch your step. Unless you're a Navy veteran, the miles of mazelike corridors can be confusing. The flight deck is three decks up, and seven decks up is the bridge—favorites for most visitors. Here, landed for the last time on this seagoing runway, are several more aircraft. The Sea Horse, a utility helicopter, looks familiar because it was in use for some time, and the same is true of the radar-equipped submarine trackers. The jets, launched by catapult down the tracks cut into the deck surface, are a little more exotic. Though they look like products of a science-fiction future, most of these Cold War–era fighters were obsolete before they were put to use.

There's a good view of Charleston Harbor from here, and powerful binoculars to aid the truly curious. *The Ships of Patriot's Point* contains a good description of what you're seeing, as well as a brief history of the harbor.

Below the hangar deck, four other tours take the visitor through a continuing labyrinth of living quarters and work areas, many of which have been turned into mini-museums and memorials. And at the very bottom is the engine room. A sign here announces that "one of the unheralded triumphs of the Navy and the young American men was being able to teach, and learn, what every pipe, every valve, every piece of equipment did and its relationship to the engineering plant as a whole." It's a triumph bordering on a miracle. A quick look at this close and complicated world of super-steam and most are ready to seek out the sunshine and sea breeze of the decks above.

In addition to the *Yorktown*, Patriot's Point is the final port of call for four other ships. The most conspicuous of these is certainly the *N.S. Savannah*. She's been called the "finest example of naval architecture to ever grace the ranks of the American merchant marines," and her sweeping lines resemble those of modern yachts and cruise ships. Named for the first oceangoing ship to rely partly on coal, this *Savannah* was the first commercial ship to use nuclear power.

She was the last as well. The cost of construction was so great that it's claimed no profit was expected. She didn't disappoint. Plagued by labor problems and a fear of radiation leaks, her operating costs continually exceeded profits, and in 1981, she was finally retired here to Charleston. There's a nautical painting exhibit in the bow, balanced in the stern by a view of atomic reactors.

Not quite so glamorous is the black-hulled Coast Guard cutter *Comanche*. (She's the only craft not open to the public.) Nevertheless, she enjoyed a far lengthier career than the *Savannah*. Serving first as an icebreaker on the Hudson River and then as a convoy escort in the North Atlantic during World War II, she ended as a pilot boat at Norfolk. A more modern cutter will soon be added to this fleet.

A visit to the submarine *Clamagore* is an experience not to be missed. A little longer than a football field, she's still hardly wider than the aisle you walk down. Entering on the stern, you step into a cramped and strange Jules Verne world where about seventy men once lived and worked. Twenty-two bunks are crowded into the aft torpedo room that we enter, and ahead, generators, air conditioners, freshwater evaporators, engines, toilets, sonar, and more bunks are all scrambled together in a baffling but no doubt lethal combination. Sadly, for all those fans of the movie *Run Silent, Run Deep*, there's no safe way to access the conning tower, so there's no periscope to peer through. You travel the length of the *Clamagore* and are reassured at the exit by a small plaque: "There are only two kinds of ships—submarines and targets."

Dwarfed by the giant carrier and pushed aside by the sub, the unimposing *Laffey* was, in fact, one of the most celebrated ships of World War II. Commissioned in February 1944, the destroyer was present at the Normandy invasion. Sent to the Pacific, she took part in several operations. Then on April 16, 1945, the ship was attacked by twenty-two kamikazes. In the nineteen-minute battle that followed, she shot down nine and assisted in downing two more, but was hit by five of the suicide squad and by three bombs as well. It was the strongest air attack on any single ship during the war, and it left the *Laffey* on fire, sinking, and with a third of her crew dead or wounded. But she survived: "The ship that wouldn't die" eventually made it back to the Pacific coast under her own power and wasn't decommissioned until 1975.

Patriot's Point entertains over a quarter of a million visitors a year and is hoping to expand its facilities even more. There's a golf course already here, and construction of a marina and harbor-side hotel has been only temporarily delayed. Group rates are available for students, and fifteen thousand scouts camped overnight on the carrier last year. In addition, two harbor tours leave from here several times a day. One goes seaward to Fort Sumter and the other

The Yorktown

upriver to the naval base. Combined with the ships, the tours can easily provide a full day of sightseeing, but after two or three hours you might be ready to give your sea legs a rest and look at something a little older—and surrounded by grass and trees.

1.1	**0.0**	**T**urn left out of Patriot's Point parking lot and retrace to first stoplight at U.S. 17 North Business.
1.7	**0.6**	**A**t stoplight, turn right onto U.S. 17 North Business / Coleman Blvd.
2.6	**0.9**	**A**fter third stoplight, cross Shem Creek Bridge.

3. OLD MOUNT PLEASANT

Before entering the old village you must cross Shem Creek (originally the Sewee Indian's *Shem ee*). Now, it's crowded with fishing boats and shrimp trawlers and lined with seafood restaurants, but a century ago, it was the port of an even more exotic fleet. Portuguese and Spanish fishing smacks were based here, and the creek was the center of a thriving oyster and terrapin business as well.

In 1793, rice mill inventor Jonathan Lucas owned a mill here; the village that grew up around it was called Lucasville until it joined Mount Pleasant in 1872. In recent years the Mount Pleasant community has grown tenfold, and the completion of the Mark Clark Expressway will no doubt mushroom it into a true city. Hidden away in one corner, however, is an old village, which in itself is a collection of villages. Actual settlement of this area began in 1680 with the arrival of an Irish soldier named Florentia O'Sullivan. Of dubious moral character and questionable ability and loyalty, he was nonetheless given "a great gun" and entrusted with the defense of this section of the harbor. Old

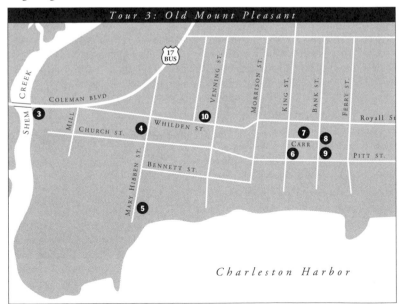

Tour 3: Old Mount Pleasant

Woman's Point, probably a corruption of an Indian name, *Oldwanus*, shows on the maps of that day, but the arrival of more settlers brought the designation of Haddrell's Point. With its high bluff and sea breeze, the area was promoted as a healthy spot by Jonathan Scott, who laid out a typical English village and was advertising lots there as early as 1766. "Extadinay [*sic*] good Water. . . A pure Air and South aspect without the least Marsh on front . . . the best Oysters and Salt Water Fish in the Province," Scott wrote, recommending it as a place of retreat "in times when contagious disease rage in town." The disease here was probably yellow fever, but planters would soon be looking for an escape from malaria as well. Entrepreneurs on both sides would follow suit during the next century, and in 1858, the results were joined together as Mount Pleasant.

Once over the Shem Creek Bridge, you enter the old village on Whilden Street. The area is primarily residential so tourists are not encouraged, but if you turn right onto Hibben Street and park at the Presbyterian church, we can keep our intrusion to a minimum.

2.8	0.2	At second stoplight, veer right onto Whilden Street.
2.8	2 blocks	Turn right onto Hibben Street.
2.9	1 block	On right is Mount Pleasant Presbyterian Church.

PARK AND WALK this tour of Mount Pleasant if the weather permits. The streets are narrow, so it can best be seen on foot.

4. MOUNT PLEASANT PRESBYTERIAN CHURCH, c. 1847
Not open to public.

The oldest in the community, this church was built by a congregation that migrated here not from Charleston but from a few miles to the north of Mount Pleasant. Before 1700, a group of New England Congregationalists was shipwrecked on the Outer Banks of North Carolina. Rescued, they settled up the coast about fifteen miles, and their descendants eventually came here to summer and then to live year-round. A chapel was built in 1827, which is a private residence today; then, in 1847, this simple meeting house was built. It's well cared for now, but during the Civil War the roof was bombed. At the war's end it was used as a schoolhouse for newly freed slaves.

2.9	50 ft.	Look right as you cross Church Street.

Look down Church Street to Shem Creek. The Georgetown Road once ended here at the HIBBEN FERRY landing, but today you'll find several seafood docks where fresh shrimp can be bought in season.

2.9	0.0	Continue on Hibben Street.
3.2	1 1/2 blocks	On left is 111 Hibben Street.

5. 111 HIBBEN STREET
The Hibben House, c. 1755
Not open to public.

This is the back entry you're looking at, disguised now by the addition of great

Victorian columns, but the simple two-story house with hip roof is still clearly evident. Jacob Motte was the builder; this was his Mount Pleasant plantation. In 1775, Colonel Moultrie erected a quick rampart in the front yard, fired on two British men-of-war, and successfully drove them from Charleston Harbor. He went on almost immediately to defend the more famous Fort Moultrie on Sullivan's Island, but he returned here to visit as a prisoner of war, and so did Cornwallis, who was using this as a headquarters. James Hibben purchased the plantation in 1803 and divided it into lots.

3.2	0.0	Continue to end of Hibben Street.
3.2	1/2 block	At end of street at the Cooper River, make a U-turn.
3.3	1 block	At stop sign, turn right onto Bennett Street.
3.5	1 block	Turn left on Venning Street.
3.6	1 block	At stop sign, turn right onto Pitt Street.

This narrow little thoroughfare leads us through what was once the business section; it was in use before the Revolutionary War.

| 3.7 | 2 blocks | Turn left onto King Street. Immediately on right facing Pitt Street is Town Hall. |

6. 302 PITT STREET
Town Hall, c. 1884
Built as a county courthouse when the village was a part of Berkeley County, this building was soon converted into a Lutheran seminary. From 1916 to 1963, it was a Baptist church, but now, it is back in government service as the arts center of the Mount Pleasant Department of Recreation.

| 3.7 | 1 block | Behind Town Hall, turn right onto Carr Street. |
| 3.8 | 1/2 block | On left is Confederate Cemetery. |

7. MONUMENT TO WAR OF 1812
This small graveyard contains the only memorial in the Southeast to the casualties of the War of 1812. See the marker for additional information.

| 3.8 | 1/2 block | At stop sign, look across Bank Street to Old Town Hall. |

8. 309 BANK STREET
Old Town Hall, c. 1890
Not open to public.
This one-story frame building served as the old Town Hall. It originally stood 50 yards northwest, facing Pitt Street, near the yellow Town Hall we just saw.

| 3.8 | 0.0 | At stop sign, turn right onto Bank Street. |
| 3.8 | 1/2 block | At stop sign, look to left at small wooden building. |

9. CORNER OF PITT AND BANK STREETS
Patjens' Post Office, c. 1880
Not open to public.

This building originally stood at the corner of Rivers Lane and Church Street. It was used as the Mount Pleasant Post Office in the late 1890s and early 1900s. The postmaster during those years was John Patjens. The building was moved to this location in 1981 and was restored by the Alhambra Garden Club.

If you are driving this tour:

3.9	0.0	Turn left onto Pitt Street.
4.0	1 block	Turn left onto Ferry Street.
4.1	1 block	Turn left onto Royall Street. At third block, Royall Street becomes Whilden Street.
4.4	4 blocks	On right is St. Andrew's Episcopal Church.

10. 440 WHILDEN STREET
St. Andrew's Episcopal Church, c. 1857
Not open to public.

The first church on this site was built in 1835 and was constructed by Bishop Theodore Dehon. The congregation outgrew the old building, and the first service in this new Gothic building was held on Christmas Day, 1857.

4.4	0.0	Continue on Whilden Street.
4.5	3 blocks	Turn right onto Hibben Street.

If you are walking this tour:

0.0	0.0	At stop sign, turn right onto Pitt Street.
0.0	3 blocks	Veer right and continue straight onto Church Street.
0.0	2 blocks	Return to parked car near Hibben Street and Presbyterian church.
4.5	0.0	Turn car around and retrace Hibben Street to stop sign at corner of Coleman Blvd. Join driving tour here.

The village has seen what many of the older residents would consider more than its fair share of changes. The broad sandy beach that ran for over a mile muddied when the harbor jetties were built. The construction of the Cooper River bridges brought residents crowding in on every side and a further subdivision of even the older section. There's still a hint of the place recalled in Miss Petie McIver's *History of Mount Pleasant*, however, so I'll let her reminiscence be the last word.

"To the villagers, their hometown was pronounced 'Mumplesson,' a creek was a 'crick,' a terrapin was a 'cooter,' and any long-legged white bird was a 'crane.' Andirons were 'dog irons,' a wharf was a 'waff,' eggplant was 'guinea squash,' lima beans were 'sibby beans,' tomatoes were 'tomattus.' Everyone said 'cyar,' 'gyarden,' and 'pam' (the resort was the 'Oil of Pams') and called their parents 'Ma' and 'Pa.'"

4.6	**0.1**	**A**t stop sign, turn right onto Coleman Blvd. / U.S. 17 North Business.
5.4	**0.8**	**T**urn left onto W 526 and continue on U.S. 17 North Business / S.C. 703.
7.5	**2.1**	**E**xit U.S. 17 North at Georgetown exit.
10.4	**2.9**	**O**n right is Christ Church. Just past church, turn right onto Old Georgetown Highway and then immediately turn right into church parking lot.

11. CHRIST EPISCOPAL CHURCH, c. 1725

Grounds open to the public.

Christ Church was one of the original ten parishes laid out by the Church Act of 1706. A wooden building erected at that time burned in 1725, and the following year this brick church was built in its place. At that time, parishioners were described as "sober, industrious, and regular attendants of public worship." This was not, however, a particularly prosperous region, boasting few wealthy planters other than the nearby Boone family. The congregation struggled to maintain services, but the building was burned by the British, and then, once rebuilt, the church was rivaled by its own Mount Pleasant Chapel. Union troops

Christ Episcopal Church

gutted the building. It was repaired once more, but services stopped in 1874. Grazing cattle knocked over tombstones, and the hubs of passing wagons wore a groove in the roadside corner of the structure. In 1923, restoration began, and in 1954 services continued.

There have been numerous changes to the little church over the years. At an early date the pews were rearranged and the side doors became windows. The cupola was added with the new roof after the Revolution and would be removed and replaced. The boxed eaves were added in this century and so was the rear addition.

Sarah Boone is buried inside beneath her pew, and other members of her family were entombed outside but close to the church. Charles Pinckney (father of the Constitution contributor) is buried at the door, the state of relative poverty he lived in elegantly defended on his tombstone. Nicolas Venning, second son of Samuel Venning who shot the British officer "Mad" Archie Campbell, rests here, and in the surrounding wooded churchyard are numerous others. Extensively restored, the little brick building was probably the vestry, but tradition says it was built to shelter waiting coachmen from rain and cold.

10.4	0.0	From church parking lot, look twenty feet to where Old Georgetown Road crosses the mounds of Fort Palmetto on both sides of road.

12. FORT PALMETTO, c. 1865

Behind the basket stand fifty yards north and just across the lane from the church is a large brush-covered mound. The lane is the Kings Highway, and the mound is a tiny section of Fort Palmetto. It once stretched across this entire neck of land and was meant to defend Charleston from invasion during the Civil War. My great-great-grandfather supervised its construction and Robert E. Lee congratulated him on a job well done, but the fort was only manned for one day. When the city was evacuated, these last-minute defenders slipped off across the Wando River. Union troops advancing from Bulls Bay stepped through the redoubt of sharpened logs and branches and bivouacked here for the night.

10.4	0.0	From Christ Church parking lot, turn left onto Old Georgetown Road.
10.4	20 ft.	Immediately turn right onto U.S. 17 North and look for basket stands.

13. BASKET STANDS

Along this section of highway you'll see dozens of "basket houses," flimsy stands made of poles and scrap lumber and tin. Here a wide assortment of sweet-grass baskets are on display and offered for sale to passing motorists. Often the basket makers can be seen practicing a craft that was brought over from Africa almost three centuries ago. The first of these early slave-made baskets were thought to be broad, shallow "fanners" that were used to fan the chaff from harvested rice. Rush, split oak, and palmetto were the materials used for fanners and several other utilitarian designs. With the end of rice cultivation about 1900, however, basket making became a more delicate and decorative artistry. Sweet-grass, sometimes accented with pine straw, became the "bundle" to be woven in place with a "binder" of narrow palmetto, and a variety of new designs was introduced. Here in the Mount Pleasant area, the work of basket makers, or "sewers," was marketed through the mail by a Charleston bookstore owner. Then, with the completion of the Cooper River Bridge in 1929, tourist traffic increased to the point that roadside stands could profitably offer the baskets directly to the consumer. Not too profitably, though. Watch the women at work and you'll realize that hours of careful craftsmanship are required to make the simplest basket—and many are far from simple. It's difficult to imagine a better souvenir of the Lowcountry or a better buy. Pieces identical to the ones hanging from these rusty nails have shown in museums all around America.

◈

10.6	0.2	Turn left onto crossover and make U-turn onto U.S. 17 South.
10.8	0.2	Turn right onto Long Point Road (just across U.S. 17 from Christ Church).
11.5	0.7	Turn right into entrance of Boone Hall Plantation.

14. BOONE HALL PLANTATION, c. 1681
Open to public.

Billed as "the most photographed plantation in America," the great white-columned Boone Hall house and formal garden wait at the end of a long avenue of majestic oaks. (It's hard to dispute the claim: On my last trip, a professional photographer and several amateurs were dodging the cars to get that perfect shot.) With the possible exception of Tara, probably no other plantation has succeeded so well in capturing the public imagination—this was the principal setting for the television miniseries "North and South," part of Alex Haley's "Queen" was shot here, and it shows up in several other movies. Boone Hall lost some pines and roof shingles to Hurricane Hugo, but it's fixed up now as good as new.

Though there is some disagreement about how much of the house is reconstruction rather than restoration, hostesses dressed in antebellum costume give an enjoyable tour of the premises. General Washington might not have sat at the dining-room table, but there's no denying that Patrick Swayze did. And there's a small display of plantation artifacts uncovered over the years.

The grounds and outbuildings of the property are certainly of interest in themselves; they tell the history of continuing use since the arrival of the first English settlers. Major John Boone was on the *Carolina* and settled on this spot in 1681. An Indian trader, he was closely linked with the resident Sewee tribe, and his purchase of Indian slaves from them and his dealings with pirates got him expelled from the colonial assembly three times. The transition to a more staid and responsible citizenship was rapid. John's son Thomas was a distinguished servant of state and church. He died in 1749 and may be buried here beside the avenue of oaks, which he first planted. John's daughter was the grandmother of two of South Carolina's most noted statesmen, John and Edward Rutledge.

The slave cabins, listed in the National Register of Historic Places, are of particular interest since few such "streets" remain. Built to shelter the house servants, the brick walls and tile roofs were a luxury, but the dirt floors, sash-less windows, and wide hearths to facilitate cooking were the norm for such quarters. Note the use of the blue "blazers"—brick singed in the kiln—as design "diapers" in the cabin wall and the especially elaborate decoration of the nearby round smokehouse.

In 1817, the Horlbeck family of Charleston bought the property. Best remembered for the construction of the Exchange Building, these master builders of Charleston operated a brickworks here and ran an extensive cotton plantation. The entrance avenue was enlarged by them in 1843, and other improvements were made. The slave cabins may date from this time as well. About the house were "miles of pasture upon which fine stock is raised . . . . the gin houses, stables, barn and dozens of little cottages where the several hundred slaves have their home—not in a negro quarter but dotted about over the country," says one account.

The scattered cottages are gone, but the remaining gin house is a gift shop and restaurant. The 1890 commissary-chapel now contains restrooms and tourist information. Fine horses, now kept in a second generation of stables and barns, still graze here, and on several Saturdays during the fall, polo is even played. (It can be watched for no extra cost.) Before the Civil War a handful of pecan trees had been planted and did well, so more were planted when the Horlbecks expanded. In 1904, Boone Hall could boast the world's largest pecan grove. Beyond the farthest of the remaining quarters is an ancient wharf that appears to have been used well into this century. Wapeckercon Creek, on which it sits, circles around the far side of the main house, and a road that can be walked or driven leads to a small black-water pond where dozens of egrets sometimes nest.

For those unfamiliar with the plantations of the Lowcountry, Boone Hall can serve as a thoroughly entertaining and unacademic beginning, and for the more serious-minded, enough original support buildings remain to satisfy. For all, there are open grounds to stroll and, of course, a valuable photographic opportunity.

———— ◈ ————

11.5	**0.0**	**R**etrace to Boone Hall entrance gate and turn right onto Long Point Road.
11.9	**0.4**	**T**urn right onto Neederush Parkway.
13.2	**1.3**	**A**rrive at Palmetto Islands County Park entrance.

15. PALMETTO ISLANDS COUNTY PARK

One of three parks run by the county, this can be the best bargain in the area. Hurricane Hugo took a thousand trees, but you wouldn't know it. More than ever, this park is a jewel. It's definitely family-oriented. There are picnic areas,

playgrounds, paddleboats, canoes, bicycles, a swimming hole, and a snack bar. On the weekends, especially during the summer, the park can get hectic. During weekday mornings (and all day during the winter), this can be a surprisingly quiet retreat. All the low palmetto- and pine-crowded islands are laced with scenic paths and boardwalks; maps are given out at the entrance. The areas at the western end (to the right of the entry) are the farthest off the beaten path, and after parking, you can begin immediately on the marsh trail that leads along the edge of Boone Hall Creek (called Wapeckercon on the far shore). Here, oyster beds show at low tide, crab-pot floats bob in the channel, and egrets and ospreys seem to be constant companions. There are plaques along the way to identify the more familiar flora and fauna, but for the most part you're left on your own to enjoy and observe.

◆

13.2	**0.0**	**F**rom park gate, retrace to Long Point Road.
14.5	**1.3**	**T**urn left onto Long Point Road.
15	**0.5**	**O**n right is Snee Farm Plantation House.

16. SNEE FARM PLANTATION HOUSE, c. 1754

Not open to public.
Through the trees you're able to glimpse the rear of the Snee Farm. Preservation groups have just succeeded in saving the house and surrounding acreage from subdivision and sale, so it will soon be open to the public. George Washington breakfasted here and, perhaps with tongue in cheek, referred to it as "Mr. Pinckney's country estate." Charles Pinckney, his host, was one of the major contributors to our country's Constitution and served four times as state governor. Since he was a strong republican and Federalist, his fellow aristocrats called him "Blackguard Charlie," but the desire to defend slavery gradually replaced his passion for a strong central government. Built in 1822, the sturdy little farmhouse with elaborately trimmed interior replaced one built by Charles's father about 1754. An Indian trader and provincial officer, he is buried at nearby Christ Church.

◆

15.6	**0.6**	**A**t stop sign, turn right onto U.S. 17 South.

16.9	1.3	Pass 526 N. Charleston exit.
18.4	1.5	Take E 526 exit on right.
20.1	1.7	At stoplight, turn left onto S. C. 703 North / Ben Sawyer Blvd.
21.9	1.8	Cross Ben Sawyer Bridge to Sullivan's Island.

17. BEN SAWYER BRIDGE, c. 1945

This bridge carries you over the Intracoastal Waterway. It was built in 1945 to replace the old trolley line bridge that you can spot on your far right, extending from Pitt Street in Old Mount Pleasant. Hurricane Hugo knocked the Ben Sawyer Bridge from its pedestal, but it was repaired quickly. Somewhere off to your distant left, a connecting bridge to the Isle of Palms is being built, but for now, this is the only link to the mainland, and the passage of a small sailboat can still back traffic up for miles.

A History of Sullivan's Island

"This island is a singular one. It consists of little else than the sea sand, and is about three miles long. Its breadth at no point exceeds a quarter of a mile. It is separated from the mainland by a scarcely perceptible creek oozing its way through a wilderness of reeds and slime." The creek has been dredged to a navigable depth now, but this description from Edgar Allan Poe's "The Gold Bug" is otherwise fitting. Poe found the setting for his gothic tale of pirates' buried treasure while he was stationed here as a young man at Fort Moultrie. He calls the architecture "miserable frame buildings, tenanted during summer by the fugitives from Charleston dust and fever." But beauty is in the eye of the beholder, for at the same time, architect Robert Mills describes it as appearing "like a city, floating upon the bosom of the wide waters, and glittering in the sunbeams."

The domestic history of the island begins in 1791. Charleston citizens in need of a place to escape the yellow fever epidemics of the city were rented half-acre lots for a penny a year. By 1800, streets had been laid out, Sunday gambling forbidden, and the pesthouse—which had previously held all the slaves entering the colony—had been closed. In 1817, the community was incorporated as Moultrieville, with its first election held in the pesthouse, now converted to an Episcopal chapel. By then, the fever epidemics of the city were so frequent that it was decided that the much-used refuge would require a police force and a school, and that only permanent buildings should be built on the lots. In 1826, Robert Mills reported two hundred houses in the village, two churches, and several excellent hotels. It was not a perfect world, however, for resident William Craft reported at about the same time that "an hour's idleness may obtain you a curlew, and having blistered your fingers you may catch a sheephead. The island air rusts metals, destroys shoeleather, and inspires verse making."

Actually, there were a few more serious problems: Hurricanes like that of 1822 did considerable damage despite the fact that many of the houses were built on piling, and the entire northern end was left abandoned because of the prevalence of malaria, or "myrtle fever." And of course, there was the Civil War, which left most of the locale flattened. Despite this, the community slowly continued to grow. Ferries had connected it with the city except during wartime, when makeshift bridges had been built. But in 1898, the development of the Isle of Palms as a resort brought with it the construction of a trolley line that crossed over from Mount Pleasant and ran the entire length of the island. (The "Station" street names are the old trolley stops.) In 1926, the system was adapted to automobile traffic and the modern world began its assault in earnest.

The island itself was inundated by Hurricane Hugo and the destruction of homes was extensive. But the islanders are gradually rebuilding—a process that's happened here more than once.

| 22.8 | 0.9 | At third stop sign, turn left on Atlantic Avenue (oceanfront). |

18. ATLANTIC AVENUE

Here we can see Victorian cottage architecture and unusual fortifications. Drive slowly; children are on the streets. During the summer, especially on weekends, the traffic is heavy.

If you want to get a good feel for the original flavor, drive down Atlantic Avenue. This was front beach once upon a time and between Station 20 and 28, there is a good concentration of turn-of-the-century cottages. Deceptively shabby (little or nothing on the island sells for under $100,000 now), these buildings ramble across small mimosa-crowded lots, with porches surrounding curious square and octagonal turrets at the corners. As a rule, at least one small wing has been added by each generation, so there's no danger of falling out of fashion. Sadly, Hurricane Hugo carried away a number of these old beauties, but fans of Victorian architecture will enjoy this street and many others inland and to the south. (Watch along Middle Street as you drive toward Fort Moultrie.) The northern end of the island contains newer homes, but many of these, like the newer houses throughout, are "tin roof" construction and blend in easily with the old.

23.7	0.9	At dead end of Atlantic Avenue, turn right onto Station 28 1/2. (Note batteries in front of you.)
23.8	0.1	At dead end, turn left onto Marshall Drive (oceanfront).
24.2	0.4	Turn left onto Station 31. On left, note batteries converted to homes.

19. BATTERIES

Scattered among all this are five tremendous batteries dating from the Spanish American War to World War II. Some have been converted into homes. One is the island library. The largest, Battery Capron or Mortar Battery, towers above the island playground. At the north end there's a good view of the ocean at Breach Inlet, but another note of caution: There's no swimming or even wading here—the inlet's currents have drowned many.

| 24.4 | 0.2 | Turn left onto Middle Street. |
| 26.1 | 1.7 | Look to the left at Station 18 1/2 for U.S. Coast Guard Station and Lighthouse. |

20. SULLIVAN'S ISLAND LIGHTHOUSE, c. 1961
Not open to public.
The old U.S. Life Boat Service buildings constructed in 1890 still stand at the base of the 1961 lighthouse. It was built as a replacement for the Morris Island Lighthouse on the far side of the harbor. At 161 feet above sea level and with 3 million candlepower, the light was the most powerful in the United States when it was built. Because of heat problems, the oxide carbon lights were replaced with a cooler system, which became automated in 1977. Boasting the only elevator and the first triangular construction, the lighthouse can be seen from fifteen miles at sea.

| 26.8 | 0.7 | Turn right into parking lot of Fort Moultrie Visitors Center. |

21. FORT MOULTRIE NATIONAL MONUMENT, c. 1809, with later additions
Fort Moultrie's History
In the first years of colonization, the notorious Florentia O'Sullivan maintained a lookout here (hence the name Sullivan's Island). For almost a century, that would be the only military function of the island. Any large draft ship wishing to enter Charleston Harbor, however, had to round the shoal, which would later be the site of Fort Sumter, and South Carolina's Revolutionary War government was quick to utilize this strategic position. "An immense pen" of spongy palmetto logs banked with sand was erected and placed under the command of Colonel William Moultrie.

Six weeks before the signing of the Declaration of Independence, the British fleet arrived and, confident of victory, crossed the Charleston Bar. Grave concern was the response of the American forces; most felt the more reliable line of defense would be that at Haddrell's Point (Mount Pleasant). "Those ships . . . will knock it down in half an hour!" a critic said of the fort. "We will lay behind the ruins and prevent their men from landing," Colonel Moultrie replied. Such drastic measures were not required, though. Nine men-of-war with three hundred guns faced off against only thirty-one cannons and four hundred men inside the fort. In the furious day-long exchange that followed, the British suffered numerous casualties and lost one ship before retreating. Charleston would not fall for another three years.

In the height of battle the Colonists' flag was shot away, and Sergeant William Jasper, under direct enemy fire, reattached it to a cannon sponge staff and raised it once more. That flag had only the crescent moon on a field of blue, but since the palmettos banked with sand had smothered the British shells before they could explode, the serviceable palm was added to the banner. And the serviceable structure was named for Moultrie.

That fort was abandoned soon after the Revolution and fell victim to hurricanes and scavengers searching for building material. A second fort built in 1804 met a similar fate, but in 1809, a new brick structure was finished. This construction, with 138 years of alterations, is what is maintained today by the U.S. Park Service.

A surprising number of celebrities passed through the fort's sally gate. Osceola, the Seminole Indian chief, is buried here. Archaeologists are certain of that because the remains had no head. It was carried off by the attending physician, supposedly for scientific reasons, but he reportedly hung it on his children's bedpost to frighten them. Edgar Allan Poe was stationed here and used the setting in his writing. Abner Doubleday, who may have invented baseball, served here under Major Robert Anderson. Once when he was moved to nearby Fort Sumter, Doubleday took aim and fired a Union cannonball into the Moultrie House Hotel. General Sherman himself was stationed here. Some say that's why he spared Charleston on his march. George C. Marshall was in charge at Fort Moultrie in 1933, and promised, "I'm going places." He was Army chief of staff six years later.

The Tour and More History

Tours begin in the new Park Service building across the street from the fort. An introductory slide show begins on the hour and a movie for the younger at heart, on the half hour. Guided tours are conducted three times a day, but you're given a detailed brochure that allows you to explore on your own. The gift shop sells a more thorough handbook, *Fort Moultrie.* On the roof, an observation platform provides a good view of the surroundings.

Fort Moultrie has been restored so that the visitor can virtually walk through time. We enter the sally gate and turn left to visit the World War II Harbor Entrance Control Post tower. Then, moving right, we come in turn to the fortification and cannons of the Spanish American War, post–Civil War, Civil War, and the early 1809 construction. Though the fort continued to serve as a principal means of coastal defense throughout this period, it was only during the Civil War that actual combat occurred. Major Anderson crossed over to Fort Sumter, and Fort Moultrie was occupied by Southern forces, who aided in the bombardment of Anderson's new stronghold. Fort Moultrie remained a key to the harbor's defense, keeping the blockading forces at bay, especially the menacing new ironclads, and guarding Charleston's flank. The fort was not abandoned until the city was evacuated in 1865.

In the years that followed, Moultrie was continually upgraded as cannons became more powerful and the concepts of coastal defense changed. Guns that disappeared from view when not being fired and the spreading of the batteries throughout the island were the last of these innovations. By the conclusion of World War II, it was obvious that the defense of mainland America could be handled best from ships and planes. Today, park visitors may watch giant black Polaris submarines slip out to sea—a defense of Charleston Harbor that now begins deep beneath the surface and thousands of miles away.

Besides the fort, the park has several less publicized amenities to offer. The best bird watching on the island can be found in the open fields and dunes in front of the fort, and paths have been made that lead to the beach. You're well into the harbor at this point, and it's a nice walk. Before the Civil War, conchologist Dr. Edmund Ravenel and the better-known Louis Agassiz had their "seaside laboratory" here, but you'll find the shells scarce today. Osceola's grave is just to the right of the sally gate. Behind the Park Service building on the back side of the island is the relocated grave of General Moultrie, and beyond that, a large concrete dock that gives a good view of Poe's "slime and reeds."

From the observation deck of the building, you can take an even better look around. Across the harbor, the well-known Fort Sumter is easy to spot, but just a few blocks to the south once stood the infamous "pesthouse"— the Ellis Island of American blacks, 40 percent of whose ancestors are estimated to have passed through quarantine here. Offshore and beneath the waves are the remains of unsuccessful blockade runners that ran aground when capture proved inevitable, and beneath the sands lie the sunken hulls of the Union's "stone blockade." The two-mile-long strips of black rock protruding from the waves are the Charleston Jetties. They're the work of Quincy Adams Gillmore, who served here in the Corps of Engineers during the Civil War and returned in 1878 to begin the seventeen-year-long project. Gillmore's plan was only an educated guess, but it proved correct. The two curved underwater sections of the jetties, beginning here and on the opposite Morris Island, allow the incoming tide to pass over, but funnel the outgoing tide in a scouring path through the channel between the visible rocks. More controversial have been the side effects: It appears that since the jetties' completion, Sullivan's Island has grown considerably, but Morris Island and Folly Beach to the south have eroded, and Mount Pleasant has lost its beach. Be that as it may, you won't find a better place than this to watch the great variety of oceangoing vessels that pass through the jetties in a steady stream.

On the far right, standing well out at sea, is the Morris Island Light. Pitch had been burned here as a signal from the earliest days, and in 1767, the first lighthouse was built. The one you see now was erected in 1870—the 264 pilings driven into rock beneath it allowed it to withstand hurricanes and earthquakes, and finally, the washing away of the island. On your far left is the new Sullivan's Island Light. Erected in 1960, its triangular shape has a steel framework covered with aluminum strips. The stairs are supplemented by an elevator and the light is aided by a radio beacon. The fort closes down at dark, so if you want to watch the light, you'll have to do it from elsewhere. And don't forget to go home eventually. As local islander and historian W. W. Wannamaher, Jr., warns, "It's a nice place to visit, but I would not want to live anywhere else."

———————— ❖ ————————

26.8	0.0	To return to Charleston from Fort Moultrie Visitors Center parking lot, turn left onto Middle Street.
28.0	1.2	Turn left onto Station 22 1/2.
28.0	1 block	Junction of S.C. 703 South; continue straight on Ben Sawyer Blvd.
30.7	2.7	At second stoplight, Ben Sawyer Blvd. becomes S.C. 703 South Business.
31.9	1.2	Cross Shem Creek Bridge.
33.3	1.4	Arrive at base of Cooper River Bridge and junction of U.S. 17 South.

ADDITIONAL READING

Surprisingly little has been written about the Mount Pleasant area, but there are Petie McIver's *History of Mount Pleasant, South Carolina*; Anne King Gregorie's *Christ Church Parish*; and W. W. Wannamaher, Jr.'s *Long Island South*. They can be found in local libraries. *The Fort Moultrie Handbook* includes a bibliography, but omits Milby Burton's book on harbor defense during the Civil War. Patriot's Point publishes a quarterly newsletter; to subscribe, write to P.O. Box 986, Mount Pleasant, S.C. 29464.

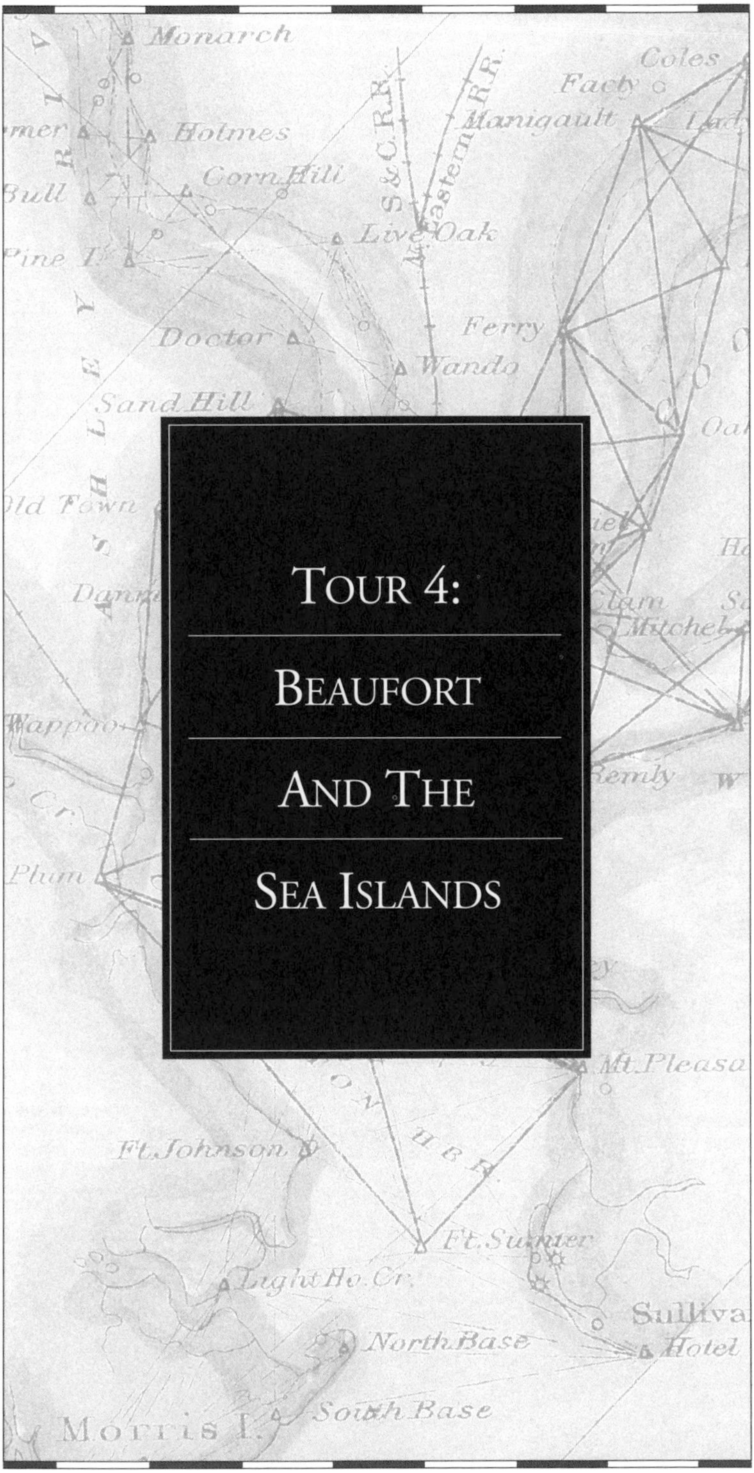

Tour 4:

Beaufort and the Sea Islands

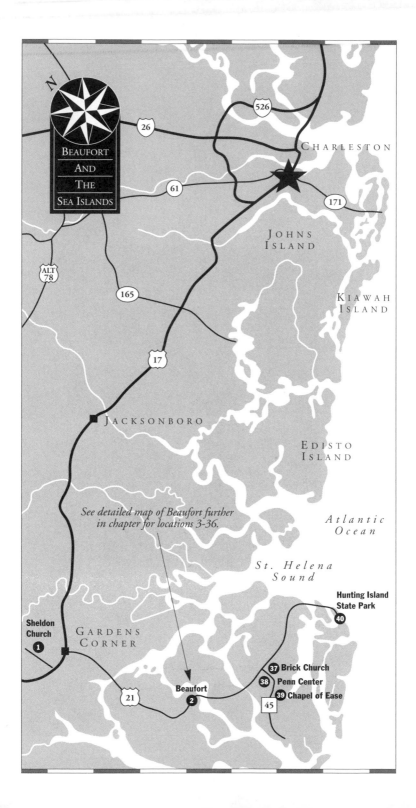

BEAUFORT AND THE SEA ISLANDS

We begin this tour by heading south on U.S. 17 for about an hour to visit the ancient and beautiful ruins of SHELDON, "the second best church in the province." Then a short drive toward the coast brings us to BEAUFORT, the second-oldest town in the state. Its architecture, especially from the Federalist and Greek Revival periods, easily rivals that of Charleston, and we're free to spend most of the day wandering the quiet streets. There's a quaint museum to visit, and two museum houses and two fine churches are open to the public. Next we cross over the Beaufort River to the once-isolated Sea Island of ST. HELENA and visit PENN CENTER, a school started for freed slaves during the Civil War that now operates as a community center. The trip ends beside the ocean at HUNTING ISLAND STATE PARK, a facility that includes a Sea Island museum, historic lighthouse, nature trails, fishing pier, and, of course, miles of beaches. To fit this tour into one day, start early and enjoy your day in the Lowcountry.

Sheldon Church, c. 1751
Open daily.

Beaufort

Founded in 1711. An active chamber of commerce offers lectures and maps. Open to the public are two antebellum houses, two handsome churches, a bayside park, national cemetery, and quaint museum. Walk or drive slowly along quiet, tree-shrouded streets to view some of the best Federalist and Greek Revival architecture in the state.

Beaufort National Cemetery, c. 1863
Open daily.

Information Center, Greater Beaufort Chamber of Commerce

Brief introductory lecture and tour maps available.

*Open daily, Monday through Saturday, 9:30 a.m. to 5:30 p.m.;
Sunday, 10 a.m. to 5 p.m.*

Henry C. Chambers Waterfront Park
Open daily.

The George Parsons Elliott House Museum, c. 1840

*Open 11 a.m. to 2:30 p.m., Monday through Friday.
Admission charged.*

The John Mark Verdier House, c. 1790

*Open 11 a.m. to 3:30 p.m., Tuesday through Saturday.
(Closed mid-December through January.)
Admission charged.*

The Beaufort Arsenal Museum, c. 1795

An entertaining collection of curious Beaufortonian collectibles.

*Open 10 a.m. to 12 noon and 2 p.m. to 5 p.m., Monday through Friday;
10 a.m. to 12 noon on Saturdays.
Admission: Free, but donations are accepted.*

Baptist Church of Beaufort, c. 1844

Open 9 a.m. to 4 p.m., Monday through Saturday; closed to public on Sundays.

St. Helena's Episcopal Church, c. 1724
Open 10 a.m. to 4 p.m., Monday through Saturday; closed to public on Sundays.
Penn Center, c. 1864
Grounds open daily. Tours available.
Museum and Library: Open 9 a.m. to 5 p.m., Monday through Friday.
Hunting Island State Park
Miles of ocean beach. Visitors center with Sea Island museum featuring exhibits on local flora and fauna, history and commercial fishing. Swimming, beach combing, cabins, fishing, nature trails, a historic lighthouse, marsh boardwalk, and fishing pier.
Open daily, daylight until dark. Admission charged.
Getting There
Though we travel U.S. 17 South on several other tours, we'll use this one to mention the historical markers passed and the other points of interest.

❖

0.0	0.0	From Charleston, take U.S. 17 South. Begin clocking mileage from south side of Ashley River Bridge.
5.9	5.9	Turn left into Clemson Coastal Agricultural Station parking lot. (Use caution when crossing northbound lane of U.S. 17.)

Clemson Coastal Agricultural Station has a small ornamental garden, which is open to the public.

5.9	0.0	From Clemson Coastal Agricultural Station parking lot, cross northbound lane and turn left onto U.S. 17 South.
9.2	3.3	Red Top Community.

Red Top was a boom town in the phosphate mining days, but the little community has calmed down since.

10.0	0.8	Cross Rantowles Creek.
10.0	80 feet	On right, William Washington Historical Marker.

William Washington, a cousin of the first president, fought the British under Tarleton at Rantowles Bridge and is buried nearby.

12.9	2.9	On right is the Tea Farm.

The Old Tea Farm at this location will soon be a county park.

14.7	1.8	To the right is a section of the Old Jacksonboro to Charleston Road, which is now eclipsed by U.S. 17.

14.7	0.0	Continue on U.S. 17 South; as you enter Ravenel, watch speed limit for 2.2 miles.
22.3	7.6	On left, note railroad running parallel to highway.

The Rail Line running parallel to the highway was completed on the eve of the Civil War, and the Union spent most of that war trying to capture it.

28.4	6.1	Cross Edisto River.
28.8	0.4	Turn right into Edisto Nature Trail parking lot; note historical marker for Old Jacksonboro.

Jacksonboro, once the capital of South Carolina, and the EDISTO NATURE TRAIL are featured in Tour 8.

28.8	0.0	From parking lot, turn right onto U.S. 17 South.
28.9	0.1	On right, in fenced-in pasture, is location of old capitol building.
35.2	6.3	Cross Ashepoo River.
35.3	0.1	On left, historical marker for Edmundbury Chapel of Ease.

The Edmundbury Chapel of Ease was named for landgrave Edmund Bellinger. A chapel was built here in 1758, which collapsed by 1810, and its replacement was burned by Union troops.

36.3	1.0	On left is turnoff for Bear Island.

Bear Island is a wildlife management area that is sometimes open to the public, and its 3,747 acres of impoundments (former rice fields) draw a large number of ducks. There are eagles and storks as well, but that's a day's trip in itself. (Please see "Additional Day Trips in the Lowcountry" on page 279 for details.)

43.8	7.5	Cross Cumbahee River Delta.

The Delta Rice Fields are on both sides of the road; the indentions and rises are the old canals and dikes. Now this area is well known for duck hunting and fishing. We're now in the vicinity of the ACE Basin. Named for the Ashepoo, Cumbahee, and Edisto rivers, the ACE Basin consists of 54,000 acres of river basin land (both state and privately owned) protected by conservation easements.

———— ◈ ————

45.1	1.3	Cross Cumbahee River.
51.2	6.1	Turn right onto Old Sheldon Church Road / S-7-21.
52.7	1.5	Pull off onto right-hand side of road and park near Sheldon Church ruins.

Sheldon Church

1. SHELDON CHURCH, c. 1751
Open daily to public.

Aficionados of ruins will find none better than those of Sheldon Church. Built under the direction of Governor William Bull, it was considered at the time "the second best church in the province and by many esteemed a more beautiful building than St. Philips." On the Sabbath, the Bull family entertained the entire congregation ("seldom less than 60 or 70 carriages") at their nearby Sheldon Plantation. England's Prince William, for whom the parish was officially named, could hardly compete. The British under General Provost burned the building in 1779, but the existing walls and columns were built upon in 1824. William Grayson reported that "they turned a beautiful ruin into a very ugly church," but this situation was remedied by Sherman's troops, who used the building for a stable and then burned it once more.

Note the six engaged columns running down each wall, for this represents the earliest attempt in America to emulate a Greek temple. The small holes you see in the walls are "put-log holes," which once held the scaffolding for the bricklayers. Repeated burnings have caused the plugs to pop out. Note, too, the brickwork. The blue glazers that are placed in a diamond pattern beneath the portico are used to spell out the date of construction on the rear wall, and on the sides are staggered as decoration. The cut bricks about head level in the attached columns are called "hogs in the wall" and suggest that at one point the columns may have been covered with stucco, which has weathered or been cleaned away.

Scattered around the grounds are about a dozen early tombs, the majority belonging to the Bull family and their descendants. Their family coat of arms, now badly worn, decorates one gravestone—an armed sword above the figure of a bull and the motto, "God is cortues," which translates, "God is gracious."

———— ◈ ————

52.7	**0.0**	**T**urn around and retrace Old Sheldon Church Road / S-7-21 to U.S. 17.
54.2	**1.5**	**T**urn left onto U.S. 17 North / U.S. 21 South.
54.5	**0.3**	**V**eer right onto U.S. 21 South.
59.0	**4.5**	**C**ross Whale Branch River.

Whale Branch River was named for an unfortunate leviathan trapped in these waters.

64.8	**5.8**	**O**n left is entrance to Marine Corps Air Station.

| 66.1 | 1.3 | Continue straight, but to right is S.C. 280 South, which leads to Parris Island Marine Base, where there is a museum. |
| 68.5 | 2.4 | Turn left into Beaufort National Cemetery. |

2. BEAUFORT

In 1520, the Spanish explored the area. Captain Jean Ribaut settled a small band of French Huguenots here in 1562, but this ended in disaster. Attempting to sail back to France in a homemade boat, the few surviving adventurers were forced to resort to cannibalism. The Spanish returned in 1566, and for twenty years maintained a fort and mission. When they left the area, they continued to consider it part of their domain. In 1663, William Hilton explored the area for the English Lords Proprietor, giving a glowing account to his employers. To posterity, he left the island name "Hilton Head." This Port Royal locale was the official destination of the English in 1670, but because of hostile Indians they chose the Charles Town location instead. A party of Scots settled here in 1685, but the Spanish destroyed their Stuart Town the following year. In 1711, two of the colony's most ambitious Indian traders, Thomas Nairne and "Tuscarora Jack" Barnwell, urged that a town be built here once more. Four years later, the Yemassee, instigated by the Spanish, killed most of the settlers in the region and burned this infant community. Most of Beaufort's occupants luckily escaped to a seized ship that happened to be in the harbor. The Indians would continue to raid the area for another dozen years, but the town was rebuilt almost immediately. Indigo production, shipbuilding, and rice planting replaced Indian trading and prosperity followed.

During the Revolution, Beaufort fell to the British. Neither partisan general Francis Marion nor his lieutenant Daniel Horry were overly impressed by the ardor or abilities of her patriots. But nearby resident Thomas Heyward had signed the Declaration of Independence, and there were enough like-minded individuals about to allow for some bitter fighting between Tories and Rebels. Sea Island cotton brought even grander wealth soon after the Revolution, along with more slaves and secessionist fever. Planters built summer homes here of grand proportion. Robert E. Lee considered the Sea Islands indefensible, and rightly so, for the two small forts at the mouth of Port Royal Sound could only slow down the Union armada for a single day. (The ninety-plus ships represented the largest concentration of firepower ever assembled by man.) Beaufort was hastily abandoned and occupied by the Union, who used it as the main base for the blockading of the other Southern harbors. The houses used for hospitals, administrative buildings, and quarters escaped destruction, but most were lost by their owners since they were confiscated for unpaid taxes.

In the years after the Civil War, a living could be made from phosphate and cotton, and the community gradually began to revive. The hurricane of 1893 swept through the area, though, killing thousands on the Sea Islands, and by 1919, the boll weevil had brought economic disaster to the region. As elsewhere, truck farming and seafood harvesting took up the slack, and the payroll from the nearby marine base gave much-needed revenue. Today, Beaufort and the surrounding islands are in the midst of a land boom, and resort communities are quickly taking the place of plantations.

3. 1601 BOUNDARY STREET
Beaufort National Cemetery, c. 1863
Open to public.

Though the world remembers Abraham Lincoln's address dedicating the Gettysburg Cemetery, many don't realize that there were nine other national cemeteries. In 1862, Beaufort fell to the Union, and the following year this plot was set aside. Bodies were brought in not only from the local battlefields and the town's own hospitals, but from all along the Southern Seaboard. Ironically, fever was the biggest killer, not bullets. The small stones radiating from the entry are usually marked with only a name and place—Illinois, Indiana, New York, Ohio—but some are more anonymous—"U.S.A. soldier," or just "U.S.A." And many are simply unknown. At the end of the Civil War there were 3,789 graves (estimates vary), but now they've been joined by almost 7,000 veterans from our country's other conflicts. Look, there in the

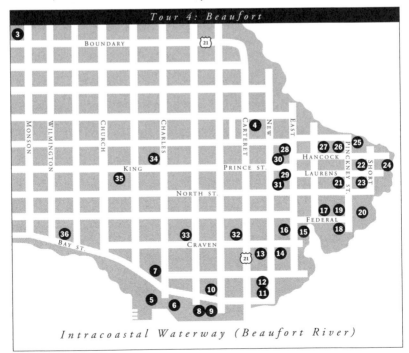

Tour 4: Beaufort

Intracoastal Waterway (Beaufort River)

distance, just beyond the center rows. Certainly unique to the Lowcountry, and perhaps to the entire South, Beaufort has a monument to the Union dead but none to the Confederate.

68.5	0.0	**R**eturn to cemetery entrance; turn left onto Boundary Street / U.S. 21 South Business.
69.0	10 blocks (0.5)	**A**t dead end, bear right onto Carteret Street / U.S. 21 South Business.

As you drive down Carteret Street, the scenery gradually shifts from aluminum and concrete to tabby, brick, and wood.

Street Names

The street names, as is often the case, can be read like a history text. Revolutionary War heroes Greene and Washington are farthest out, and then we'll see names "emblematic of British royalty"—Duke, Prince, and King. Carteret was a proprietor patron at the time of settlement, as was Craven, and elsewhere are streets named for American statesmen like Laurens, Baynard, and Hamilton. But a few have been changed from the original, for following the Civil War, people complained of names "swept away by the ruthless hands of the late tax commissioners who . . . seem to have taken fond delight in the over-throw and eradication of everything." We'll walk down Federal Alley later in the day.

69.2	3 blocks	**O**n left is The Old Beaufort College.

4. 800 CARTERET STREET

The Old Beaufort College Building, c. 1852

Open to public.

This unusual Greek Revival building is now being used by the University of South Carolina. The original college started as a preparatory school in 1795 and moved to these new quarters in 1852. After the Civil War it was used by the Freedman's Bureau, then as a private school, and then a public one before getting its current tenants. Still bemoaned today is the loss of the college's library. Saved from marauding treasury agents, this war booty was stored in the Smithsonian Institution for safekeeping, but that section burned and the books and papers were lost.

Books

Books were serious business in Beaufort in times past, as Robert Barnwell explains in his best-known poem:

> *On summer morns they loved to read;*
> *On summer eves to float,*
> *Woe to the man who had no books*
> *Or chanced to have no boat!*
> *For Beaufort was a strange old town*
> *In those old days remote,*
> *One had to have a library;*
> *One loved to have a boat.*

69.6	**7 blocks**	Turn right onto Bay Street.
69.8	**3 blocks**	Turn left into Information Center, Greater Beaufort Chamber of Commerce. (Information Center has 15 minute parking, but there's free 2 hour parking farther down Bay Street.)

5. 1006 BAY STREET
Information Center, Greater Beaufort Chamber of Commerce

Look alert. The receptionist admits she judges her audience by body language and tailors her lecture to suit the attention span of the listener. In addition, there are several good books for sale here, probably the most essential being *A Guide to Historic Beaufort*. It has a map and short history of ninety places of interest. The buildings are beautiful and interesting and the live oaks are as sprawling and moss-draped as any in the world. Though it is possible to drive, walk through the town as much as possible.

69.8	**0.0**	Behind the Information Center and next to the water is the Waterfront Park.

6. HENRY C. CHAMBERS WATERFRONT PARK

This six-acre waterfront park is just behind the chamber of commerce building. You'll find a brief history of the area cast in brass, and for the less studious there's a seawall promenade, as well as picnic tables, a playground, and even porch swings.

69.8	**0.0**	Walk across Bay Street from the Information Center parking lot to Elliott House.

7. 1001 BAY STREET
The George Parsons Elliott House Museum, c. 1840

Open to public.

This Greek Revival mansion is a good example of what has been referred to as the "Beaufort style" of architecture. Built by Elliott on the eve of the Civil War, it was occupied by one of the community's richest men, Dr. W. J. Jenkins. Confiscated and used as an Army hospital, it was then sold for taxes. A century later, the Bank of Beaufort purchased the home and arranged for it to become a house museum operated by The Beaufort Historical Foundation. The floor plan is the traditional Georgian one with a central hallway containing a fine staircase. The ceilings are high and decorated with gilded cornices and moldings. The mantels are of Italian marble. Much of the furniture is from the period when Dr. Jenkins shared the house with his wife and eight daughters, and all of it is considered exceptionally fine. From the outside the house can be enjoyed for its fanlight door and original iron banister and, of course, the massive columns, which are a hallmark of the Beaufort style.

The Beaufort Style

Just as Charleston's population made use of its location and climate by developing the familiar single and double houses, here in Beaufort a distinctive accommodation evolved that was best suited to the surroundings.

Beaufort

These houses are usually free-standing, on relatively large lots, on high foundations, and face directly into the southerly breeze. The floor plan is often T-shaped, with a wing off the back, and two small projections off the side to bring the breeze into the rear rooms. The roof is shallow and hipped and often eclipsed completely by the giant porticoes of the front. These great Greek Revival columns had been preceded by the much lighter construction of the Federalist period and then by piazzas stacked on smaller columns of "superimposed orders." Most houses did have double piazzas, but be on your guard, architecture buffs, for changes have been made. The Elliott house began with only one piazza. The second-story porch was added about 1900, and alterations to other houses are even more dramatic. The impulse to conform to the Beaufort style has been so great that Federalist, Italianate, and Victorian buildings have sometimes been completely refaced.

69.8	**0.0**	**A**fter visiting Elliott House, cross the street and turn left on Bay Street. Enter business district.
70.0	**1 block**	**O**n right is the John Cross Tavern.

8. 808–812 BAY STREET
The John Cross Tavern
Open to public.

There's no exact date, but the tavern has been around for a very long while (or at least the name and site have). Pirates dropped by. Methodist founder John Wesley spent the night here in 1735. Biographer Parson Weems, who invented the story of George Washington and the cherry tree and took even more liberties with Francis Marion, died in one of the upstairs rooms. A tavern, a bookstore, and a restaurant now occupy the building.

70.0	**Same block**	**N**ext door, on right, is 802–806 Bay Street.

9. 802–806 BAY STREET
The Rhodes House, c. 1800
Not open to public.

A thriving shipyard was once run here, and the three-story building also saw service as a customhouse, hotel, and commissary before becoming a Belk's department store. It now awaits an uncertain future.

| **70.0** | **Same block** | **O**n left of Bay Street and across the street is 801 Bay Street. |

10. 801 BAY STREET
The John Mark Verdier House (The Lafayette Building), c. 1790
Open to public.

The Historic Beaufort Foundation did a wonderful job of restoring and furnishing this home, and its guide gives an excellent tour. The son of Purrysburg Huguenot immigrants, builder Verdier was only twenty-six when he made this architectural statement—success attained. (He later moved to Charleston and went bankrupt.) The house was a Union headquarters during the Civil War, and in later years was used as a fish market, icehouse, law office, and barbershop. The telephone office was in the grand second-story drawing room. In 1942, the structure was condemned, but the Marquis de Lafayette, on his tour of the South, had briefly addressed the citizens from this portico, so "The Committee to Save the Lafayette Building" did just that, and the foundation took over in 1968.

Note the woodwork of the interior, the graceful stair, and the familiar Federalist Venetian or Palladian window. Upstairs there's one strangely rustic bedroom, and then a second-story drawing room with elaborate Adam brother mantels. Upstairs entertaining was still in vogue, but not for much longer. Imagine the dancers at the ball, the Union officers staring at the harbor, the telephone operators listening in.

Beaufort and the Adam Brothers
The Adam brothers, Robert and James, had contributed dramatically to English architecture thirty years earlier when they turned from the massive decoration of Italy's Palladian villas to what they claimed were the more delicate and graceful lines of true Roman design. Interiors were affected most, but exteriors changed as well, and much of what we think of as Federalist (1780–1830) is Adam inspired. The double portico of the Verdier house has been altered slightly since 1865, but take a good look at it anyway. We also see this on Drayton Hall, then refined on Charleston's influential Miles Brewton home, until finally here in Beaufort the central bays (the fanlight door and glass door) are framed by a far more delicate but still perfectly proportioned portico. These porticoes are almost as distinctively Beaufort as the double piazzas. There are four more houses in town like this, two of them of tabby. Judging by their interiors and apparently early construction dates, Mills Lane writes, "Beaufort was ahead of Charleston in adopting the new Adam style."

Tabby
You'll notice that many of the house foundations like this one are of tabby—an aggregate of broken oyster shell and oyster-shell lime. It was a favorite in fort construction, but not so often used in houses. Here on the Sea Islands, clay for bricks wasn't as plentiful as on the mainland, but the Beaufort residents seem to have used tabby even when brick was available. Building with it was an art. Forms like those used in modern concrete work held the mixture while it hardened; the forms were then raised higher and higher until as many as three stories

had been built. The recipe still exists, but no one has had much luck in duplicating it, and even here you'll notice that salt or chemical reaction breaks down the shell. Still, these buildings are probably the best preserved in the country.

70.0	**0.0**	After visiting the John Mark Verdier House, continue on Bay Street.

At this point, you may want to return to the parking lot and continue the tour in your car, but I hope you will want to continue walking, as the town is so beautiful when viewed on foot.

70.1	**1 block**	Cross over Carteret Street, and on right is The Point.

The Point

You're entering an area thick with moss-draped oaks, flowering shrubs, and grand old homes. If you have only a limited time, the chamber suggests you spend it here. This was once called Black Point, and then Sams Point after the family that had settled on nearby Dawtah Island. The first, William Sams, was a Tory seeking a "healthier climate," but he arrived just in time to begin planting Sea Island cotton. His two sons would grow rich and proliferate, and the family would build fine town houses. It's just "The Point" now, though; the "Sams" has been dropped, and the first two houses only date from 1907—the year a raging fire got this far.

70.1	**Same block**	Last house on left is 601 Bay Street.

11. 601 BAY STREET
Lewis Reeve Sams House, c. 1852
Bed-and-breakfast.

Built by Lewis Reeve Sams, this particularly fine example of the Beaufort style was saved from the 1907 fire when the workers in a nearby cotton gin formed a bucket brigade. Note the marble entry stairs and the use of Doric and Ionic columns rather than the single pillar, soon to be popular. If you're spending the night, you can see black marble mantels and exceptional plaster work.

70.1	**0.0**	At end of Bay Street, turn left onto New Street.
70.1	**1 block**	On the left is 214 New Street.

12. 214 NEW STREET
The Thomas Hepworth House, c. 1717
Not open to public.

Built by the chief justice of the colony, Thomas Hepworth, this is the oldest house in town. It's said the slits in the foundation were for Indian fighting, which is probably true. This corner was the first four lots to be granted after the massacre by the Yemassee. The Proprietors were requiring thirty-by-fifteen-foot houses to be built within two years of lot purchase, and that's probably what lies at the center of this little "Dutch building." Note the massive chimney. It appears to have four flues but is actually only one.

This interesting little house has an interesting history; Whitney's cotton gin was demonstrated inside. Called "the Temple of the Sun," it was long associated with the Masonic order and also shows up as "the Republican headquarters." There are several other houses in the neighborhood, some of them two-story, that are almost as old, but this is the only "Temple of the Sun."

70.2	1 block	On left is 310 New Street.

13. 310 NEW STREET
The Berners Barnwell Sams House, c. 1818
Not open to public.

Here's another Sams house, but this one was built by an earlier generation. Dr. Berners Sams's slaves constructed it in 1818. The original was only one room deep and had a parapet around the roof. It was used as a hospital for freed slaves during the Civil War.

70.2	Same block	Turn right on Craven Street.
70.2	1st block	On right, see Rainbow Row / 506–510 Craven Street.

14. 506–510 CRAVEN STREET
Rainbow Row, c. 1870 to early 1900s
Not open to public.

These Victorian homes with their ornate gingerbread, towers, and turrets are getting overdue praise and attention. Since they're painted different colors, the neighborhood is sometimes referred to as "Rainbow Row."

70.3	1 block	Turn left on East Street. On right facing Craven Street is 411 Craven Street.

15. 411 CRAVEN STREET
The Castle, c. 1850
Not open to public.

There were several "castles" in Beaufort, but only this one survives. It has been described as Italianate, Greek Revival, even Medieval: Six massive hexagonal columns, five-foot parapet, and great chimneys above that are all coated with a mottled stucco that shifts from pink to tan to gray, depending on the day's mood. Yes, it's the perfect castle for a ghost, and this one is a dwarf who came ashore four centuries ago with the French Protestant Jean Ribaut. The builder, Dr. Joseph Johnson, saw him enter the basement one day and was told by his gardener that the little man lived there. A few others would see him pass from the creek edge into the house, but nowadays, only children can spot him. He appears for believers every day at two o'clock.

70.3	1 block	On left is 412 East Street.

16. 412 EAST STREET
The Henry Farmer House, c. 1810
Not open to public.

Builder Farmer was still working well within the traditions of the Federal period. Note the traditionally proportioned portico (far wider than that of the

Verdier house) and how it extends to include two side windows as well as the doors. The next owner, widow Charlotte Beadon, married her lawyer, Dr. Thomas Fuller, and together the couple traveled through Europe gathering exotic plants for this garden.

70.3	**0.0**	**A**t end of block, turn right on Federal Street / S-7-165.
70.4	**2 blocks**	**O**n left is 315 Federal Street.

17. 315 FEDERAL STREET
The John Blythewood House (Cassina), c. early 1800s
Not open to public.

Margaret Blythewood, daughter of builder John, and her husband John Bell were living here when the Civil War started. A former slave of theirs, Mary Belle, bought the Beaufort-style house in 1863, and it was still in the hands of black owners when the storm of 1893 brought flood waters up to the front porch. Boatloads of refugees from the exposed islands stepped directly onto the porch and found refuge inside. Much of the roof blew off and still hadn't been replaced when the house was sold five years later. This was Federal Alley then, not the respectable street of today.

70.4	**Same block**	**L**ast house on right is 302 Federal Street.

18. 302 FEDERAL STREET
The William Fripp House (Tidewater), c. 1830
Not open to public.

The Fripp family had been in the area for over a century when William, a wealthy St. Helena planter, built his traditional summer home, Tidewater, in 1830. Legend has it that the house was disassembled elsewhere and put back together on this site upside down—the top story on the bottom. While it's true the second-story ceilings are six inches higher, modern engineers have determined that each floor is where it belongs.

Fripp gave generously to the poor, helped build the Beaufort Baptist Church, and almost single-handedly saw to the construction of another church on St. Helena. "So well known were his benevolences and purity of life that he was known all over the state as 'Good Billy Fripp.'"

70.4	**0.0**	**A**cross Federal Street is 303 Federal Street.

19. 303 FEDERAL STREET
The James Rhett House, c. 1884
Not open to public.

James Rhett's house is something of an architectural novelty. The story goes that the young man was out to win the hand of a lady who was demanding the finest house in Beaufort. He intended to make the house two rooms deep, but ran out of money and built what you see. It's called "Rhett's Folly," a reference apparently to both love and architecture.

70.4	**0.0**	**A**t end of Federal Street is Marshlands (501 Pinckney Street).

20. 501 PINCKNEY STREET
The James Robert Verdier House (Marshlands), c. 1814
Not open to public.

The single encircling veranda of Marshlands is said to show Barbadian influence, but otherwise the structure is typically Federal in design. Builder Verdier was a doctor noted for his work with yellow fever patients. The house is the fictional setting for Francis Griswold's *Sea Island Lady.*

70.4	0.0	Turn left onto Pinckney Street.
70.5	2 blocks	On left is 604 Pinckney Street.

21. 604 PINCKNEY STREET
The Edward Means House, c. 1853
Not open to public.

Colonel Means's house is one of the few built of brick and also one of the few entered from the east or street end. An occupying Yankee reporter wrote, "The splendor of the houses and furniture and the beauty of the place have been exaggerated, but the house of Col. Edward Means would be called handsome in any town in the North."

70.5	0.0	Turn right on Laurens Street.
70.5	1 block	On left is 201 Laurens Street.

22. 201 LAURENS STREET
The Berners Barnwell Sams House, c. 1852
Not open to public.

This Regency structure is the second home built by Dr. Berners Barnwell Sams. Remember, the first was the modest wood frame home back on New Street—a far cry from this great columned Greek Revival brick dwelling. Sams was a successful cotton planter, but was educated as a doctor. He spent a good part of the year in town practicing medicine on his friends and relatives. The large open square in front of the house is actually part of this property and is called "the Front Green." The doctor's son recalls that this was a favorite turn for carriages in the evening, and he and his brother would catch on behind for sport and drop off in front of their father's office. But they were finally caught. "The next carriage that drove by was not troubled by outriders. Here were right and wrong. Father was right and we were wrong."

70.6	1 block	Second house on right is 100 Laurens Street.

23. 100 LAURENS STREET
The Paul Hamilton House (The Oaks), c. 1856
Not open to public.

Paul Hamilton's was one of several Italianate houses built in the neighborhood. Note the decorative brackets beneath the eaves and compounded columns of this romanticized Italian villa. At the end of the war, Hamilton was given three days to go to Charleston and raise the money to redeem the house. When the sale took place on the second day instead, irate neighbors led by a Northern merchant bought it for Hamilton. "We shook hands with the

Northerner that night," Hamilton's daughter wrote, "though up to that time we had said we would never shake hands with any Yankee."

70.6	**Same block**	At end of Laurens Street on left is 1 Laurens Street.

24. 1 LAURENS STREET
The Edgar Fripp House, c. 1856
Open to public.

The Edgar Fripp home also started out as an Italianate villa and even boasted Romantic turrets and wings. Badly damaged in the hurricane of 1893, however, it was reconstructed as you see it now. This one, too, was about to be sold out of the family at the war's end, but a Frenchman seeing the owner in tears bought it for him, kissed him on both cheeks, and departed. True story; it's documented.

If the house looks vaguely familiar, it should. Author Pat Conroy's *The Great Santini* was filmed here. That's the same basketball hoop under which Robert Duvall bullied his son. Yes, and besides that, they made *The Big Chill* here. William Hurt and Kevin Kline played football on that lawn; Glenn Close watched from the porch. The present owners aren't overjoyed by this notoriety. Remember, you're blocking the narrow lane that leads into their driveway. (Since our last visit, Beaufort has hosted another movie production—Conroy's well-known *The Prince of Tides.*)

70.6	**0.0**	Turn around and return one block to Short Street.
70.6	**1 block**	Turn right onto Short Street.
70.7	**1 block**	At stop sign, turn left on Hancock Street.
70.7	**1/2 block**	On right is 207 Hancock Street.

25. 207 HANCOCK STREET
The Elizabeth Hext House, c. 1720
Not open to public.

Set well back from the road, this little two-story house was once considered to be "in the country." Elizabeth, an only child of the pioneer builders, married a grandson of "Tuscarora Jack" Barnwell, William Sams. They started the local Sams dynasty, but this house went out of the family's hands when the Union sold it for taxes.

70.7	**1 block**	On corner of Hancock and Pinckney streets, on right, is 804 Pinckney Street.

26. 804 PINCKNEY STREET
The Johnson House, c. 1850
Not open to public.

Dr. John Johnson's home is similar to the home of Edward Means in that the entrance is to the side, but this house is slightly smaller and made of painted brick. Both houses were constructed by Johnson's brother-in-law, Franklin Talbird, a builder of lighthouses. In 1873, the doctor wrote a good reminiscence, quoting in hindsight, "Thrice happy the farmers, did they but know their own blessing."

70.8	**Same block**	On right is 313 Hancock Street.

27. 313 HANCOCK STREET
The Henry Talbird House, c. 1786
Not open to public.

Henry Talbird sold his home to a Sams, who sold it back to a Talbird. A descendant of both families lives there now. The house is unusual because the second story is only one room wide.

70.8	**1 block**	Facing you at the dead end of Hancock Street is 708 East Street.

28. 708 EAST STREET
The Tree House, date unknown
Not open to public.

Tradition has it that this house was cut in half when it was moved here so that it could slip in beside the giant oak. The family of the famous slave pilot Robert Smalls did the moving in 1910 and it's still called the "Tree House."

70.8	**0.0**	Turn left onto East Street.
70.8	**1 block**	Turn right onto Prince Street.
70.8	**Same block**	First house on left is 502 Prince Street / S-7-110.

29. 502 PRINCE STREET
Pretty Penny, c. 1885
Not open to public.

Builder George Doane had a lumberyard that allowed him to put only the choicest of woods into his Victorian dwelling. The low lot was filled with palmetto logs before construction began. "Pretty Penny"—well built and well named.

70.9	**Same block**	On right is 511 Prince Street.

30. 511 PRINCE STREET
The Henry McKee House, c. 1834
Not open to public.

Though the exterior and interior trim of Henry McKee's home suggest a continuing line to the earlier Federalist period, the twelve-foot ceiling and great windows suggest Greek Revival proportions. It's a house with a history of unusual occupants. Robert Smalls was born a slave in a cabin behind the house and, for service to the Union, would win fame and the money to buy this house at a tax sale. The DeTreville family, who had lost the house, carried the suit to regain it all the way to the Supreme Court and lost. The wife of the original owner, McKee, when old and confused, wandered into the house thinking it was hers. She was placed in her old bedroom by Smalls and remained there as "mistress" of the house until she died.

70.9	**0.0**	Turn left on New Street. On left is 601 New Street.

31. 601 NEW STREET
First African Baptist Church, c. 1865
Not open to public.
Built by freed slaves, this was originally called "the Praise Church." The balconies of even the largest antebellum churches could not accommodate three or four thousand slave members. Even before the Civil War, many blacks met in their own little "praise houses" or "praise churches."

There are dozens more homes scattered about, and you'll find them written up in several places, but now for a change of pace.

70.9	**0.0**	Continue on New Street.
71.1	**2 blocks**	Turn right onto Craven Street.
71.2	**2 blocks**	On right is Beaufort Arsenal Museum, 713 Craven Street.

32. 713 CRAVEN STREET
The Beaufort Arsenal Museum, c. 1795
Open to public.
An 1852 face-lift gave the Arsenal the appropriately Gothic fortress facade it now enjoys. Two small cannons seized from the British currently guard the entrance to the embattled museum on the second floor. Take a look: This is one of Beaufort's hidden treasures. Sheriff McTeer, "the High Sheriff of the Low Country," got together with seven friends and donated what was of interest to them. Their intent: to "increase and diffuse knowledge by maintenance and development of a general museum and library of art, science, history, and industry." It's an eclectic collection, and the visitor can't help feeling that he or she has wandered into an attic—the collective attic of the entire town.

Kentucky long rifles hang above a World War I machine gun. There are stuffed animals, African kudus, an Alaskan brown bear, and local nine-foot rattlesnakes. A shrimp boat model sits beside an early sewing machine, next to ice skates and needlepoint. Then, there are modern-day paintings and a warthog head. The artifacts of Beaufort-area Indians are here (disorganized but extensive), along with early photos, Civil War memorabilia, McTeer's voodoo idol, and Alice Smith's watercolors. Spanish olive-oil jugs from 1566 and a 1562 French sword from Parris Island coexist with the skull of a twenty-foot alligator shot in nearby Dale. All that and much more, all cluttered together and waiting to be discovered. But the building is slated for renovation, and the nonprofit organization and its loyal curator could end up on the street. No admission, but donations are happily accepted.

71.2	**0.0**	Continue on Craven Street.
71.3	**2 blocks**	On right is 907 Craven Street.

33. 907 CRAVEN STREET
The Tabernacle Baptist Church, date uncertain
Grounds open to public.
It's said that a temporary schism in the Baptist congregation caused this church to be built sometime before the Civil War, but the split healed quickly and it became a meetinghouse and lecture room. At the war's end, five hun-

dred black members of the congregation withdrew and bought the church. The storm of 1893 did severe damage to the building, but it was rebuilt close to the original style.

The grave of Robert Smalls is here, and a bust and plaque commemorating him. Born a slave in Beaufort, Smalls had been illegally taught to read and write, and when war broke out, he was working as a coastal pilot. Putting his family aboard the steamer *Planter*, he boldly passed through the Confederate lines and went into the service of the Union. He returned to Beaufort and served in Congress during the Reconstruction era, asking for his people only "an equal chance in the battle of life."

If you're tired of walking, this is a good opportunity to turn left, return to the Information Center office, and get your car. Otherwise, continue by turning right and go two blocks to the corner of King and Charles streets.

71.3	1/2 block	Turn right onto Charles Street.
71.4	2 blocks	Turn left onto King Street.
71.4	20 feet	Turn left into the Baptist Church of Beaufort's parking lot.

Beaufort and the Revivals

Resident William Grayson reported in the years following the Revolution that in Beaufort "religion was very little regarded . . . . Sunday was a day of boat racing, foot racing, drinking, and fighting." There were exceptions, of course, but the town was in need of the revivals that passed this way like "comets." The first, he recalls, was followed by the terrible hurricane of 1804, which swept away the old barbecue house that had been the scene of much merriment. But the grandest revival of all was that of 1832. Reverend Daniel Baker, a Savannah Presbyterian, preached to all with such fervor that "the hardest natures were softened. Ancient quarrels were reconciled. The lion and the lamb lay down together." Six members of one law firm gave up their practices to become priest and preachers.

34. 600 CHARLES STREET

Baptist Church of Beaufort, c. 1844

Open to public.

This great Greek Revival building is considered by many to be one of the finest Baptist churches in America, and can certainly be considered a monument to perseverance. Besides its having to overcome a general indifference to spiritual matters, early Baptist opposition to slavery made the denomination unpopular among the Lowcountry aristocrats, and its later evangelistic work among blacks was not always appreciated, either.

The First Baptist Church in Charleston had established a mission in nearby Euchaw, and this was to serve a tiny Beaufort congregation until an official church was organized here in 1804. The old foundation of this meetinghouse still remains, and it must have been reasonably well attended even before the Great Revival. In 1826, the Baptists were recorded as the majority in Colleton District. It was a converted lawyer, Reverend Richard Fuller, however, who saw to the construction of this impressive building. Midway through, a sudden need for more funds sent him soliciting in the community and won him the not-so-holy title of "the prince of beggars." It was for a good cause.

Robert Mills may have helped with the architecture, in a way: It's possible Fuller borrowed the plans of Mills' Charleston Baptist Church. Some major changes were made, though, for the attic story has been omitted and part of the portico area is enclosed. The result is more typically Greek Revival, but as the first building in the area to use the massive columns, it was considered a bold departure at the time. Notice, then, that the addition of a grand steeple in the mid-twentieth century made the structure less a pagan temple and more a proper church. The interior is exceptional. Supported by finely worked Doric columns is a three-sided balcony once used by the slave membership, and high above that is a cove ceiling with plaster rosettes that make it the finest such decoration in Beaufort.

In the Civil War the church was used as a hospital for black soldiers, and a temporary walkway connected the side balconies. The communion table had been carried off to Charleston and the pews scattered, but all this was retrieved. The communion silver had been hidden by a black deacon and so was safe. The black membership, however, had dropped from 3,557 to 3; the white from 182 to 20. The church survived and is growing still.

71.4	**0.0**	**F**rom the Baptist Church parking lot, turn left onto King Street.
71.5	**2 blocks**	**T**urn left onto Church Street.
71.5	**1/2 block**	**O**n left is St. Helena's Episcopal Church.

35. 501 CHURCH STREET
St. Helena's Episcopal Church, c. 1724
Open to public.

This substantial church began in 1724 as a small thirty-by-forty-foot brick building on the very edge of the frontier. By 1712, the parish of St. Helena had been laid out, and Presbyterian and Anabaptist ministers had already come and gone. It was in this year that Reverend William Guy took over the parish, and he was the only man of God about—a fortunate one, for he escaped the attacking Yemassee. In the century following, church historian Frederick Dalco reports a high turnover of priests, poor health and death being the usual causes of change. The Wesley brothers visited this building in 1736, but as with the Baptists, it was Dr. Baker's revival of 1832 that put new life into the Episcopal efforts. By then the building had been enlarged and a great 118-foot steeple added, but further additions were made in 1842, extending it to the present size.

During the Civil War the church became a hospital. The pews and galleries were stripped away and a second story was hung inside between the galleries. Tombstones were brought in to use as operating tables. At the war's end the tottering steeple with its London clock was taken down; the present

Christopher Wren–like substitute didn't replace it until 1942. It's been a gradual process, but the building has been restored inside and out, and you're allowed to see the interior and stroll through the grave-crowded grounds.

St. Helena's has had some illustrious and adventuresome members. Captain John Bull, whose wife was taken by the Yemassee, gave the silver service that's still used on occasion. "Tuscarora Jack" Barnwell was buried here in 1724. Indian trader, mapmaker, and co-founder of the town, he's best known for leading the successful campaign against North Carolina's Tuscarora Indians in 1712. (They killed our first naturalist, John Lawson.) Two Confederate generals rest here, and just inside the entry gate lie two English officers who got a Christian burial from the men who bested them in Revolutionary War battle. Dr. Perry, fearing he'd be buried alive, had his tomb furnished with bread and water and an axe for escaping. The suicides and dueling dead are plotted across the street by the parish house where a mysterious mass burial of twenty-five was recently discovered. Not all so dramatic—those familiar with the region will find in these beautiful, quiet grounds familiar names of the ordinarily departed.

71.5	**0.0**	Continue on Church Street.
71.6	**1/2 block**	Turn right onto North Street.
71.8	**3 blocks**	Turn left on Monson Street.
71.8	**1 block**	Turn left on Bay Street.

36. 1411–1103 BAY STREET
Bay Street Residences, c. 1786 to 1900
None open to public.
From the outside, this three-block-long collection of nine houses offers an interesting commentary on the Beaufort style, or styles.

The first, 1141 BAY STREET, was a Victorian house remade completely into a Beaufort-style mansion.

The next, 1405 BAY STREET, had its slender columns and double piazzas replaced with these grander columns.

The third, 400 WILMINGTON STREET, is unchanged, but note the front door. It's fake. The front windows open as doors, but the real entry is on the side, so the house doesn't get a Bay Street address.

The next, 1307 BAY STREET, is a rather modest home built in 1883 by a Connecticut foot soldier who decided to remain here.

Stephen Bull had a small cottage here at 1305 BAY STREET, but this big house dates from 1900.

The home at 1301 BAY STREET is pre-Revolutionary, but was moved here from St. Helena Island in 1850. The rector of Sheldon Church, Charles Heverett, managed to reclaim it after the Civil War.

The tabby manse at 1211 BAY STREET is next—a graceful Adam brothers–Federalist building, similar in feel to the Verdier house, but made completely of tabby. Thomas Fuller built it in 1786, and Baptist lawyer convert

Reverend Richard Fuller lived here. It's said that he gave one last party for his friends at this home before renouncing worldly ways.

Robert Means, merchant and planter, built the home at 1207 BAY STREET in 1790. The classical columns were added in this century.

Built in 1810, the John Cuthbert House at 1203 BAY STREET has been given additional porches and bay windows. Tradition says the family sawed this house in half and moved it here from an "unhealthy" location.

The building at 1103 BAY STREET is a pre-Revolutionary home that got a substantial face-lift during this century. William Elliott—sportsman, poet, politician, and essayist—lived here. One of the few to oppose secession, he still kept the respect of his fellow citizens.

And for good measure, here's a tenth. Just next door at 1113 CRAVEN STREET is the "Secession house." Originally it was an early tabby house; Milton Maxcy replaced the top tabby floor with two floors of wood in about 1800, and opened a school for boys. In 1861, Edmund Rhett rebuilt the 1800 addition in the familiar Greek Revival tradition. The first secession ordinance in South Carolina was drawn up here. This is it—the first house to leave the Union, and, judging by its closeness to the bay, probably one of the first to get back in.

72.2	**5 blocks**	**O**n right is Information Center of Greater Beaufort Chamber of Commerce.
72.2	**0.0**	**F**rom the chamber of commerce parking lot, turn right on Bay Street.
72.4	**4 blocks**	**T**urn right onto Carteret Street / U.S. 21 South Business. Cross Beaufort Bridge and continue on U.S. 21 South.
76.5	**4.1**	**C**ross onto St. Helena Island.

St. Helena Island

Like Edisto, St. Helena was in many ways a world unto itself. Not forty years after Columbus's discovery, the Spanish dropped by and named it. The settlers on the *Carolina* voted not to settle on it, but the English soon returned to run cattle here. Next, they planted indigo, and finally, cotton, which made them suddenly rich. In 1815, St. Helena's citizens, assuming they were the only island of the name in existence, protested to the British government when they heard that Napoleon was to be exiled to St. Helena. Other outsiders came instead, and on January 16, 1865, the southern tip of St. Helena, now divided into three thousand lots of the new "City of Port Royal," went on sale. This utopian get-rich-quick project went nowhere, but there were a few who were not land speculators or soldiers or dreamers, and they intended to give practical aid to the newly freed slaves.

78.7	**2.2**	**T**urn right onto Martin Luther King, Jr. Drive / S-7-45 at Frogmore.
79.1	**0.4**	**O**n left is Brick Baptist Church.

37. BRICK CHURCH, c. 1855

Not open to public.
"Good Billy Fripp" built this church for the few white and many black Baptists on the island. His freed slaves didn't recall him as being particularly good to them. They took possession of the church in 1862, and it's still in the hands of their descendants and others.

79.1	**0.0**	**C**ontinue on S-17-45.
79.2	**0.1**	**J**ust 60 feet before historical marker, turn right into parking lot of Penn Center.

38. PENN CENTER, c. 1864

Open to public. Tours available.
Once a school for freed slaves, this facility is now operated as a community center, Peace Corps volunteer training site, and museum/library for the study of black history and Sea Island culture.

Two Pennsylvania women, Laura Towne and Ellen Murray, arrived on the island in 1862 and were joined soon after by the first black teacher, Charlotte Forten. They began to instruct and provide health care for the newly freed slaves. First, classes were in a nearby plantation, then in the Baptist Church across the street. In 1864, a small prefab schoolhouse was set up on the present site. All that remains of this first school is the bell tower and the model of the Liberty Bell it held. They've been moved into the trees on the far side of the road. These other buildings date from this century when Penn School switched over and became an industrial and agricultural school, teaching not only reading and writing but homemaking, midwifery, carpentry, black-smithing, basketry, farming, and more. Most of these structures were, in fact, built by the students.

On your far right and farthest back is the industrial arts shop that has been turned into a cultural center and museum. Visitors and scholars are welcome. There are oral histories and photographs in the archives, and farm implements and examples of the industrial school work on display. If you want to get an idea of how radically things have changed on the island, just flip through the photographs of Edith Dabbs's *Face of an Island.*

In 1951, Penn School became Penn Community Center, and its concern became to improve the living conditions of the poor and make them self-reliant. Martin Luther King came here on retreat during the early 1960s because it was one of the few biracial meeting places in the South (the cottage he stayed in is still here), and it has been used for many other conferences since then. Peace Corps volunteers train here now, as well, but the school needs a renovation, and there are plans to make a further record of the island's rich but vanishing culture and broaden the role that Penn Center plays in Lowcountry and national affairs.

———————— ◈ ————————

79.2	**0.0**	**F**rom Penn Center parking lot, turn right onto S-7-45.
80.0	**0.8**	**O**n left is Chapel of Ease to St. Helena's Church (the White Church) ruins.

39. CHAPEL OF EASE TO ST. HELENA'S CHURCH (THE WHITE CHURCH) RUINS, c. 1730

Open to public.
Built originally as a Chapel of Ease for the Beaufort Church, it's constructed of tabby and brick combined. There had only occasionally been Methodist preachers on the island before the Civil War, but at its end, the chapel was reported to be in their hands. It burned in a forest fire in 1886.

———————— ◈ ————————

80.0	**0.0**	**F**rom Chapel of Ease parking lot, turn right onto S-7-45 and retrace to U.S. 21.
81.3	**1.3**	**A**t stop sign, turn right onto U.S. 21 South.
90.3	**9.0**	**A**rrive at Hunting Island State Park.
91.5	**1.2**	**T**urn left into park entrance gate/S-7-762.
91.8	**0.3**	**P**ass through entrance gate and turn right into Visitors Center parking lot; pick up map.

40. HUNTING ISLAND STATE PARK

Hunting Island State Park is a busy one, handling a million visitors a year. On the August afternoon we arrived, though, it didn't seem particularly crowded. Stop at the new VISITORS CENTER just inside the entry. Enjoy the exhibits of the SEA ISLAND MUSEUM and get further information and a map that will guide you about this largest of the beach parks.

The roads are narrow and one-way. They twist and turn through old dunes grown thick with palmetto and slash pine—it's the largest natural stand of the pine in South Carolina. To the left, or north, you'll find the HUNTING ISLAND LIGHTHOUSE. It was built of cast iron so it could be moved back as the beach eroded. A wise decision: Built in 1875, it was moved here only fourteen years later. At the base of the light is an interesting display giving the history of lighthouses in general and particularly in South Carolina. You're welcome to walk to the top. The winding cast-iron

steps seem to get steeper as you go, but you're rewarded finally with a bird's-eye view of the island, ocean, shoals, back bays, and distant St. Helena.

Here at the lighthouse is a NATURE WALK not yet on the map. It's a mile long (thirty minutes) and carries you through the maritime forest out onto a dune edge thick with sea oats. You can return by way of the beach. There's swimming and beach combing here, but remember, a million others have come before you, and the gradual slope means gradual waves, so few shells find their way ashore. Turtle nests are monitored and protected, and there are one or two supervised night walks during the summer. As with other parts of the island, bird watchers are advised to come in October or later; the crowds are much smaller and the birds more plentiful.

The SECOND NATURE WALK is to the middle of the island and follows an old roadbed down to the edge of a tidal lagoon. For those unwilling to leave their cars (you might be tired by now), the narrow winding roads with browsing areas planted for deer offer a good look at the jungle-like flora and tropical lagoon.

91.8	**0.0**	**A**fter touring park, return to park entrance.
94.8	**3.0**	**A**t the entrance gate, turn left onto U.S. 21 South.
96.5	**1.7**	**T**urn right into Marsh Boardwalk parking lot.

Outside the park's main entrance there are two more nice spots. The first is the MARSH BOARDWALK. A good lesson in salt tolerance, three wooden walkways connect low sandy islands of stunted pines and cedars. There are fiddler crabs running everywhere at low tide, and at the boardwalk end is a small tidal creek.

96.5	**0.0**	**F**rom Marsh Boardwalk parking lot, turn right onto U.S. 21 South.
97.0	**0.5**	**T**urn left, just before bridge, into parking lot of Paradise Fishing Pier.

At the very end of Hunting Island is the state-owned PARADISE FISHING PIER stretching out into the inlet. Many sections of the beach and the lagoon are set aside for fishing as well, but here you can rent a rod and reel for a modest $1.50 or just walk out and watch others for free. Now, whiting is a favorite catch, but these waters were once famous for their schools of tremendous drum. Here sportsman William Elliott once harpooned devilfish—manta rays larger than his boat. Nice place to end the day—probably a very long one if you got this far.

97.0	0.0	From pier parking lot, turn right onto U.S. 21 North.
114.1	17.1	Continue straight on U.S. 21 North Business.
115.7	1.6	Return to Beaufort and continue on U.S. 21 North to U.S. 17 North.
131.0	15.3	Veer right and continue on U.S. 17 North to Charleston.
183.0	52.0	South side of Ashley River Bridge.

ADDITIONAL READING

A lot has been written about this area, so this is far from a complete list. The local library has three manuscript memoirs: John Grayson's *Autobiography,* John Johnson's *Beaufort and the Sea Islands,* and Lena Lengnick's *Beaufort Memoirs.* The old standby is Nell Grayson's *Tales of Beaufort.* Mary Hilton did the excellent but out-of-print *Old Homes and Churches of Beaufort.* Look for Katherine Jones's *Port Royal Under Six Flags* and William Elliott's *Carolina Sport.* If you're interested in St. Helena, try Edith Dabb's *Sea Island Diary,* Ted Rosengarten's *Tombee,* and Ronald Daise's *Reminiscences of Sea Island Heritage.* Check the Penn Center Library for other titles.

NOTES

Tour 5:

Awendaw To Georgetown

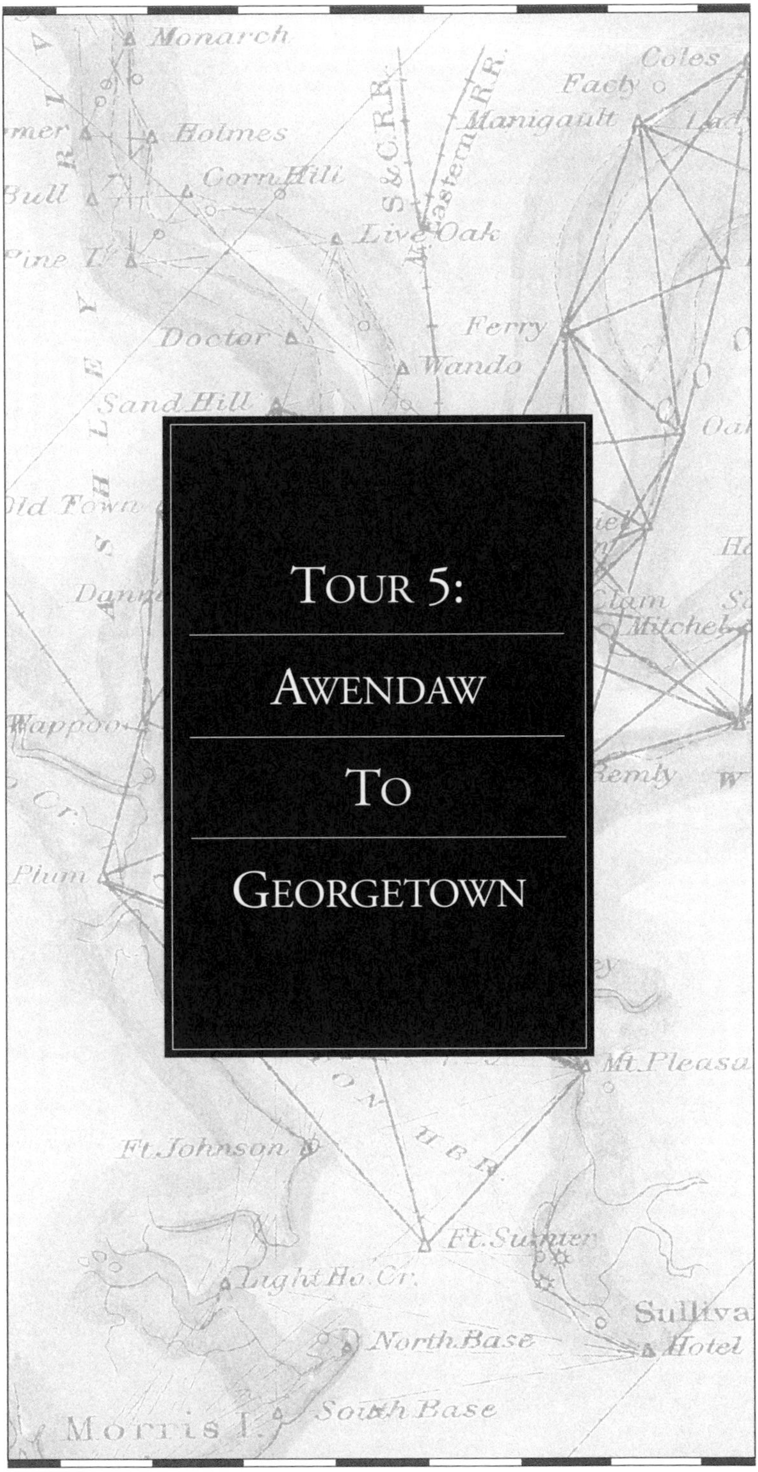

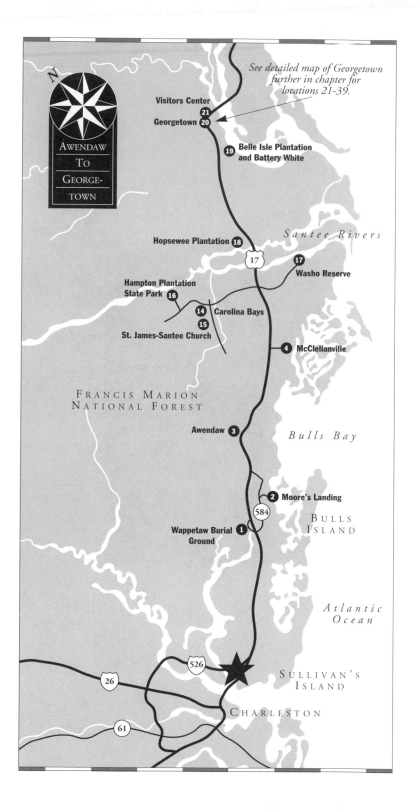

N

AWENDAW
TO
GEORGE-
TOWN

See detailed map of Georgetown further in chapter for locations 21-39.

Visitors Center **21**
Georgetown **20**

19 Belle Isle Plantation and Battery White

Santee Rivers

Hopsewee Plantation **18**
17

17 Washo Reserve

Hampton Plantation State Park **16**
14 Carolina Bays
15
St. James-Santee Church

4 McClellanville

FRANCIS MARION NATIONAL FOREST

Awendaw **3**

Bulls Bay

2 Moore's Landing
584
BULLS ISLAND

Wappetaw Burial Ground **1**

Atlantic Ocean

526

26

SULLIVAN'S ISLAND

CHARLESTON

61

AWENDAW TO GEORGETOWN

This tour continues north and along U.S. Highway 17 through the Awendaw community and on to Georgetown. We start with the eighteenth-century burial ground of WAPPETAW. The pier at MORRE'S LANDING is an interesting stop for nature lovers where off in the distance you can see Bull Island, a hurricane-battered but still beautiful barrier island. A visit there takes an entire day. Heading north again, we pass through THE FRANCIS MARION NATIONAL FOREST, which offers much to wilderness-oriented visitors. We tour the little "fishing village" of MCCLELLANVILLE. Next is a distinctive 1768 Anglican church, ST. JAMES–SANTEE. Close by is HAMPTON PLANTATION STATE PARK, offering tours of poet Archibald Rutledge's Colonial mansion and the surrounding gardens and wilderness. Close to the plantation is the beautiful nature walk of the WASHO RESERVE, and a grand place for a picnic lunch. We cross the Santee Delta to tour the house, grounds, and outbuildings of HOPSEWEE PLANTATION—the birthplace of Thomas Lynch, signer of the Declaration of Independence. We end our tour in GEORGETOWN, one of the oldest communities in the state. It boasts ancient houses and churches, museums, and other points of interest, and if you choose, tram, boat, and walking tours help you find your way. If you want to fit your tour into one day, take your time and go home when the sun goes down.

Wappetaw Burial Ground, c. 1800
Open daily.

Moore's Landing
Open daily.

McClellanville
Open daily.

St. James–Santee Church, c. 1768
Open daily.

Hampton Plantation State Park
Guided tour of restored plantation house, c. 1736, extensive garden, resident naturalist, picnic area, restrooms.
Open Thursday through Monday, 9 a.m. to 6 p.m.
House tour: Saturday, 10 a.m. to 3 p.m.; Sunday, 12 noon to 3 p.m.;
Thursday and Friday, 1 p.m. to 4 p.m.
Admission charged.

Santee Coastal Reserve–Washo Reserve
Nature trail through and around an ancient rice planting reservoir.
Open February 1 through October 31. Saturday, 8 a.m. to 5 p.m.;
Sunday, 1 p.m. to 4 p.m.

Hopsewee Plantation
Guided tours of c. 1740 Colonial house. Self-guided tours of outbuildings and grounds.
Open Tuesday through Friday, 10 a.m. to 5 p.m.
Admission charged.
Grounds and cabin: Open daily. Admission charged.

Belle Isle Plantation and Battery White
Open daily.

Georgetown

An active chamber of commerce. Town founded in 1732. Many Colonial and antebellum structures. Rice museum, house museum, guided tours, boat trips, and more.

Georgetown County Visitors Center
Open Monday through Friday, 9 a.m. to 5 p.m.
Telephone: (803) 546-8436

Georgetown Tours

Capt. Sandy's Tours. 709 Front Street. Call (803) 527-4106. Boat tours leave from Riverfront Wharf and times vary from season to season, so call for general information. Listed below is the spring 1992 schedule.

HISTORIC SEAPORT TOUR: *Port of Entry 1732, fishing fleet, shrimp boats, stories, and sunken ships. History and legends. Monday through Thursday; 1 hour. Admission charged.*

PLANTATION EXCURSION: *Rice planters' mansions. Monday through Thursday, 1 p.m. 3 hours. Admission charged.*

SHELL ISLAND TOUR: *Visit a pristine barrier island and enjoy shell collecting. Friday and/or Saturday, depending on demand, 9 a.m. 4 hours. Admission charged.*

ISLAND QUEEN PLANTATION TOUR: *Leave from Land's End Marina on U.S. 17. May to November, Monday through Saturday, 2 p.m.; 2 hours. Admission charged.*

RICE MUSEUM: *Monday through Saturday, 9:30 a.m. to 4:30 p.m. 30 minutes. Admission charged.*

KAMINSKI HOUSE: *House museum with exceptional furnishings. Monday through Friday, 10 a.m. to 4 p.m. Tours on the hour; 45 minutes. Admission charged.*

MISS NELL'S PERSONAL WALKING TOURS: *Tuesday and Thursday, 10:30 a.m., 2:30 p.m. Saturday and Sunday, 2:30 p.m. to 4:30 p.m. Admission charged.*

Bull Island

A separate day trip to a barrier island with nature trails and a pristine beach; a mecca for bird watchers. Tour departs from Moore's Landing. *(Please see "Additional Day Trips in the Lowcountry" on page 279 for information.)*

———— ◈ ————

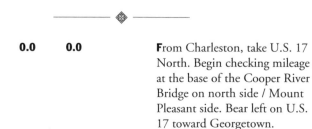

| 0.0 | 0.0 | From Charleston, take U.S. 17 North. Begin checking mileage at the base of the Cooper River Bridge on north side / Mount Pleasant side. Bear left on U.S. 17 toward Georgetown. |

| 14.6 | 14.6 | Turn left onto 15 Mile Landing Road / S-10-584. |
| 14.7 | 0.1 | On right, Wappetaw Cemetery. |

1. WAPPETAW BURIAL GROUND, c. 1800

Grounds open to the public.

Thirty-five gravestones, all dating from the eighteenth century, are all that remain. But in 1695, a group of New England Congregationalists were shipwrecked on the outer banks of North Carolina. Befriended by the Hatteras Indians, fifty-two were rescued by the governor of Carolina and landed near here on Seewee Bay. Separated from Reverend Starbo's Charleston-based Presbyterian congregations, they built at least one church on this site. Badly vandalized by Union troops, it collapsed in 1897. By then, the members had moved on.

Hurricane Hugo

The area of the coast we are about to drive through took the brunt of Hurricane Hugo in late September 1989, a fact that should quickly become obvious. Through all of the Awendaw community and on to McClellanville, the bulk of the pine trees have been snapped off at a height of about twenty feet. This in itself is an impressive, if tragic, sight. No doubt, time will mellow the situation. The broken stumps will rot and tumble over to be covered by the beginnings of a new forest. For now, be prepared for a shock.

There is a silver lining. As a result of the storm, the United States Forest Service, the custodian of most of these woodlands, has accelerated its program of recreational land use. Here in the vicinity of Iron Swamp a large interpretative center is being built. Inside, the visitor will be treated to natural history exhibits and explanations of local land use—from antebellum rice planting to present-day time management. The United States Fish and Wildlife Service will also have an exhibit area here. The Cape Romain Wilderness area adjoins the National Forest, and this complex treasure of protected seaside ecology will also be explained. We'll return to this subject a few miles down the road, but for now there's a bit of history to tend to.

◈

14.7	0.0	Turn around.
14.8	0.1	Retrace to U.S. 17.
14.9	0.1	Cross U.S. 17 and continue straight on Sewee Road / S-10-584.
18.2	3.3	Turn right onto Bull Island Road / S-10-1170.
19.7	1.5	Arrive at Moore's Landing pier parking lot.

2. MOORE'S LANDING

Moore's Landing was ground zero for Hurricane Hugo. A twenty-foot surge of water came ashore here, and the damage it did should be obvious for many years to come. Currently, however, the landing is still the headquarters for the sixty-four-thousand-acre Cape Romain National Refuge. With the exception of Bull Island, the Refuge, with its vast expanse of saltwater marsh, creeks, and bays, has been declared a National Wilderness Area, which guarantees that whatever industry eventually moves this way will be non-polluting. The original intent was to preserve migrating duck populations, but the Refuge turned out to be a fortuitous home for much else, especially the loggerhead turtle. Cape Romain is now one of the best protected and most productive nesting areas for this endangered species. The Landing's concrete pier extends well out into Sewee Bay and is a good spot to look for shorebirds, especially the bright-billed skimmers.

❖

19.7	0.0	From Moore's Landing parking lot, retrace Bull Island Road / S-10-1170.
21.2	1.5	At yield sign, turn right onto Seewee Road / S-10-584.
24.8	3.6	At stop sign, turn left onto Doar Road.
24.9	0.1	At stop sign, turn right onto U.S. 17 North.
28.6	3.7	U-turn onto U.S. 17 South.
28.7	0.1	Turn right into Francis Marion National Forest Swamp Fox Hiking Trail parking lot.

A Brief Comment on the Surrounding Area

The FRANCIS MARION NATIONAL FOREST covers over a quarter of a million acres and includes practically all the land on the left side of the highway for a distance of up to forty miles. At the center is a broad and vaguely defined area called Hell Hole, which from the earliest days of settlement enjoyed a reputation as a haven for criminals and runaway slaves, a reputation only worsened during our twentieth-century experiment with prohibition. (The name Hell Hole did not, however, refer to hell-raising. The first settlers coming across the great open bays of the area considered them the work of the devil—"hell-holes.") In 1935, this land and more was bought as part of the New Deal effort to save the South. Up until then, what remained of the woodlands was being burned yearly in order to grow grass for freely roaming cattle and hogs. It was hoped that a well-managed forest would encourage a substantial capital investment in nearby mills and thus bring jobs. Civilian Conservation Corps crews came in, roads were constructed, and animals were removed. Pulp mills were built and they, together with lumber mills, still depend heavily on the forest.

Though it fulfilled its original promise, the forest has become a subject of growing controversy, for concepts of land use have broadened, and many feel that this federal agency isn't doing all it can to comply with the theory of "multiple uses." As it stands now, endangered wildlife like the swallow-tailed kites and red-cockaded woodpeckers are sheltered while the plentiful deer and turkey are hunted on a limited basis. Fragile Carolina bays are protected, but elsewhere hardwoods are to be completely replaced with pines. There are some trails for hikers and others for motorbikes. Broad paved roads for loggers run beside wilderness areas crossed only by paddleboat. It's a delicate balancing act to say the least, but one that the Forest Service is managing. As stated earlier, Hurricane Hugo so destroyed the pines that even greater emphasis is now placed on recreational use. It may look bad from the

Francis Marion Forest

highway, but the National Forest still contains some truly beautiful spots. Thousands of acres have been set aside to protect endangered plants and animals and to entertain the wilderness-oriented visitor. Interested? For information on hiking, camping, canoeing, and more, contact the Wambaw Ranger District in McClellanville or the Witherbee Ranger District in Huger.

3. THE AWENDAW COMMUNITY

When explorer-naturalist John Lawson passed this way in 1700, he mentioned only two small plantations here at Avendaugh-bough. The name has been shortened to Awendaw, and the community is now spread out thinly along miles of highway. On crossing the Awendaw Bridge in 1926, however, Dr. William Johnson saw little change from Lawson's day, and reported, "There is much about these parts that makes me think of wild men of ye olden times."

---◈---

28.7	**0.0**	**E**xit parking lot to right onto U.S. 17 South.
28.8	**0.1**	**M**ake left U-turn at first paved crossover onto U.S. 17 North.
38.7	**9.9**	**P**ass the caution lights and turn right onto McClellanville's Pinckney Street / S-10-9.

4. McCLELLANVILLE

Hurricane Hugo inundated this village, severely damaging practically every home and leaving most of the shrimp fleet well ashore, leaning against broken trees and houses. Much has been repaired, but 167 years of false optimism has ended.

A History of McClellanville

After the great hurricane of 1822 swept away the summer colony at the mouth of the Santee River, Archibald McClellan leased out lots here to half a dozen families. Then, in 1852, R. T. Morrison bought the adjoining land and began to divide it. The Civil War brought a sudden influx of refugees to the little

"Santee seashore" village, and in the years after, impoverished planters and
their descendants gradually came to live here on a year-round basis. When it
was incorporated in 1926, the town had a population of five hundred and

there were twenty-two stores on the main street where
there now are four. By then, farming, lumbering, and
oystering were the chief sources of income, freight came
in from Charleston by boat, and on Friday and Saturday
people came to town to buy their weekly provisions. It
was expected that the completion of the Cooper River
Bridge and the paving of U.S. 17 would bring long-
awaited "boom times," but instead, customers drove out of town to do their
shopping, stores closed, and by 1970 the population was down to 350. It's
been growing slowly ever since, and now the citizens, used to their solitude,
feel threatened by the prospect of being further "discovered." This entry didn't
take much research: I spent my summers playing in the town creek and have
lived here for the last twenty years.

39.5	0.8	On right is McClellanville Public School.

5. McCLELLANVILLE PUBLIC SCHOOL, c. 1925
Not open to public.
This substantial piece of monumental architecture dates from the time when
the village had political clout. In 1916, three of Charleston County's state leg-
islators came from here. The building has been restored and is now
McClellanville's middle school.

39.5	200 ft.	On right is New Wappetaw Presbyterian Church.

6. NEW WAPPETAW PRESBYTERIAN CHURCH, c. 1877
Not open to public.
Some descendants of the Congregationalists stranded on Hatteras almost three
centuries ago ended up here. (Remember, their graveyard was our first stop.)
Originally, the building had a Victorian tower and belfry set to one side.

Roadside Plantings and Architecture
Note the smaller live oaks and great wisteria bushes beside the road. This thick-
et was planted as part of a WPA project and guarantees that the village won't
ever go without shade or flowers. Most of the large white frame houses date
from the 1890s on. A good many were first intended only as summer homes.

39.6	0.1	On left, just beyond Oak Street, is McClellanville Methodist Church.

7. McCLELLANVILLE METHODIST CHURCH, c. 1900
Not open to public.
The building dates from the turn of the century, but these Methodists probably
got their start in the 1830s when the Episcopal congregation closed their church
and followed their priest to a Methodist meetinghouse on the Santee River.

39.8	0.2	On right is Dupre House.

8. 423 PINCKNEY STREET
The Dupre House, c. 1850
Not open to public.

This gray-shingled, raised cottage is the oldest building in town. It was taken apart and floated down the Santee in the first year of the ill-fated rebellion. The marsh in that day came up to the front yard; everything beyond is dredge fill.

39.8	200 feet	Turn right into parking lot of Municipal Offices, Government Dock.

9. 405 PINCKNEY STREET
Government Dock

This is the old site of the Cape Romain Wildlife Refuge headquarters. The concrete block house with red tile roof was a 1935 triumph in the type of utilitarian design championed by Frank Lloyd Wright. Cold and damp. (I was born in this one, or at least at a nearby hospital.) The "Government tower" beside it was built to guard the refuge from poachers, but soon after was turned over to the Forest Service. A new town hall has been built next door, and you can stop by there if you have any questions.

39.8	0.0	Turn around in Government Dock parking lot; turn left onto Pinckney Street.
40.1	0.3	Turn left onto Oak Street / S-10-71.
40.1	100 ft.	On left is Deer Head Oak.

10. DEER HEAD OAK

A favorite of children and photographers, it's hard to miss the Deer Head Oak, but, sadly, this landmark is dying.

40.2	0.1	On left is Chapel of Ease, St. James–Santee Chapel.

11. ST. JAMES–SANTEE CHAPEL OF EASE, c. 1891
Open to public.

In 1891, the Episcopal congregation moved their services from the old "Brick Church" on the Santee to this shingle-sided, Gothic Chapel of Ease. Planter Alex Lucas designed it, and four local black craftsmen did the work, cutting by hand the intricate scrollwork of the chancel screen.

40.2	0.0	On right, diagonally across the street, is R. V. Morrison House.

12. 142 OAK STREET
The R. V. Morrison House, c. 1870
Not open to public.

R. V. Morrison and his wife Aletha raised 11 children in this ancient little square two-story house. In later years, Aletha spent her mornings in the garden, indiscriminately kissing each youngster that passed, and then inquiring, "And whose child are you?"

The Rest of Oak Street

This was once called Water Street, and the "dock"—the large ditch on your left—was deep enough to float small freight boats. Since then, dredge fill has drastically altered the shape of things all over town. The white board-and-batten cottage facing the water was hastily built in 1861, but not completely finished until a few years ago. Several of the houses on your right once doubled as inns. In those days this was a sandy beach, but it and the rest of the swimming spots have fallen victim to modern times. At the end of Oak Street once stood R. T. Morrison's wharf. A turpentine works was here, and they loaded pulpwood onto barges at this spot when I was a boy. They had the "fish houses" by then, too, and that's what you'll find today.

40.3   0.1   On left are the Shrimp Docks.

13. SHRIMP DOCKS

Many of the shrimp boats, clam dredges, and smaller oyster boats dock here. Seafood is "packed out" and sold. Forklifts and moving boats are only the most obvious dangers on the waterfront, even in those spots open to the public, so be careful.

"An Old-Time Fishing Village"

That's the description given most often of McClellanville, but, except for oysters and terrapins (in 1900, McClellanville was the nation's largest exporter), there was practically no commercial fishing here before World War II. Now, however, you're almost certain to see at least one or two of the dozens of shrimp trawlers that pack out here. Before entering the ocean, the large outriggers are lowered, and the large wooden doors you see in the racks pull the nets to the bottom and spread them wide. A "tow" lasts two hours. A shrimper's day is twelve to sixteen hours, and trips of a week or longer are common. The last few seasons have been bad and competition from foreign shores makes things worse. Not quite so conspicuous but more profitable have been the small clam dredges you see tied up here, as well. The long conveyor is lowered to the bottom of the creek bed and its sled-like head driven forward by the boat as a large pump washes clams and oysters up onto the moving belt. A crew waiting topside picks these off as they pass. Assembly-line work, freezing weather, and daylight till dark, but the pay was good until pollution of the major beds meant

Shrimp Docks

that everything had to be replanted in another location for two weeks and then harvested a second time. During the winter months you can usually buy oysters at one of four docks. Most of these are brought in by crews often working singly in the twenty-foot wooden bateaux you may see tied along the creek edge. They're towed out to work, some even farther than Moore's Landing, and then separate to work the tide down and up, pitching the shellfish from the banks and creek bottom into these boats. A good day's work used to be a hundred bushels, but, like everything else these days, there are fewer oysters to go around.

The docks themselves have changed. Thirty years ago the language of the workers was an even faster and thicker form of Gullah, and the women still sang occasionally when they headed shrimp. When the North Carolina–based Wells Brothers' fleet of Yellow Riggers (so called because of their rustproof paint) packed out on September nights, Captain Happy's deaf-and-dumb "striker," or assistant, would juggle five empty Pepsi bottles and laugh silently. The legendary Doonie Watts told us unprintable stories about foreign ports of call. It's still exotic, but not that exotic: too much stainless steel and too many fluorescent lights.

------ ◆ ------

40.3	**0.0**	**T**urn around and retrace Oak Street to Pinckney Street.
40.5	**0.2**	**A**t stop sign, turn left onto Pinckney Street / S-10-9.
41.5	**1.0**	**A**t stop sign, turn right onto U.S. 17 North.
47.3	**5.8**	**T**urn left onto Rutledge Road / S-10-857.
48.7	**1.4**	**T**urn left onto Old Georgetown–Charleston Road / S-10-1335 (dirt road—if very wet, may not be passable).
49.0	**0.3**	**O**n right, small black-water pond, Carolina bay.

French Santee

This area was originally called "French Santee." The French Huguenots probably arrived here shortly after 1685, and laid out their village of James Town fifteen miles to the north. Paddling up the Santee River in 1700, explorer John Lawson reported them well situated and doing a brisk business with the Indians. "The French being a temperate industrious People . . . have out-stript our English," he writes. "'Tis admirable to see what Time and Industry will (with God's Blessing) effect." In 1706, when these settlers asked to be included as an Anglican parish, there were 100 French and 60 English families living here on the south bank of the Santee. Fortunes would soon be made in rice planting.

Young men once raced their thoroughbred horses in the straightaways of this sandy road and stagecoaches passed daily. It was "the King's Highway" then; it's quieter now.

14. CAROLINA BAYS

On your right, you'll see a small black-water pond. That's probably the deeper portion of a Carolina bay. These mysterious elliptical depressions are scattered over much of the Southeastern seaboard, but are most prevalent in the Carolinas. The name "bay" may refer to the sink, but more likely, it refers to the evergreen bays that early naturalists found growing in these depressions. Because of the uniform alignment of the "craters," it's been suggested that they were formed by a meteorite shower, a reasonable but controversial argument now being eclipsed by a more urgent concern for the bays themselves. Many, like the great one off to your left, are no longer recognizable for they've been drained and planted in pine.

50.8   1.8   Pull off the road on right for St. James–Santee Church.

15. ST. JAMES–SANTEE CHURCH, c. 1768
Open to public.

This is the fourth church to serve what was originally a largely French Huguenot congregation. A surprising departure from the rural church design of the day are the classical porticoes attached to the north and south faces. Long noted for their architectural distinction, these entries probably had a utilitarian and political function: Even at this late date, the French congregation was arriving from the north along a road now almost vanished, while the English, coming along the King's Highway, entered through the south doors. By 1847, such distinctions had been abandoned, the French entry was bricked up to make a vestry, and the altar occupied this portion of the aisle. The high-backed pews are probably original, though.

During the Revolution, the silver altar service, a gift from Thomas Lynch, was carried away permanently, but the Bible and prayer book given by Rebecca Motte were found in an English bookstore and returned. The entry door bears what might be a hastily scratched Masonic seal, but that didn't keep Union soldiers from destroying the pulpit and chancel. The finely crafted pulpit you see today was the work of a modern-day priest and stands before a newly restored Palladian window. This congregation migrated to McClellanville, but the building is being preserved and services are held here once a year.

Judging by early church records, far more people died than are accounted for in this little cemetery. Perhaps they were buried on plantations, or had cypress markers that have disappeared. Look for the stone of Samuel Warren and his son, which was moved here from the earlier Euhaw site. Samuel was the priest here before the Revolutionary War and broke with superiors, friends, and relatives in order to return to his rebel congregation. His son lost a leg in the battle for Savannah, and tradition has it that he mailed the appendage to two English aunts who had wished him ill. The obelisk you see here was originally placed at nearby Waterhorn in 1820, and commemorates Huguenot Daniel Huger and his Horry descendants. Alexander Watson rests to the left of the church. His history is clear reading, but they left off the fact that he took a slave for his second wife and left his fortune to their mulatto children. After a bitter court fight, the children won the inheritance and ended up in Washington, D.C., under the care of "The Great Compromiser," statesman Henry Clay. Their case prompted a further tightening of the manumission laws.

50.8	0.0	**T**urn around and retrace S-10-1335.
52.9	2.1	**A**t stop sign, turn left onto Rutledge Road / S-10-857.
53.3	0.4	**T**urn right into entrance gate of Hampton Plantation State Park.

16. HAMPTON PLANTATION STATE PARK, c. 1736

Open to public.

The Hampton Plantation house has been carefully restored with portions of the walls left exposed so visitors may "read" the story of the house for themselves. As was often the case, each new resident made some changes, often grand ones. This site was probably acquired by Huguenot Elias Horry between 1700 and 1730, and when he died of "country fever" in 1736, the house may have already existed in a much smaller form. His son Daniel, however, may have built it as late as 1750. In any event, this first version is the central portion of what we see today—a small saltbox dwelling whose main entrance was on the water. (Notice that the stairs originally faced the opposite direction. The paneling with unusual feathering probably dates from this early date as well.) Rice cultivation on the river and adjoining Wambaw Creek increased the family's fortune considerably, and after Daniel's marriage, changes were made. The massive portico and two large wings (one containing a great blue-ceilinged ballroom) were added sometime before the Revolution and may have been due to the influence of Daniel's mother-in-law, Eliza Lucas Pinckney. Eliza, famous for her indigo cultivation, had stayed for some years in England, where she was a fan of actor David Garrick. She visited his home at Hampton and saw there a similar Adam-style portico. It's thought she brought both name and column design back to the Santee. After the death of Horry, his wife Harriet continued to operate the plantation successfully on her own, as her mother once had. She and Eliza, wearing sashes painted with the president's likeness, stood on these steps to greet George Washington and preserved the large oak on the lawn because he recommended it.

Despite these early and colorful residents, however, Hampton is still best known as the home of the state's poet laureate, Archibald Rutledge. He grew up on the plantation during the difficult years following Reconstruction. The family home, and most especially the woods around it, remained a constant inspiration and source of material for the naturalist, hunter, poet, essayist, and short-story writer. He returned whenev-

Hampton Plantation

er possible; in 1936, he retired here for good and, with the help of the loyal black residents, set about rescuing the house and grounds. Two collections of essays followed, *Home by the River* and *The World Around Hampton.* Certainly some of his best and most popular writing, they give a good account of the struggle to reclaim house and land and the accompanying delight in nature; also, they mark the end of the romantic plantation era.

He's passed on now, but, occasionally, visitors were lucky enough to get Will Alston to show them around. A hunting companion of Archibald Rutledge in his youth, Will was a gifted storyteller in his own right. "Washington oak," he'd say. "That the backyard. That be saved by President Washington. Little bitty oak. Washington ask 'um not to let'um clear it down." Once inside, he'd continue: "That call the 'never finish room.' Nursery beyond that. Nail here from grandfather time. Peg from great-grandfather time. All this handwork. Axe and hacket. You take your time and look." Good advice.

The camellia garden, with its path that leads to the creek, is ancient. The avenue of 154 hollies and the 800 dogwoods was added by Archibald Rutledge in the 1930s. A park naturalist-interpreter is on hand to introduce you to the flora and fauna and explain construction methods. Hopefully, a boardwalk will soon lead into the nearby abandoned rice fields. The hurricane did damage here, incidentally, but the park staff has worked diligently, so it's very hard to spot.

We'll let Dr. Archie have the last wistful word here: "Though the civilization that it cradled and nourished has passed away, the charm survives. The home remains lovely after the guests are gone."

53.3	0.0	Return to main gate, turn left onto Rutledge Road / S-10-857.
55.1	1.8	At stop sign, cross over U.S. 17 and continue straight on South Santee Road / S-10-857.
56.6	1.5	Turn left onto Santee Gun Club Road (dirt road).
59.2	2.6	On right, Washo Reserve bulletin board with tour guide folders.

17. SANTEE COASTAL RESERVE–WASHO RESERVE

Two severe hurricanes during the 1890s put an end to rice planting here, and a group of wealthy northern sportsmen bought Washo and a half-dozen other places to form the Santee Gun Club. Grover Cleveland hunted here in times when a hundred-duck day was not uncommon, but those days passed, and in 1974, the entire twenty-four thousand acres was donated to the Nature Conservancy, which in turn passed all but the thousand acres surrounding the Washo Reserve over to the state's wildlife department.

This is one of the prettiest spots on God's green earth, but, especially in the summer months, the mosquitoes and deerflies can defy description. Fortunately, the Reserve is now open to the general public from February 1 through October 31, so plan accordingly. A three-mile course, the Washo Trail starts out along a slave-built dike. The impoundment to the right is thick with cypress and tupelo gum; at times, the black water is coated a brilliant green by aquatic vegetation. A boardwalk extends into this area. This is a famous rookery for wading birds; look for them, as well as ospreys and alligators, as you continue to walk the edge of the reserve and around the perimeter of a newer impoundment. On my last visit, at the very end of September, we saw none of these. Only two deer, an otter, four wood ducks, a red-shouldered hawk, and picture-book forests of cypress, hollies, and live oaks—and mosquitoes and deerflies.

59.2	0.0	Retrace Santee Gun Club Road to paved South Santee Road.
61.8	2.6	Turn right onto South Santee Road / S-10-857.
63.3	1.5	At stop sign, turn right onto U.S. 17 North.
64.2	0.9	On both sides of U.S. 17 is Santee Delta.

The Santee Delta

As you're about to cross the first bridge over the Santee River, Peachtree Plantation, which is not open to the public, is on your left. This was where inventor Johnathan Lucas built the rice mill "that would do for rice production, what Eli Whitney's gin did for cotton." On your right is Fairfield (not open to the public), the home of statesman Thomas Pinckney. Although the many mansions were on the river bank, the wealth came from the delta that we're crossing.

In 1700, John Lawson reported this area to be a great swamp forest "affording vast Ciprus-trees, of which the French make Canoes, that will carry fifty or sixty Barrels." It would remain a cypress swamp until after the Revolution. Then clearing, ditching, and diking converted forest to field, and by 1830, rice was being grown all the way to the ocean's edge. The spots where the rush appears particularly thick are old canals, and the dikes are sometimes marked by low growths of cedars. On the small islands and in the marsh itself were slave communities complete with barns, mills, and meetinghouses, and, in some places, large brick hurricane towers that gave refuge from storms. Though not connected to the mainland, most of these parcels were referred to as separate "plantations." We're looking at Tranquility, Blackwood, Indianfield, and dozens more.

| 66.5 | 2.3 | Turn left across U.S. 17 South into Hopsewee Plantation. |

| 66.7 | 0.2 | Arrive at Hopsewee Plantation parking lot. |

18. HOPSEWEE PLANTATION, c. 1740

Open to public.

We start the tour by parking beside the unusual outbuildings. Note the wide overhang and graceful fascia of the kitchens, suggesting a Caribbean influence. Inside you'll find a typical Lowcountry cooking arrangement of great open fireplaces. Besides the utensils for cooking, there's also a display of early agricultural implements—hoes, scythes, tillers, and mortar. Next, you're invited to walk the half-mile nature trail along the high bank of the North Santee River, or simply sit on the dock. Four days a week the main house is open for a hospitable tour. The interior, now carefully restored, has its original candlelight molding and especially wide pine flooring. Note the typically Georgian layout of rooms, but the central hall probably came later and the stairs are in the house's new "front" entry. The exterior siding is beaded; the foundation stuccoed and scored as block. Expanded and embellished by consecutive owners, this house, like Hampton, is a far more authentic mansion house than some of its better advertised rivals.

Hopsewee Plantation is best known as the birthplace of Declaration of Independence signer Thomas Lynch, but actually it was the builder, Thomas Lynch, Sr., who intended to sign. "He is a solid, firm judicious man," wrote John Adams of the older Lynch, who, sometime around 1740, crossed the Santee from Fairfield and built the main portion of this house. His son was born here in 1749, and at the age of fifteen was sent off for seven years of English education. Both father and son were involved in the events leading to the Revolution, and both attended the Second Continental Congress. Thomas Sr. apparently suffered a stroke just before the signing of the Declaration and died on the way home. Thomas Jr., in poor health for some years, was sailing for France in 1779 when he disappeared at sea. In 1762, the house was bought by Robert Hume, whose son John was said to have turned down a Scottish earldom just to remain an "Earl of Marshmud" here at Hopsewee. Grandson John Hume Lucas (also grandson of the inventor Johnathan) rebuilt the neglected house in 1846, adding the functional double piazzas across the front. He's probably also responsible for the distinctive kitchens that you park beside.

66.7	0.0	From Hopsewee Plantation parking lot, retrace drive to U.S. 17.
66.9	0.2	At end of drive, cross U.S. 17 South and turn left onto U.S. 17 North.
72.9	6.0	Turn right onto S-22-23.
75.4	2.5	At stop sign, continue straight and cross S-22-18.

75.4	**50 ft.**	**A**t stop sign, turn right onto Belle Isle Road / S-22-295.
75.6	**0.2**	**F**ollow road uphill to the left.
76.0	**0.4**	**A**t stop sign, go straight to Belle Isle Villas gatehouse and through gates.
76.2	**0.2**	**O**n left is Battery White.

19. BELLE ISLE PLANTATION AND BATTERY WHITE

This boyhood home of Francis Marion and the site of a Civil War battery is a pretty spot and offers a good view of Winyah Bay. Here on North Island in front of the Battery White is the June 13, 1777, landing spot of the Marquis de Lafayette and Baron de Kalb, who came to offer their services to the nation. Both served as major generals in the American Revolution.

◈

76.4	**0.2**	**C**ontinue to parking lot and Mini Museum.
76.4	**0.0**	**F**rom parking lot, retrace to gatehouse and Belle Isle Road.
76.8	**0.4**	**A**t gate, go straight on Belle Isle Road/S-22-295.
77.4	**0.6**	**A**t stop sign, turn right onto South Island Road / S-22-18.

A Short History of Georgetown

If we discount an ill-fated 1526 settlement by the Spanish, then the history of this area begins in 1705 when the English Proprietors granted the land. Within fifteen years, enough settlers had arrived to warrant an Anglican parish called Prince George–Winyah: "George" for the Old World king and "Winyah" for the soon-to-disappear Indians. As elsewhere, ship stores—tar and lumber—were produced here, but they had to be shipped through the Port of Charles Town. From the Santee north, there was discontent over this trade monopoly, and in 1732, Georgetown became an official port. It was already a "city" by then, the third oldest in the colony. Elisha Screven had laid out a town grid with lots set aside for churches, markets, jail, and school. His original streets constitute the historical district today, but his plan was disrupted when the hundred-acre common was claimed by others. As a consequence, the churches weren't built on Church Street, and the stores now crowd a waterfront that was meant to be open.

Located at the junction of six rivers, it was almost inevitable that Georgetown would prosper as a trading center. Ship stores and shipbuilding, and the planting of indigo and rice, made early fortunes, so when the Revolution came, many of the town's satisfied merchants and planters remained loyal to the king. The community survived this indiscretion amazingly well, and soon after the war enjoyed a wealth few could have imagined.

Expanding rice cultivation made this one of the richest sections in the nation. Georgetown was not a particularly healthy spot to summer in, but planters built town houses and public buildings that still remain.

80.6	**3.2**	At yield sign, go straight onto U.S. 17 North.
81.0	**0.4**	Cross Sampit River Bridge. Visible to right is downtown Georgetown.

20. GEORGETOWN

Crossing the river named for the Sampit Indians, you get a good view of the town. On your right, ships are docked and imported salt is stored in that great dome. On the left is the paper mill—a pulp-processing plant that International Paper started back in 1936. Georgetown has depended on mills since the turn of the century, when the Atlantic Coast Lumber Company began what would become the largest lumber mill on the East Coast. It went bankrupt during the Depression, so the paper mill was a welcome source of revenue. A little more controversial is the Georgetown Steel Mill on your right. It came in the late 1960s bringing much-needed jobs, but as you'll notice, the discharge from its stack has coated the town with a light brown soot that gives a distinct "Rust Belt" look to this side of the community. Don't let that spoil your trip, for just a few blocks to the right is a 250-year-old village that's enjoying a long-overdue comeback.

81.0	**0.0**	Continue on 17 North.
83.6	**2.6**	Turn left into Days Inn / Georgetown County Visitors Center.

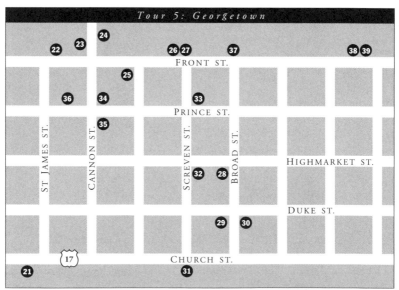

Tour 5: Georgetown

21. GEORGETOWN COUNTY VISITORS CENTER

Information is available here on all the local tours and spots of interest. Front Street flooded during Hurricane Hugo, but the houses here are high and well built. The damage was minor and is now repaired.

First, enjoy a drive through this historic area. Later, you'll have an opportunity to park and visit some of these sites.

83.6	**0.0**	From Days Inn / Georgetown County Visitors Center parking lot, turn right onto U.S. 17 South.
83.8	**1 block**	Turn left onto St. James Street / S-22-80.
84.2	**4 blocks**	Turn right onto Front Street.
84.2	**20 ft.**	First house on left is 405 Front Street.

22. 405 FRONT STREET
The Withers-Daley House, c. 1737
Not open to public.
The oldest house in town, it originally was only one room deep with porches front and back. It may have served as an inn.

84.2	**1 block**	Turn left onto Cannon Street.
84.3	**1/2 block**	The building on left is 16 Cannon Street.

23. 16 CANNON STREET
The Red Store–Tarbox Warehouse, pre-Revolution
Not open to public.
Silk, indigo, and fine wines were stored in this colonial warehouse. The town's finest inn once adjoined the building. Theodosia Burr Alston sailed from here on the *Patriot* and was never seen again.

84.3	**0.0**	Across street on right is 15 Cannon Street.

24. 15 CANNON STREET
Heriot-Tarbox House, c. 1740
Not open to public.
Indigo built this fine house. Sections of the vault-like foundation served as summer cool storage. Candles lit in the dormer "candle windows" notified the community that the woman of the house was alone and should be protected. Builder Heriot was loyal to the king, one of whose soldiers was shot on this front porch by Marion's raiders.

84.3	**1/2 block**	At dead end, make U-turn and retrace to Front Street.
84.3	**1 block**	At stop sign, turn left onto Front Street.
84.4	**1 block**	Sixth house on right is 528 Front Street.

25. 528 FRONT STREET
The Man-Doyle House, c. 1760

Not open to public.

This "grand old mansion house of the village" is a typical Georgian double house with the double-tiered front portico. Built or purchased by Miss Mary Man of nearby Mansfield Plantation in about 1775, the building once enjoyed a prestigious view of the water and no doubt was the mansion against which others were measured. Note the wood of the pediment simulating stone, the ornate cornice molding, and beaded siding. Prominent in Georgetown's history, the house is a fine example of pre-Revolutionary construction.

84.5	**1 block**	Continue on Front Street. On left is 633 Front Street.

26. 633 FRONT STREET
Kaminski Building, c. 1842

Open to public.

Now an annex of the rice museum, this building began as a hardware store in 1842. The cast-iron front went on in 1859, and Heiman Kaminski added the distinctive three-story light well after the Civil War. Just inside the door is a model of the Brown's Ferry vessel. Dating from 1730, this fifty-foot freighter was rescued from the bottom of the nearby Black River and is the oldest example of American shipbuilding ever found. It is hoped that the original can be stabilized and displayed. An art gallery fills the rear of the store.

84.5	**25 feet**	Next building on left is the Rice Museum.

27. CORNER OF FRONT AND SCREVEN STREETS
The Rice Museum, c. 1841

Open to public. Short lecture. Small admission charge.

Since the Revolution, this has been the site of the town market, but the present Greek Revival building wasn't constructed until a fire swept the waterfront in 1841. Three years later the distinctive clock tower was added. The second floor, once the town hall, is now the Rice Museum. Here in the flood plain of these half-dozen rivers, forty thousand acres of rice were planted in 1850. The amount of work required to lay out these fields has been compared to the building of the Great Pyramids. Since the slaves did the work in this boggy terrain, usually without even the help of animals, much of the museum bears witness to their reluctant labor. In paintings and glass-cased models or dioramas, we see the land being cleared, ditched, and diked. At times, it was necessary to flood and drain the land, so a series of water-control structures, or trunks, were installed. Visitors see demonstrations of harvesting, winnowing, and milling the grain, along with the tools used: hoes, mortars, wooden shovels, and fanner baskets. An intricate little gear-filled model of a rice mill represents the full-sized machines that once stood beside this river. There's also a display on indigo production.

A good selection of books and pamphlets are for sale; for touring the town, you should at least have *A Guide to City of Georgetown Historic District.*

| 84.6 | 1 block | Turn right onto Broad Street / S-22-379. |
| 84.8 | 3 blocks | On right, in third block, is Prince George–Winyah Episcopal Church. |

28. PRINCE GEORGE–WINYAH EPISCOPAL CHURCH, c. 1753

Open to public.

The British burned this building after using it as a stable, so a new roof and pews were added then; the tower was added in 1824. The windows of the chancel addition were taken from one of the slave chapels built by Ploden Weston. Over the years a small army of inattentive boys scratched a great fleet of rice schooners and other graffiti into the sides of the box pews. See if you can find "Yes, mama." The churchyard has stones dating back to 1767. Governor Robert Alston is buried here, and the founder of Porter Military Academy, Anthony Toomer Porter.

| 84.9 | 1 block | On right is Hebrew Cemetery. |

29. 400 BROAD STREET
HEBREW CEMETERY

Open to public.

The Jewish community in Georgetown is the second oldest in South Carolina and probably predates the earliest grave here, dated 1762. In overall appearance, there's little to set it apart from the neighboring graves of the Episcopalians, but a close look shows Hebrew inscriptions and stars.

| 84.9 | 0.0 | Across street on left is 417 Broad Street. |

30. 417 BROAD STREET
Bethel African Methodist Church, c. 1882

Open to public for tram tour.

Organized as a congregation in 1865, freed slaves built this AME Church in 1882, and in 1908 it was remodeled and bricked over. The hand-painted windows can be appreciated from the outside, but the tram guide has to show you the unusual crimped tin ceiling of the interior.

| 85.0 | 1 block | Turn right onto Church Street. |
| 85.1 | 1 block | Turn right onto Screven Street, noting Baptist Cemetery on left. |

31. CORNER OF CHURCH AND SCREVEN STREETS
Baptist Cemetery, c. 1804

Open to public.

Elisha Screven set aside this lot for construction of a Baptist church that wouldn't be built here until 1804. In the midst of the early graves is a monument to William Screven, founder of the Baptist Church in South Carolina. This statue to the Confederate War dead stood originally at the corner of Broad and Highmarket, but it was moved out here when traffic patterns shifted.

| 85.2 | 2 blocks | On right at corner of Screven and Highmarket streets is Prince George Parish Hall. |

32. CORNER OF SCREVEN AND HIGHMARKET STREETS
Prince George Parish Hall, c. 1818
Open to public.
This was the three-story county jail until 1950. Now, with a top story removed, the two-foot-thick walls of this 1818 structure shelter the parish hall.

| 85.2 | 0.0 | Continue on Screven Street. |
| 85.3 | 1 block | Turn left onto Prince Street, noting on right the yellow Georgetown County Courthouse. |

33. CORNER OF SCREVEN AND PRINCE STREETS
Georgetown County Courthouse, c. 1824
Open to public.
This yellow building was designed by Robert Mills. The Greek Revival structure is fronted by the massive pediment and columns that we associate with South Carolina's best-known architect. The annex on the left is a 1948 addition.

| 85.5 | 2 blocks | On right is 501 Prince Street. |

34. 501 PRINCE STREET
Winyah Society Hall, c. 1857
Not open to public.
Indigo planters meeting socially paid for their drinks in indigo, and the surplus went to finance a school for the poor. This red brick hall with stucco trim and stately portico was designed by leading Charleston architect Edward Bickell White.

| 85.5 | 0.0 | Across the street is 502 Prince Street. |

35. 502 PRINCE STREET
The Morgan-Ginsler House, c. 1825
Not open to public.
To all appearances, it's just a conventional town house, but this one is haunted. It was a Union hospital: Blood still stains the dining room floor, and the bumps at night are said to be the sound of "the devil herding the bluecoats back."

| 85.6 | 1/2 block | On right is 417 Prince Street. |

36. 417 PRINCE STREET
The Cuttino-Turner House, c. 1790
Not open to public.
Just as in Charleston, Georgetown had her single houses. This one and the one next door were built by William Cuttino for his two daughters. Both houses have had additions and repairs, but the original structures, with their narrow sides to the street, are easy to identify.

| 85.6 | 1/2 block | At stop sign, turn right onto St. James Street. |

85.7	**1 block**	At stop sign, turn right onto Front Street.
85.9	**3–4 blocks**	In the next few blocks, park and visit Rice Museum and River Walk behind buildings on left as well as houses open to the public.

37. RIVER SIDE OF FRONT STREET
The River Walk

Restaurants and shops along this boardwalk face the water, and several small city parks are located along the high ground. Shrimp boats dock nearby. A part of the town's revitalization project, this once-derelict waterfront has been successfully refurbished.

85.9	**2 blocks**	On left is 1003 Front Street.

38. 1003 FRONT STREET
The Kaminski House, c. 1760
Open to public.

This was the town house of the Alston family (the Brookgreen Plantation Alstons). Heiman Kaminski, returning from four years of Confederate service with only two silver dollars, made a fortune with his hardware store in the lean years that followed the war. Heiman's son Harold, a retired naval officer, and his wife Julia Pyatt enlarged this house and furnished it. In 1972, it was willed to the City of Georgetown.

The house has been drastically altered over the years, so it's difficult to say what is original, but inside you'll find a remarkable collection of antiques. "Eclectic" is the word used by the custodians, but for the most part these furnishings are American. You'll get a thorough and entertaining tour. There's a three-hundred-year-old Spanish trousseau chest just inside the door; then English clocks, Persian prayer rugs, and Charleston Chippendale, portraits, and petit point. Master furniture designers Duncan Phyfe and Thomas Elfe are represented. Upstairs is a 1760 Chippendale-style commode, and in the next room, Art Deco beds. It all blends together in a curious, comfortable, and elegant whole, so if you're interested in antiques and interior decoration, you won't want to miss the home of Harold and Julia Kaminski.

85.9	**0.0**	On left is 1019 Front Street.

39. 1019 FRONT STREET
The Pawley House, c. 1790
Not open to public.

You only have a view of the rear, but that shows some interesting brickwork, and George Washington slept here.

ADDITIONAL TOURS (Organized or Otherwise)

You've probably noticed by now that the buildings in the town that are listed on the National Register of Historic Places have numbered plaques giving the builder, current owner, and date of construction. Besides the "Guide" already mentioned, a single sheet, "Historic Trail," provides a map and one- or two-sentence entries about the fifty-eight sites listed. Also available is a cassette walking tour of several downtown blocks.

The Swamp Fox Tram offers an enjoyable introduction to the area. This open carriage is pulled about the streets by a jeep, while the guide gives you a bit of history and points out the highlights. You stop to enter the Prince George Church and the AME Church across the street. (This is the only way you'll get inside the AME Church.)

If you like to walk, Miss Nell Cribb promises real Southern hospitality, history, legends, and ghost stories, and maybe even lemonade on the front porch. For the starting point of "Miss Nell's Tours," check at the chamber of commerce.

Two tour boats cruise the surrounding waters and their skippers give accompanying lectures on everything under the sun. The first boat, the *Island Queen*, leaves from the Land's End Marina across from the Visitors Center office. The second, Captain Sandy's *Osprey*, starts out from the Riverfront Wharf at 600 Front Street. Both tours are good; try not to leave Georgetown without taking at least one.

Plantation Tours of the Waccamaw River

The *Island Queen*, a large, steel-hulled passenger boat, is closed enough to protect passengers from the weather and there are restrooms and refreshments on board. We went up the Waccamaw on our afternoon tour. Captain Richard spoke of the great plantations of the rice culture and the famous men of the day. The lecture is thorough, prepared by several local historians. The boat often moves close to shore so that you can get a good look at the abandoned rice-field dikes and the wildlife now in residence.

The *Osprey*, an open pontoon boat, gives a comfortable, relatively quiet ride. The captain has spent most of his life on the water and much of it in this area, so no matter what the official name of the tour you've chosen, you'll be hearing an easy blend of history, natural history, and present-day matters. The captain recaps the history of the port from day one to the present as we leave the Sampit for the Waccamaw. Osprey are spotted quickly; royal terns feed on schooled mullet as we are shown the hangar from which Belle Baruch flew her plane to harass poachers on her Hobcaw Barony. We

 are told about indigo and the War of Jenkins's Ear and rice from Madagascar. There is a lecture on caviar and "cow sturgeon" as the boat slips by abandoned rice fields and second-growth cypress. Then, easing into narrow Jericho Creek, we begin a sort of *African Queen* passage through a close world of hibiscus, cypress, and butter cups. The boat reaches the Peedee River and we see the copper-roofed house of Arundel on the bank. Built in 1841, it got a face-lift this century, but the great oaks crowding about suggest that it has looked that way forever. Another Scottish homeplace, Direlton, shows well

from the river. Not typical, it's an early Victorian version of a Georgian plantation home. The boat slips through a world of crowding, thick vegetation that gradually gives way to the open Waccamaw, the distant stacks of the steel mill, and the rest of the twentieth century.

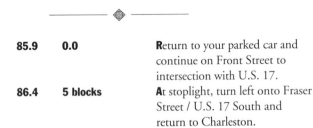

85.9	**0.0**	**R**eturn to your parked car and continue on Front Street to intersection with U.S. 17.
86.4	**5 blocks**	**A**t stoplight, turn left onto Fraser Street / U.S. 17 South and return to Charleston.

LAFAYETTE MEMORIAL HIGHWAY

This highway from Georgetown to Charleston is named in honor of the Marquis de Lafayette, who landed on North Island near Georgetown on June 13, 1777. He was accompanied by a small group of volunteers, including Baron de Kalb, a native of Germany. They promptly went to Charleston and thence to Philadelphia, where they offered their services to the nation. Both Lafayette and de Kalb served as major generals in the American Revolution. Both were famous for their gallantry. De Kalb gave his life at the Battle of Camden, South Carolina, in August 1780.

In 1824 Lafayette returned to the United States, hailed during his tour as a hero of the nation. While in South Carolina he laid the cornerstone for the monument to de Kalb in Camden.

> *South Carolina is proud to honor the memory of*
> *Lafayette and his Gallant Comrade in Arms.*
> *June 13, 1977*

(From marker on U.S. 17 South of Georgetown, South Carolina)

142.4	**56.0**	**N**orth side of Cooper River Bridge.

ADDITIONAL READING

David Doar's *Sketch of St. James Santee Parish* is still in print. Michael Frome's *Battle for the Wilderness* says bad things about the U.S. Forest Service. Thomas Clark's *The Greening of the South* says good things. Hampton Plantation has a selection of Archibald Rutledge's work and other related works. *The History of Georgetown County* by George Rogers and Alberta Lachicotte's *Georgetown Rice Plantations* are both back in print. "That We Should Have a Port," a good short history by Ronald Bridwell, is sold at the tour center. The Rice Museum has a good selection of books on related topics.

NOTES

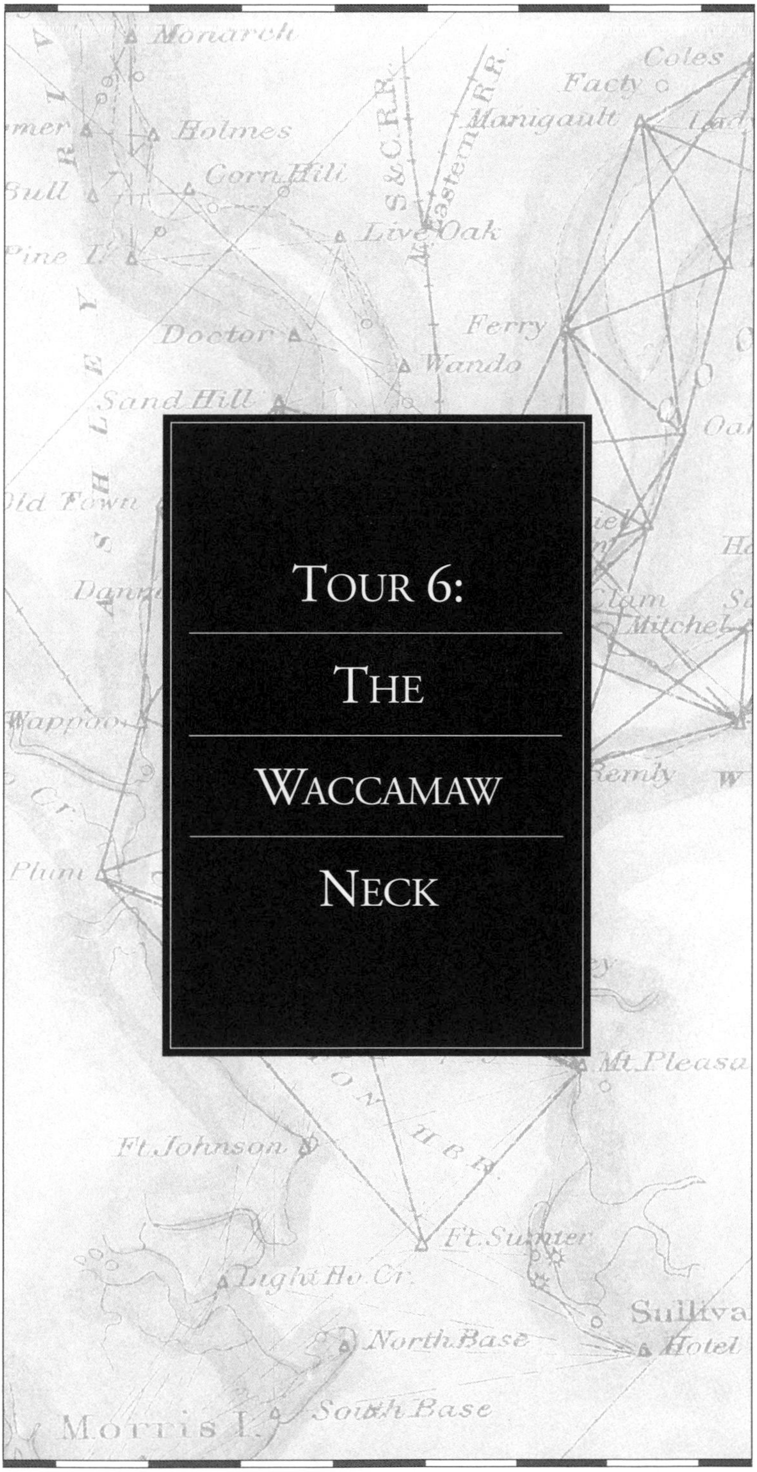

Tour 6: The Waccamaw Neck

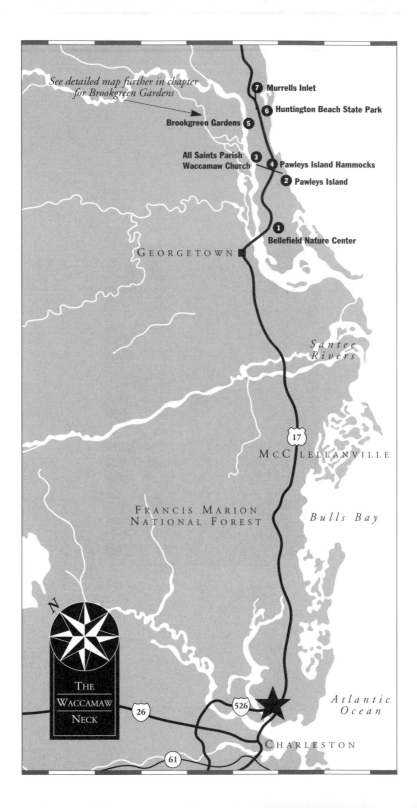

See detailed map further in chapter for Brookgreen Gardens

7 Murrells Inlet

6 Huntington Beach State Park

Brookgreen Gardens **5**

All Saints Parish
Waccamaw Church **3**   **4** Pawleys Island Hammocks

2 Pawleys Island

1

Bellefield Nature Center

GEORGETOWN

Santee Rivers

17

McCLELLANVILLE

FRANCIS MARION
NATIONAL FOREST

Bulls Bay

N

THE
WACCAMAW
NECK

26   **526**

61

Atlantic Ocean

CHARLESTON

THE WACCAMAW NECK

This tour begins just beyond Georgetown and continues north along U.S. 17 to the community of Murrells Inlet. We start at the BELLEFIELD NATURE CENTER—a part of the Belle W. Baruch Foundation—with a small but entertaining display of natural history and archaeological treasures. Then we visit the two-hundred-year-old seashore retreat of PAWLEYS ISLAND. Just inland we look at the three Anglican church buildings of ALL SAINTS PARISH WACCAMAW CHURCH—side by side but very different. We continue up Waccamaw Neck to BROOKGREEN GARDENS to see one of the finest exhibitions of American figurative sculpture in the country. The garden itself is a botanical museum, and there's a wildlife park as well. Directly across the road is HUNTINGTON BEACH STATE PARK, a mecca for bird watchers and ocean bathers. A couple of miles up the highway is the MURRELLS INLET community, famous for its seafood restaurants. If you want to fit this into a single day, start early. If not, take your time and come back another day.

Bellefield Nature Center

Open 10 a.m. to 5 p.m., Monday through Saturday.
No admission charge.

Pawleys Island

All Saints Parish Waccamaw Church, c. 1917

Church grounds open during daylight hours. (Two related churches across road.)

Brookgreen Gardens, c. 1929

Open 9:30 a.m. to 4:45 p.m.
Admission charged.

Huntington Beach State Park

Twenty-five-hundred-acre park with three miles of broad ocean beach. Activities include swimming, fishing, camping, and nature walks. Excellent birding. Naturalist on duty during summer months. Also a trading post, picnic area, and restrooms.

Open daily, 9 a.m. to 6 p.m.
Admission charged during season.

Atalaya, c. 1938

The Moorish-style beach house built by Archer and Anna Huntington, now a part of Huntington Beach State Park.

Interior tours daily at 11 a.m. and 1:30 p.m.

Murrells Inlet

Old summer retreat now famous for its seafood restaurants.

———————— ❖ ————————

0.0	0.0	From Charleston, take U.S. 17 North; begin clocking mileage at north side (Mount Pleasant) of Cooper River Bridge.
13.1	13.1	Look on left for Kiwi Farm.

Kiwi fruit has been grown at this farm for about ten years. "Kiwi" is the nick-
name for the people of New Zealand, the country where the fruit was first
established as a commercial crop. The fruit, also called Chinese gooseberry,
grows on vines and has a fuzzy brown skin and soft green pulp, similar in taste
and consistency to white grapes.

16.5	**3.4**	**O**n both sides, Francis Marion National Forest (see Tour 5).
33.5	**17.0**	**O**n right, McClellanville (see Tour 5).
40.8	**7.3**	**S**antee River Delta (see Tour 5).
42.8	**2.0**	**L**ook on left for Hopsewee Plantation (see Tour 5).
54.5	**11.7**	**C**ross Sampit River; look to right for downtown Georgetown (see Tour 5).
57.1	**2.6**	**C**ross Pee Dee River and Black River bridges.
57.7	**0.6**	**S**outh side of Waccamaw River.

Travel and Tourism

North of Georgetown, the two bridges we crossed replaced the ferry in
1935 and allowed the automobile to replace the boat as the main means of
transportation for the citizens of the Waccamaw Neck. When visitors
began to pass through, it was the beginning of a "recreation explosion"
that is now booming stronger than ever. Now, many who once only vaca-
tioned here come to stay year-round. This southernmost tip of the
Waccamaw Neck is called Hobcaw Barony and was actually settled long,
long before.

A History of Hobcaw Barony

The first European colony on the North American continent is thought to
have been started here in 1526 under the direction of the Spaniard Lucas
Vásquez de Ayllón. His five hundred settlers were plagued by starvation
and fevers. Ayllón died, mutiny followed, and the slaves revolted. Building
a ship, 150 of the original party managed to escape back to Cuba. In 1718,
the site was granted to one of the Lords Proprietor, John Carteret, and the
fourteen-thousand-acre Hobcaw Barony remained in one block until it was
divided into rice plantations just before the Revolution. In 1905, entrepre-
neur and statesman Bernard Baruch began purchasing the individual plots,
reuniting the property and using it as a place to relax and entertain friends,
among them Sir Winston Churchill and Franklin Roosevelt. His daughter
Belle inherited the land and willed the Barony to the state for use as a
teaching and research center.

59.3	**1.6**	**T**urn right into Hobcaw Barony: The Belle W. Baruch Foundation Institute—home of The Belle W. Baruch Forest Service Institute of Clemson University, Belle W. Baruch Institute for Marine Biology and Coastal Research of the University of South Carolina, and Bellefield Nature Center.

1. BELLEFIELD NATURE CENTER

The natural history displays in the small Bellefield Nature Center building are excellent. Just inside is a "touch table," fun for adults as well as children. You're asked to identify and speculate on a variety of nature's pieces and parts, ranging from pine cones to wild boar skulls. Next is a display case of archaeological finds—from Indian projectile points dating to 13,000 B.C. through the rice hoes and dispensary bottles of comparatively modern times. In the center, several saltwater and freshwater aquariums and containers hold a variety of local animals that you might not be lucky enough to spot any other way. They've got a chicken turtle, an old-time delicacy no longer on supermarket shelves. There are snapping turtles, snakes, and much, much more.

❖

59.3	**0.0**	**F**rom Bellefield Nature Center parking lot, turn right onto U.S. 17 North.
66.1	**6.8**	**V**eer right onto S-22-266.
67.3	**1.2**	**A**t Pawleys Island stop sign, turn right onto S-22-10.
68.2	**0.9**	**A**t stop sign, turn left onto S-22-265.
68.2	**1 block**	**A**t stop sign, turn right and follow S-22-265.
68.9	**0.7**	**D**ead-end at south end of Pawleys Island.

2. PAWLEYS ISLAND

Four miles long and no more than a quarter-mile wide, Pawleys Island today enjoys an almost mystical reputation as a genteelly shabby vacation spot. Three Pawley brothers took out a grant for this land in 1711, but it probably wasn't occupied even as a summer retreat until after the Revolution. In 1845, future state governor Robert F. W. Allston built a causeway and moved his family onto the island for the malaria season. "The vehicles, horses, cows, furniture, bedding, trunks, provisions" were brought from nearby plantations on great flats. Summer residents were well attended by servants and free to catch up on visiting and enjoy the seashore recreations. Nine houses and a school (studies continued even here) to accommodate forty white residents were soon reported; a church, a rectory, and more homes fol-lowed. About a dozen of these old structures remain and can be glimpsed occasionally through the thick growth of stunted oaks and cedars.

Protected by its high dunes, Pawleys Island escaped the great 1893 storm with the loss of only two houses, but the Gray Man, a mysterious ghost, is said to appear to warn of approaching storms and other catastrophes. (He must have had his work cut out for him during the late 1950s: A storm tumbled over much that was built on this newly washed-up sliver of land on the south end.) In 1902, the Atlantic Coast Line Railroad ran a train from the Waccamaw ferry landing over to the island. It washed away four years later, but its southern causeway is still traveled by automobiles. The orchestras of the 1900s were replaced by the rock-and-roll bands of the dance pavilion, but that too is gone. Summer visitors no longer line up shoulder to shoulder with pitchforks and prong every flounder in the creek, either.

Hurricane Hugo cut the island in half and many houses were lost. People are rebuilding quickly, though, and Pawleys Island continues to enjoy a reputation for relaxed fun. Houses can be rented and several inns offer old-time hospitality. The little chapel is non-denominational, and the front is all glass so you don't have to give up the marsh view even for that one hour a week.

———— ◈ ————

68.9	**0.0**	**R**etrace S-22-265 to S-22-10; continue straight through intersection of S-22-266.
70.6	**1.7**	**C**ontinue straight north on S-22-10.
71.3	**0.7**	**T**urn left onto S-22-46.
71.7	**0.4**	**A**t stoplight, continue straight across U.S. 17 onto S-22-46.
73.5	**1.8**	**A**t stop sign, turn right onto S-22-255.
73.7	**0.2**	**O**n left, All Saints Parish Waccamaw Church, turn into the parking lot on the right side of the road.

3. ALL SAINTS PARISH WACCAMAW CHURCH, c. 1917

Grounds open to public.

Separated from Georgetown's Prince George Parish in 1767, this new parish, like most after the Revolution, had to struggle simply to maintain services. In 1832, however, Reverend Alexander Glennie brought about a revival of interest and expanded the church's ministry into the slave community. In 1844, the old church was taken down and a new "building of colonial design, with massive columns on the front porch" took its place. The Civil War brought an end to Reverend Glennie's ministry for both whites and blacks, and in 1915 the church burned. Similar in style to "the old church" but on a slightly smaller scale, this new one is the fourth on the site. It was built with the aid of generous contributions.

The cemetery contains the remains of Westons, Wards, Allstons, Alstons, and numerous others that live on in local history and legend. Notice the graves of the victims of the great 1893 storm, and that of Plowden Weston. Reverend Glennie had been brought here from England to be Weston's tutor and in later life would have in the planter his staunchest ally. Sally Flagg rests here, as well, but she isn't the one famed as the ghost in Murrells Inlet. Unfortunately, her gravestone suffered the attention of this notoriety, all the same.

Across the street is the new All Saints Church. The parish house to the left was built in 1975 to match the existing 1917 church. The house was struck by lightning and burned before it could be used, which is why, when it was rebuilt the following year, lightning rods went on its roof and on all the buildings in the church grounds. The low buildings to the rear are the kindergarten, and the tremendous new temple to the right is the church. Based on the design of the earlier buildings, it is unusual because, as in a true Greek or Roman building, its columns actually support (or appear to support) the portico and the sides as well.

Beyond the kindergarten buildings is one of the thirteen slave chapels that Reverend Glennie built. This one has been moved about the countryside three times and saw service as a summer church, library, and community center before ending up here as a youth center.

73.7	**0.0**	**F**rom church parking lot, turn left onto S-22-255 and retrace.
73.9	**0.2**	**A**t stop sign, turn left onto S-22-46.
75.7	**1.8**	**A**t stoplight, turn left onto U.S. 17 North.
76.0	**0.3**	**T**urn right into parking lot of Pawleys Island Hammock Shop.

4. PAWLEYS ISLAND HAMMOCKS

This type of rope hammock was invented by Joshua Ward of nearby Brookgreen Plantation and successfully duplicated and marketed by his brother-in-law, A. H. Lachiocotte. Cool and comfortable, it's truly a sinister device, for once hung and occupied, it can cause even the most strong-willed person to "lose a crop." Purchase at your own risk from the original Pawleys Island Hammock Shop or the other gift shops in this area. (A small branch of the Georgetown Chamber of Commerce operates behind the Pawleys Island Hammock Shop.)

| 76.0 | 0.0 | From the Hammock Shop's parking lot, turn right onto U.S. 17 North. |
| 81.2 | 5.2 | Turn right onto U.S. 17 North. Turn left into Brookgreen Gardens. |

5. BROOKGREEN GARDENS, c. 1929

Waccamaw Neck was the land of the rice princes, a place rich in history and myth, and Brookgreen Gardens is particularly noteworthy. It's made up of Brookgreen and three other plantations, which, like others in the area, originally ran from the ocean to the rice fields of the Waccamaw River. Local travel

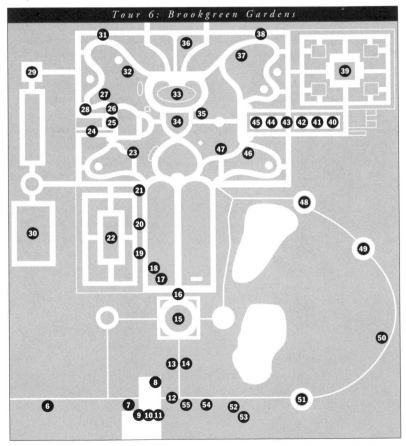

Tour 6: Brookgreen Gardens

in that day, of course, was by ferry—Dover and Calais were the Waccamaw River ports of this provincial neighborhood. More than one resident, however, ventured out into the world or at least made a mark upon it.

The owner of Brookgreen Plantation, William Allston, was a captain under Francis Marion. Showing great promise, his son Washington Allston left home to study art abroad. A friend of Samuel Coleridge, Washington Irving, and Samuel Morse, he became a leading artist of the day and, because he used color in the manner of that Renaissance master, was known as "the American Titian." The Oaks Plantation, located nearby, was the home of Joseph Alston and his wife, Theodosia Burr. She was the daughter of Aaron Burr and would remain closely attached to her controversial father. After Burr ended his political career by killing Alexander Hamilton in a duel, Alston helped finance his father-in-law's attempt to establish an empire in Mexico. This last adventure prompted charges of treason against Burr, but the three remained close, doting on the Alstons' one son and planning the future around him. Joseph was elected governor in 1812, but tragedy soon followed. The son died of malaria, and Theodosia, journeying to see her father, disappeared at sea, leaving behind two heartbroken men and a romantic legend. Adjoining Laurel Hill was the home of Plowden C. J. Weston, the student and supporter of Reverend Glennie, best remembered even into this century for the kind treatment he gave his slaves. The Ward family had bought Brookgreen early in the 1800s, and Joshua John Ward discovered and propagated world-famous "Carolina Golden Big Grain Rice." At Brookgreen and seven other plantations, he grew almost four million pounds of rice in 1850, and by some estimates was the wealthiest planter in the country.

The Civil War brought a sudden end to this golden age of golden rice. The planting did continue at Brookgreen under the ownership of the Hasell family, and they and the related Willetts and the two Dr. Flaggs maintained a school, a church, and an infirmary for both blacks and whites in the community. In 1920, the collection of plantations was sold to Dr. D. J. Mood, who ran it as a hunting club. His daughter, Julia Peterkin, would add one more page to this colorful history, for she used this locale in her novels, the best known being the Pulitzer Prize–winning *Scarlet Sister Mary*. The Depression arrived, and Waccamaw Neck grew poorer still. Brookgreen and the other three plantations went on the market and the Huntingtons bought them.

The Huntingtons

The Huntingtons were interesting people. Archer Milton Huntington's father went west for the Gold Rush and ended up in the hardware business in Sacramento. This was just a steppingstone for organizing the Central Pacific Railroad. More railroads came, and a shipyard in Newport News, along with a mistress and an illegitimate son, Archer. On the death of his wife, Archer's father married his mother, but the preceding fourteen-year gap of impropriety marked the boy and made him secretive and retiring in later life. Under his mother's direction, however, he received a uniquely free-form, globe-trotting education. He read much and traveled widely; Spain and its literature became his greatest love. At thirty-three, he completed a translation of the El Cid epic that's still the standard text today. Successful, rich, and witty, he was not particularly happy, says family member A. Hyatt Mayor, and when

Brookgreen Gardens

Archer's wife ran off with a theatrical producer, he became desperate to the point of suicide. It was then that he was rescued by and married to the sculptor Anna Hyatt. He was fifty-three and she was forty-seven.

Anna Hyatt was born and raised in Cambridge, Massachusetts. Her father, a Harvard professor and noted paleontologist, encouraged her early interest in living animals. Her older sister, already a sculptor, introduced her to what would be the avocation and vocation of a very long life. She understood the skeletal structure of animals (her paleontologist father's legacy) and was gifted with an extraordinary sense of observation and memory. After a few months of training at the Art Student League in New York, she made the domestic animals of a Maryland farm and the wild animals of the Bronx Zoo her textbooks. Animals would remain her specialty, but she's best known for two figures with animals—an equestrian statue of Joan of Arc unveiled in 1915, and *Diana of the Chase*, done in 1922. The following year she married Archer Huntington.

They were happy; they shared an intense interest in the arts and their seemingly dissimilar personalities complemented each other. A prolific period for the sculptor followed; then she contracted tuberculosis and had to spend a year in a Swiss sanitarium. Returning from Europe in 1929, Archer decided that his stocks were overvalued and sold them, so the couple was still very rich when they saw the newspaper ad for sixty-six hundred acres of South Carolina rice plantations. They visited Brookgreen, decided it would be a good place for Anna to regain her health, and bought the property. Soon they were planning a sculpture garden on the site of the Brookgreen house. This 1901 dwelling was torn down, and the plantation's beach house was dismantled to make room for their residence, Atalaya.

Wherever he set his foot, Archer Huntington declared, a museum sprang up, and this was to be no exception. At first it was to contain Anna's work only, but they quickly decided to make the collection representative of the history of American sculpture. The garden, embellished with verses from appropriate poets, would contain Southeastern flora and fauna, and the surrounding nine thousand acres would be a wildlife refuge.

Anna designed a garden for the site in the shape of a butterfly and Georgetown horticulturist Frank Tarbox, Jr., took charge of planting. Archer saw to the building of brick walls and fountains. His wife sculpted, other artists were generously supported, and Brookgreen took shape. The paving of Highway 17 in 1935 brought a sudden increase in visitors. The Huntingtons continued to return during the winters, but during World War II their beachfront home was turned over to the Army for coastal defense. The couple came to stay in 1946 and 1947, and then retired to the North for good. Archer died in 1955, but Anna maintained an active interest in Brookgreen for many more years. She sculpted until she was ninety-five and died in 1973 at the age of ninety-seven, leaving its trustees to exhibit and preserve Brookgreen for the enjoyment and instruction of all.

81.2	50 ft.	At Brookgreen Gardens entrance, No. 1, *Fighting Stallions*.

Guide to Statues Along Entrance Road

NO. 1. *Fighting Stallions*—Done by Anna Hyatt Huntington when she was seventy-five, this tremendous aluminum casting was placed here at the entrance in 1951 to catch the eye of passing motorists. It proved so successful that it became the symbol of the Gardens.

NO. 2. *Plaque and Entry*—Just beyond, a plaque announces the formation of the gardens by the Huntingtons in 1931 "for the appreciation of American sculpture and the preservation of Southeastern Flora and Fauna." The road is shaded by longleaf pine, oaks, and hollies and leads past historical markers for the Alstons and Allstons already discussed. We pay the attendant and are soon driving between four animal groups by Huntington. In the fork ahead is a larger work.

81.8	0.6	Ticket booth and gatehouse. (NOTE: When we last visited Brookgreen Gardens, new road construction was under way that may affect the next two entries.)
82.0	0.2	In triangular median, No. 3, *Diving Eagle*.

NO. 3. *Diving Eagle*—Notice the American flag nearby and the wreath that the eagle is delivering to the waves. This six-foot bronze was added in 1980. It was cast from the first enlargement, but an earlier eighteen-foot version is located at Battery Park in New York and dedicated to those lost at sea during World War II.

82.0	0.0	Veer right onto Allston Circle Drive as indicated by sign.

Metal Staues

For metal pieces like this *Diving Eagle*, cast in bronze, foundries usually produce the final product working from a smaller model done by the artist. This one was probably cast in sand in several pieces that were then welded together. (We'll get back to the "lost wax" method later.) Once here at Brookgreen, metal pieces are washed periodically with mild soap and water and usually waxed to ensure preservation.

82.1	0.1	Veer left as indicated by the sign for the Sculpture Garden and Visitors Pavilion. On right, No. 4, *In Memory of the Workhorse*.

No. 4. *In Memory of the Workhorse*—This 1964 piece gives you some idea of the length and breadth of Huntington's career; it was inspired by a small piece, *The Storm,* that she had modeled in France fifty-seven years earlier. She loved all animals, but horses were a favorite subject.

Stone Statues

In this medium, most artists create a half-size or smaller model in clay and then turn it over to master stonecutters who produce the statue. A large work can take two or three people several years to complete. Like the metal pieces, the stone and marble works are washed periodically and, once dry, are coated with a silicon finish to protect them from the elements. Unfortunately, acid rain is a problem here, and the stone can even be stained by leaves and bird droppings, so don't take the pristine condition of these outdoor displays for granted.

82.1	**0.0**	**C**ontinue on Allston Circle Drive.
82.3	**0.2**	**O**n right, No. 5, *Youth Taming the Wild.*

No. 5. *Youth Taming the Wild*—Done by Huntington in 1931, this was one of the earliest pieces placed at Brookgreen. The struggle depicted may represent intellect against animal strength or a youthful country taming its frontier, but the viewer is allowed to bring to it whatever meaning he or she likes. This piece was shipped from New Jersey, and when Brookgreen's laborers coaxed it off the barge they sang, "Come on, Horse, come on, Horse, we got a stable all fixed for you." And here it is.

82.4	**0.1**	**C**ontinue on Allston Circle and veer right following signs for Sculpture Garden and Visitors Pavilion.

The Visitors Pavilion

Close to the first parking lot is the sculpture garden reception area. Restrooms are here, and during the warm months a small snack bar opens. Next is a gift shop and indoor sculpture gallery. Between this and the parking lot you'll pass two works.

82.9	**0.5**	**T**urn left into the parking lot for the Sculpture Garden and Visitors Pavilion. Park and walk to Visitors Pavilion. No. 6, *Spirit of American Youth* is temporarily moved and wrapped in tarp.

No. 6. *Spirit of American Youth*—The original of this "young man reaching for the heavens" was done by Donald DeLue to keep watch over ten thousand Allied soldiers buried at our cemetery in Normandy. (Notice that the title, artist, material, and date of completion are given on a small plaque at the base of each statue.)

		On right, No. 7, *End of the Trail.*

No. 7. *End of the Trail*—One of the most popular of all American sculptures is this 1915 piece by James Earle Fraser. Though working out of a European classical tradition, American sculptors were looking to their native land for subject matter—a vanquished and vanishing subject, in this case. This probably looks familiar to you, but Fraser did one even more popular: He put the Indian on the buffalo nickel.

> Enter covered space, on left, the Visitors Pavilion Museum Shop.

Museum Shop

Two good books on the garden and its sculptors are sold here: *A Century of American Sculpture*, with color photos and five essays, and the more academic *Brookgreen Gardens Sculpture* by Beatrice Proske. There's also a brochure guide, dozens of pamphlets, and short natural history studies. Cassette tours can be rented and you can sign up for tours by well-informed guides. You're welcome to abandon this text now, for the following is a purely subjective rambling that leaves out most of the 450 statues that can be seen. We start here in the gift shop.

> Temporarily inside Museum Shop, No. 8, *The Huntington Busts*.

No. 8. *The Huntington Busts*—Though the Garden doesn't otherwise include portrait busts of individuals or commemoratives to them, an exception was made for the founders. Anna's sister sculpted her portrait and Anna did her husband's bust. "We are classicists," he declared at one point, but it's obvious from the eclectic range of these works that he did not mean this in the narrowest sense. Craft was important, and the end product of this craft should be something recognizably human or animal.

> Return outside and cross to The Carl Paul Jennewein Gallery; inside are No. 9, *Iris*; No. 10, *Debbie II*; and No. 11, *Toro Bravo*.

The Carl Paul Jennewein Gallery

All the sculptors at Brookgreen are American by birth or naturalized. Carl Jennewein came here from Germany as a young man. No. 9, *Iris*, by Jennewein greets us at the door. She's the goddess of the rainbow and descends to bring the messages of gods to men.

While in the gallery, take a look at No. 10, *Debbie II*. This isn't a goddess, just a thoroughly realistic naked woman. Debbie wore clothes in an earlier work—a sweater so finely ribbed that sculptor Isidore Margulies was accused of literally casting her from life. The artist explains that such realism is really an illusion. "I want the viewer's eye to fill in those details that I left out." We can guess that the glowing flesh of this National Sculpture Society's 1980 gold medal winner is bronze, but amazingly enough, so is the green ribbon about her hair.

NO. 11, *Toro Bravo*—Charlotte Dunwiddie left Germany just before World War II and lived for some years in South America. Here she presents the bull at the moment just before he enters the bull ring. He has stood in darkness until now and suddenly, blinded by the light, pauses a moment before charging.

Leave Jennewein Gallery by the door through which you entered.

Turn right; step between a pair of *Lions*, No. 12, by Anna Hyatt Huntington.

NO. 12. *Lions*—Bronze by Anna Hyatt Huntington done in 1930, the year the Huntingtons bought Brookgreen.

Turn left as you continue. On left is No. 13, *The Thinker*.

NO. 13. *The Thinker*—We're going to see a lot of animals but most are treated in a more realistic fashion than this chunky little ape. Marshall Fredericks' style is distinctively his own. Lighthearted and deceptively simple, his works are favorites of children, and we'll find him well represented when we finish up in the open ground to our right.

Directly across the walk is No. 14, *Flying Wild Geese*.

NO. 14. *Flying Wild Geese*—*The Thinker* pulls in upon himself, in part, a collection of short, slightly curved, but well-defined interlocking planes. In this Fredericks piece we see a completely different use of the almost flat surfaces— broad and rounded and silhouetted against the sky.

Continue, and in center of pool is No. 15, *Diana of the Chase*.

NO. 15. *Diana of the Chase*—One of the best known of Huntington's works, this 1922 piece was cast a dozen times. Diana, goddess of the woods, huntress queen, is often depicted in the midst of chase, but here the pursuit is up instead of forward, a shot at waterfowl rising from the surrounding water.

Diana's Pool

The pool serves several purposes, probably the most important being to reflect light upward. I asked the Gardens' director, Gordon Tarbox, why people have been throwing pennies in there all these years, and he laughingly admitted that he had no idea, but says the bank hates to see him coming with those bags of "dirty money." What happened to the goldfish that were here for so long? Herons and egrets ate most of them, and then an otter waited until the pool froze over, broke a hole in the ice, and pretty well finished the job.

Continue through gates on far side of pool. On gate post, No. 16, *King Penguin and Owl*.

NO. 16. *King Penguin and Owl*—Decorating the gatepost are two of the ten playful birds Paul Manship did for the Bronx Zoo gates in 1932. Minnesotan

Manship's early discovery of archaic Greek sculpture would influence him greatly and he in turn would influence many of those working in the twenties and thirties. His distinctive sculpture is well represented here at Brookgreen.

The Live Oak Walk

Brookgreen is actually not one garden but several, for its spaces are laid out much like a house, with each room or section given a distinctive planting and thus a different setting for the sculpture. These live oaks, originally the entry to the plantation, were incorporated into the Huntingtons' plan from the beginning and make this the most canopied of areas. The serpentine pieced brick walls allow light through but at the same time provide a soft gray backdrop for the works.

The Botanical Museum

The oaks and ivy are easy to identify and their influence is obvious, but much of the other planting, along the sidewalk's edge, requires a more studied appreciation. The sculpture garden now contains over 2,000 plant species and cultivars. The plants themselves are actually a museum. Each is labeled with a small plaque that gives the genus, the species, the family, and (at the bottom) the common name. And just as in any museum, the displays have been numbered and catalogued. Interesting for botanists and gardeners, the numerous plantings also provide almost constant change in color, texture, and setting.

The Verses

Archer Huntington selected these and friend R. A. Baillie chiseled the letters. A poet at heart, Huntington endowed the poetry chair at the Library of Congress. (South Carolina's own James Dickey was a recipient.) These poems are usually romantic and occasionally whimsical. Dixon Lanier Merritt's "A wonderful bird is the pelican, His bill will hold more than his belican," is no longer anonymous. Walt Whitman's line, "and a cow crunching with depressed head surpasses any statue," is given a place of honor. For a modest sum you can buy a copy of them all at the gift shop.

> Just through gates, turn left; first sculpture on right is No. 17, *Narcissus*.

No. 17. *Narcissus*—A young faun made of Tennessee marble takes delight in its own reflection. German-born Adolph Weinman has several other pieces with similar classical themes, including the mammoth *Riders of the Dawn*. Fauns, fawns, and sylvan situations, this garden is brimming with them, so I won't repeat myself by mentioning another.

> Continue on walk; turning the corner to the right on left against the wall is No. 18, *Reaching Jaguar*.

No. 18. *Reaching Jaguar*—Based on "Senior Lopez," a particularly large and ferocious resident of the Bronx Zoo, this work was modeled in 1907. Huntington went each morning to watch the animal step down for its morning meal and worked from memory of these brief moments. This natural, sketchlike treatment of the poised cat is a tough act to follow for any of the other "animaliers," including Huntington herself.

Continue on walk. Next on left is No. 19, *The Puritan.*

NO. 19. *The Puritan*—Surrounded by a billowing cloak, this hard-faced Calvinist takes a bold step forward, or does he? In fact, the figure is executed in relatively low relief. Nineteenth-century sculptor Augustus Saint-Gaudens is often called "the father of American sculpture" because of his break from the Neoclassical tradition in favor of realistic treatments like this one. Look across the garden to the far wall. The cloaked angel steps forward in a similar manner, but its face is indistinct and shadowed—an abstraction. That's *Benediction*, designed for a war memorial by Daniel French. Incidentally, French was capable of rendering the realistic as well as the symbolic—he sculpted the Lincoln in the Lincoln Memorial.

Continue on walk; next on left is No. 20, *Zeus.*

NO. 20. *Zeus*—The raised thunderbolts are given additional meaning once we know that this was meant for the top of the AT&T Building in New York. Best known for his architectural work, Robert Aitken also did the reliefs in the pediment of the United States Supreme Court building. Here in South Carolina, he did *The Marine* on Parris Island.

At walk intersection, turn back to left into Palmetto Garden, then veer right.

Palmetto Garden

Alleyways of palms and great ceramic jars give this bright open "room" the Moorish feel that Archer Huntington greatly enjoyed.

First on right is No. 21, *Primitive Man and Serpent.*

NO. 21. *Primitive Man and Serpent*—Roland Perry studied abroad and traveled through Germany and Norway. "Unrestrained naturalness and liveliness of expression," says Proske of his work. Originally, the title was *Thor and the Midgard Serpent.* The Norse god battled continually with the serpent at the center of the earth, and in their final encounter both perished.

Continue on walk, turning left to pool. In center is No. 22, *Samson and the Lion.*

NO. 22. *Samson and the Lion*—In the center is a similar but one-sided struggle. Christian sculptor Gleb Derujensky shows Samson rending the young lion, but it seems neither unrestrained nor natural. The effusive *Ecstasy* in the far corner is his as well. A little lively for my staid taste. As you continue to walk in the Palmetto Garden, note the war memorial by Daniel French and the complex sundial by Paul Manship. Also the unusual planting of this Mediterranean "room." That low, square hedge at the center is yaupon—the red-berried cassina that we usually see growing wild in the coastal forest.

> Go out the side gate through which you entered.

This is the lower left-hand corner of the giant butterfly designed by Anna Huntington. Great oaks and magnolias circle much of this enclosure, but the center where the house stood, though thick with shrubbery, is open to the sky.

> Continue straight out gates; to left is white figure, No. 23, *Maidenhood.*

NO. 23. *Maidenhood*—Marble has a much finer texture than limestone because the gases have escaped before it solidifies. Sculptor George Barnard said of this study in serenity, "I finished the marble in a way I finished no other flesh." In later years, the model who posed for this piece was the cause of a scandalous murder.

> Turn left; at end of walk turn right, and 2 ft. later to left. On right is No. 24, *L'Après-midi d'un faune.*

NO. 24. *L'Après-midi d'un faune*—I said I wasn't going to mention another faun, but Percy Baker did this delicate carving himself. Ordinarily, a piece of these proportions would be done in bronze, but Anna Huntington requested marble. It was broken during delivery.

> To your right is a green wooden kitchen building. Turn around and walk to its front door, on your left will be No. 25, *My Niece.*

NO. 25. *My Niece*—Jo Davidson was the most famous of American portrait sculptors, but he still had time to do a few figure studies like this one.

The Kitchen

Plantation kitchens were placed away from the main house to prevent fires, but this one survived instead of the house. It was used as a clinic when the Huntingtons first arrived. Today, it houses a collection of local shells, plantation tools, guns, and a finely made cypress dugout. The boxwoods growing in front are all that remain of the Wards's extensive antebellum garden. The bell tower was built around the stump of a West Coast cedar that dated from their time.

> From exit door of kitchen, turn left; on left wall is No. 26, *Jaguar Eating.*

NO. 26. *Jaguar Eating*—That's Senior Lopez again, and the companion piece of the first Huntington cat. It's breakfast time at the Bronx Zoo.

> Continue straight on winding walk, and to right in center of garden is No. 27, *Man Carving His Own Destiny.*

No. 27. *Man Carving His Own Destiny*—"Struggling to hack out his own character, carving his own future by the effort of his will" is how Czech-born Albin Polásek described his work. We'll see pictures of this later in the small statue gallery.

Continue straight on walk; next on left is No. 28, *Shark Diver.*

No. 28. *Shark Diver*—"Only within the suspension of water can the human form be released to its ultimate flow of grace and action," wrote sculptor Frank Eliscu. To suspend a figure in this manner required a masterful refinement of the lost wax process.

The Lost Wax Process

Bronze and other metals are cast using this method. The work is modeled in wax, with a core of some other material. Then a silica (ceramic or sand) mold is formed around this. As melted bronze is poured in—the casting—the wax liquefies, exiting through "gates." After cooling, the mold is broken away and the surface of the casting is smoothed. If cast in sections (remember *Diving Eagle*), these are then welded together. Finally, the patina, or permanent color, is put on with a chemical bath.

Just after *Shark Diver*, bear left and then right, and turn left through the next gates to reach No. 29, *Pegasus.*

No. 29. *Pegasus*—When the blood from the severed head of Medusa fell into the sea, it produced the winged horse Pegasus, who, once caught and tamed, was given to the Muses. Laura Fraser presents this "symbol of inspiration" carrying its artist-rider above the clouds. The sculptor worked on the model for five years and then the stonecutters took over. This began as about forty tons of granite in the quarry at Mount Airy, North Carolina. They brought it here in three pieces and whittled half of that away. Still, little chance of it getting airborne.

To left at end of green is No. 30, *Fountain of the Muses.*

No. 30. *Fountain of the Muses*—This is a fairly new addition by Swedish-born Carl Milles. There were nine Muses, the daughters of Jupiter and Mnemosyne, goddess of memory, but these aren't they. The figures dancing across the pool are five artists who have been inspired, and a faun, a centaur, and a goddess are keeping them company. Those strange little things spurting water are fish. Milles is an undisputed giant of twentieth-century sculpture, and this display came here by way of the Metropolitan Museum of Art. But like winged Pegasus, the pleasure and purpose of this one evades me.

Return to No. 29, *Pegasus*, and look straight ahead to marsh.

In front of us are old rice fields, filled in in some spots and returning to cypress in others.

> Turn right, return through gates and turn to left. At dead end turn to right, and first on left is No. 31, *Diana.*

We're once more in the upper left-hand corner of the butterfly.

No. 31. *Diana*—The most hunterlike of the Gardens' Dianas, this one is set off by the wilderness of abandoned rice fields beyond. The companion to this is the *Actaeon* at the far end of this walk. Silhouette-like and angular, the enameled eyes and stylized hair show the influence of archaic Greek sculpture.

> As you face *Diana*, do an about-face and turn left onto circling walk. Second on right is No. 31, *Mares of Diomedes.*

No. 32. *Mares of Diomedes*—Hercules tamed these man-eating mares, but this wasn't the title selected by sculptor Gutzon Borglum. He had Old West horse-stealing in mind. He is best remembered for carving the four presidents on the face of Mount Rushmore.

> Continue straight to pool.

The Alligator Pool

Archer Huntington designed this pool to act as a reservoir for several surrounding fountains. Note how the overflow spills into a surrounding trough that leads to other lower fountains. The sunning alligators were sculpted by his wife.

> In center of pool is No. 33, *The Alligator Bender.*

No. 33. *The Alligator Bender*—Nathaniel Choate carved the original statue out of mahogany. Then in Italy (he liked to be where the marble was), Choate did this Seminole Indian version.

> Walk to right around pool, and on far side turn right to gold No. 34, *Dionysus.*

No. 34. *Dionysus*—The sculpture of eighteenth-century France inspired Edward McCartan. "The forms are purified and the lucid composition polished to a glowing brilliancy of line," wrote Proske. This one gets special care for its gold leaf over bronze. Dionysus was the god of wine, but also a promoter of civilization, lawgiver, and lover of peace. Bright and elevated, he occupies a commanding position in the Gardens' main axis—a landmark for wandering visitors. But take a close look, and you'll see that Huntington's *Diana* is centered on the far end, next to rice fields. With upward-springing hound at her feet, the dark, twisting huntress shoots heavenward. This gleaming god and accompanying panther are turning decidedly downward.

> Continue around No. 34, *Dionysus,* and on right is No. 35, *Long Lost Thoughts.*

NO. 35. *Long Lost Thoughts*—You're on the left edge of what's unofficially called the baby garden, so there's stiff competition for this recent work by Charles Parks. Still, this child of the twentieth century (he's wearing clothes and isn't gleefully squeezing some small animal) is the winner: It's one of the most popular pieces in Brookgreen. Note the tree stump base; that, too, is a welcome relief from the conventional.

> Continue turning to right at the edge of the fountain; third figure on right is No. 36, *St. Francis.*

NO. 36. *St. Francis*—Architect and sculptor Julian Harris writes, "He was not a powerful man; he was an ethereal man. Everything was simplified in his life, so in doing this work I tried to express what I saw in reading and studying St. Francis." A short verse accompanies the saint who seems a worthy enough companion of gods and alligator wrestlers.

> Look behind you toward the rice field at gates and stairs.

Stairs

In plantation days these steps led down to the boat landing; you can still follow them down to the creek edge. The pillars are topped by two more of Manship's Bronx Zoo birds.

> Continue on walk past *St. Francis* to second figure on right, No. 37, *Sea Horse.*

NO. 37. *Sea Horse*—Seen across the hedge and opposite walk is Joseph Kiselewski's strange creature. He specializes in religious sculpture but has done several pieces for the young and young at heart. This unlikely sea horse appears to be at least half porpoise.

> Next on left, No. 38, *Actaeon.*

NO. 38. *Actaeon*—And here is the soon-to-be-deceased companion of Manship's *Diana*, at the far end of this walk. Actaeon spied on the goddess while she was bathing in her secret pool. In revenge, she turned him into a stag and his own dogs tore him apart.

> Continue to right and follow path around corner. Enter the Dogwood Garden to left. In center of pool is No. 39, *Riders of the Dawn.*

NO. 39. *Riders of the Dawn*—You'll be happy to see that Weinman's forty-ton stampede has been placed here where it can balance the equally monumental *Pegasus* and assure that Brookgreen doesn't tip over.

Dogwood Garden

The theme of this room seems to be people with animals. There's a particularly strange piece by Alexander Calder, the father of the mobile-making Calder, and a particularly nice old woman in the far right corner. That's *Communion* by Brenda Putnam. The real stars, though, are the dogwoods themselves.

As you face No. 39, exit garden to right. Pass restrooms. Turn right, again right, and right again into building.

The Museum of Small Sculpture

Inside the old caretaker's cottage that fronts this building, you'll find a display of the stonecutter's tools, and photographs of the methods by which measurements are transposed from model to stone, and of the cutting itself. Stonecutter R. A. Baille is pictured working on *Man Carving His Own Destiny*. Its creator, Albin Polásek, had left only a plaster model, but Baille thought such stonecutting was no different from conducting another man's symphony. Ironically, though, he died while carving this other man's destiny and the statue was finished by others.

Some of the statues you'll find inside the adjoining walled area were models for larger works; others were meant to be small. A fourth of the Gardens' collection is in this roofless, gray brick room; I'll mention just a few.

On each side of door into outside display area are No. 40, *The Cid Campeador and Joan of Arc.*

No. 40. *The Cid Campeador and Joan of Arc*—Just inside the door are small models of the two great equestrian statues for which Anna Huntington is most well known—liberators of Spain and France.
No. 41. *Persephone*—This may be the only human figure that Fredericks has here. (He did the thinking ape at the beginning.) Queen of the realm of the dead, this goddess was allowed to wake each spring and let life begin once more. This statue is also in the Gibbs Art Gallery garden.
No. 42. *Driller and the Rigger*—The working man was often celebrated in the art of the twenties and thirties, but works like these aren't likely to lend themselves to garden settings.
No. 43. *Bronco Buster*—This was the first attempt at sculpting for illustrator Frederic Remington. Needless to say, the 1895 work proved to be a tremendous success.
No. 44. *Venus and Adonis*—Located at the far end, this is one of the happiest (and funniest) works in Brookgreen, for Frederick MacMonnies blessed his two classical beauties with a realistic spontaneity. Victorian Americans weren't fooled by the title. They understood the all-too-human proposition and covered this impudent piece with a cloth when it was exhibited in New Rochelle.
No. 45. *Rain*—The crouching figure with headdress of rain is in the popular Art Deco style of the day.

Return to entrance of Museum of Smaller Sculpture and turn left; 40 feet at split of walk is No. 46, *Voratio.*

NO. 46. *Voratio*—This strange caterpillar by Jane Armstrong is the closest thing to abstraction we'll come across. Presumably, the title is a godlike reference to the animal's appetite. Touch it; it won't bite.

Turn to right of *Voratio* and first on right at pool is No. 47, *Night.*

NO. 47. *Night*—Compare the caterpillar to this Neoclassical piece by Czech-born Mario Korbel. Which is better? Which do you want in your garden?

Do an about-face, walk about 25 feet and exit through a gate to the left; in front of you will be a large pond. Bear left and at end of walk is a reflection pool with No. 48, *The Thinker*, in the center.

NO. 48. *The Thinker*—Take a good look at Gaston Lachaise's floating *Swans*, and then brace yourself for Henry Clews's *The Thinker*. I used to laugh at this and now I don't. The old man is attempting to come up with a new thought, a vanity indicated by the peacock feathers. From top to bottom, it's packed with symbolism, a searing indictment of a materialistic society, the same spiritually barren society that was feeding the sculptor. Clews finally got so disgusted he went to France and fixed up an abandoned château on the Riviera.

Continue on walk curving to right, and 200 feet on, in center of a very large green, is No. 49, *Time and the Fates of Man.*

NO. 49. *Time and the Fates of Man*—We're in the wide-open spaces now, and Paul Manship makes good use of the sunshine. Three women—young, middle-aged, and old—are spinning out the passage of time while the sun marks the hour in the grass about the flower-encircled base.

Continue, and on left is No. 50, *Mother and Baby Bear.*

NO. 50. *Mother and Baby Bear*—Back to back, these two squat on the side of the path like giant children's toys. It's not surprising, then, that this work is a favorite of children. Sculptor Marshall Fredericks says, "I love animals of all kinds and I did this group basically for children because I'm very fond of children. I love a child's reaction to a sculpture because it's such an honest reaction."

Continue to next pool and No. 51, *Gazelle Fountain.*

NO. 51. *Gazelle Fountain*—A wheeling gazelle crowns the top of this final pool. Another work by Fredericks, this one is as graceful and full of motion as the mother bear is stolid, but they have lightheartedness in common.

At next opportunity veer left, No. 52, *Don Quixote*, with No. 53, *Sancho.*

NO. 52. *Don Quixote*—This is rocky ground for the Spanish knight-errant, tilter at windmills. For Anna Huntington, he's a sad figure, depressed. His horse Rocinante was modeled here at the Atalaya studio from an animal so poorly it had to be hung from a sling, but given a little attention the model gained a new lease on life. Rocinante seems to have been a particular favorite of Archer Huntington; he named his yacht for him and found in the poor horse's "stumbling up to God" a triumph as grand as Napoleon's.

NO. 53. *Sancho*—Huntington gave the honor of doing this knight's companion to Jennewein, who created this well-fed and content retainer. No rocks beneath his feet.

Return to main walk and bear left. On both sides of walk, No. 54, *The Baboons*.

NO. 54. *The Baboons*—We started out a few feet from here, stepping between Fredericks's ape and geese, and now we end between his baboons. The sculptor's fame began with his *Baboon Fountain* at the 1939 World's Fair, and here are two cast from the half-size originals and presented to Brookgreen in 1985. "Understated" is the term used to describe them, so understated they'll remain.

Continue straight on. On left is No. 55, *Len Ganeway*.

NO. 55. *Len Ganeway*—This old farmer reading his paper on the park bench is a favorite of visitors, and you may have to wait your turn to sit beside him. There's no danger that he's been "cast from life," but note the detail in the rubber boots, overalls, and worn face with ample mustache. We assume this is a portrait of a real person, probably the artist's neighbor, but actually, *Len Ganeway* is the pen name of the editor of the newspaper that commissioned the work. Sculptor Derek Wernher explained, "He's just a little guy reading a newspaper. Once I got the head, I got the person and the rest of it fell into place." Wernher is one of the few sculptors to do his own foundry work.

We're through: the three-hour Brookgreen. Actually, that's not much better than the famous "three-minute Louvre," but there's no law that says we have to see it all. Still, I'll venture to complain that there are too many statues. Most museums show only a small portion of their collections at any one time, which allows them the luxury of removing pieces that are no longer timely or appreciated or popular. Brookgreen doesn't; they say permanent and they mean it.

So now we are left to sit beside Len Ganeway and mutter to ourselves that last retort of all Philistines, "We know what we like." But do we? We can't respond as children do by climbing into the lap of the mother bear. Did you find a dozen works that brought you genuine pleasure? If so, return and you're sure to find a dozen more. I'll let Derek Wernher have the last word. He said this about his old farmer Len Ganeway: "If they don't know who the person is, then they don't know humanity. And if you can't feel it, well, I'm sorry." And here's what he said about people who write tours of sculpture gardens:

"They want all this verbiage. They want to know what you feel is the essence. Well for Christ's sake, there it is. You can go through stylistic interpretations and blah, blah. But an art work is a helluva lot more than that."

| 82.9 | 0.0 | From parking lot, turn left onto Allston Circle Drive. |
| 83.4 | 0.5 | Turn left into Nature Wildlife Park and Educational Center parking lot. |

The Nature Wildlife Park

This natural history exhibit actually begins at the Educational Center. You'll find only native animals and plants in this section of Brookgreen, but it, too, is a museum. Sometimes you have to look closely into the wilderness, but 123 different plant species have been labeled with both Latin and common names.

The volunteer tour guide gives a surprisingly complete introduction to the Huntingtons and Brookgreen, warns of fire ants, and then leads us down the trail. We pass by live oaks and Spanish moss, then enter less well-known terrain. Beauty berry, black cherry, bladder pod, and fiddlehead, the first of the dozen ferns, are here. Lichens brought out by the rain give color. Soon we've reached the wildlife column done by Huntington when she was eighty-four.

The Aviary is ninety feet high, made of soft netting suspended on great posts. (It has become the model for several others.) The freshwater tide moves in and out of this swamp bottom where ibis and egrets are the most obvious of the six enclosed species. Many people don't like to see animals in captivity, but we're told these birds and other animals in the park have been brought in injured or raised as pets so, with the exception of the alligators, they'd have a difficult time making it in the wild.

We see cypress and cypress knees up close and then head for the otters. There's a display board here giving general otter information. There's a male called Tramp and a small female who swim and slide and playfully wrestle each other for our entertainment.

The alligators are decidedly more sinister. Cold blooded, they wallow out muddy holes in summer and winter, but on this September day four are on very visible display.

Foxes and raccoons don't live in harmony in the wild, but since they're well fed, they are getting along. The red fox is thought to have been brought over

from England for fox hunting when the native gray fox kept climbing trees to escape the hounds.

There's another aviary for birds of prey, and the next stop is the deer savannah. This twenty-three-acre enclosure is surrounded by moat and high fence. Usually about forty deer are kept; today, five of them are fawns and all are close to the visitors. The bucks have already taken on the gray coat of winter, but most remain summer brown. Like all the animals, they seem tame and content enough with their surroundings. We follow the edge of the fence for several hundred feet and a sign directs us to the parking lot.

83.4	**0.0**	**F**rom Nature Wildlife Park parking lot, turn left onto Allston Circle Drive and continue to U.S. 17.
85.1	**1.7**	**A**t U.S. 17 stop sign, continue straight across U.S. 17 into entrance of Huntington Beach State Park.

6. HUNTINGTON BEACH STATE PARK

Actually, the tour starts as you enter the park. A small brochure is given out at the gate, and there is a part-time naturalist on the staff to help with questions.

After a loop through the mainland forest, the park road crosses a causeway dike that offers a dramatic introduction to the environs.

85.8	**0.7**	**O**n right is the Mullet Pond.

The Mullet Pond

The Mullet Pond is a freshwater to brackish lagoon that's home to about one hundred alligators. Unless it's deep winter, you'll see the eyes and noses sticking above the water. These are about five feet long, with a few babies from last year mixed in. The real old-timers retired to the far end after public feeding was stopped. DON'T FEED THE ALLIGATORS! THEY CAN BE DANGEROUS. Banana waterlily and cattail are the most noticeable of the plants here, but storm tides sometimes cross over and kill them back. The duckweeds, widgeon grass, and other rushes are a more tolerant food supply for waterfowl. Year-round you'll see gallinules, coots, and grebes, and during the winter, a great variety of migrating ducks. The herons and egrets, of course, work both sides of the causeway.

By now, old friends of Huntington Park don't have to be told how badly it was damaged by Hurricane Hugo. The loblolly forest once seen on the far shore was completely killed. Still, nature—with a little help from the park staff—is repairing the damage.

85.8	**0.0**	**O**n left is Tidal Salt Marsh.

Tidal Salt Marsh

On your left is a tidal salt marsh. Low tide exposes an extensive mud flat with broad oyster beds. At high tide, only the top of the marsh shows—a fertile cycle which we can examine up close from the MARSH BOARDWALK.

86.8	**1.0**	**A**t stop sign, turn left.
87.0	**0.2**	**T**urn left into Marsh Boardwalk parking lot.

Marsh Boardwalk

On this day seagulls are feeding in Oak Creek where the Marsh Boardwalk pier ends, and on the far shore a variety of wading birds are roosting.

87.0	**0.0**	**F**rom parking lot, turn left.
87.8	**0.8**	**O**n right is Hot and Hot Fish Club historical marker.

Hot and Hot Fish Club, Drunken Jack Island, and the Flagg Storm

A historical marker on the northern end of the island commemorates the Hot and Hot Fish Club. This famous fish fry was originally held on Drunken Jack Island, just inland from where we stand. The day's catch was brought ashore and cooked all during the afternoon, so there were at least two courses—hot and hot. The honorary president provided a ham or roast, and the vice president, the wine. My host for this portion of the Waccamaw tour was local folklorist Genevieve Peterkin, and she explained how Drunken Jack Island got its name. When his mates came ashore to bury treasure, a pirate named Jack wandered off drunk and was marooned. His skeleton was discovered years later, still clutching a rum bottle. That's just a legend, but the truth that Genevieve suspects may be just as strange. It's thought that early in the nineteenth century, a "yard axe" (self-proclaimed) preacher named Jack would row out here when the urge for demon rum got the better of him.

87.8	**0.0**	Continue straight to parking area.
87.8	**200 ft.**	Park in this North End parking lot.

North End and Jetty

Since the hurricane, the dunes have been fenced off to hasten their rebuilding process. Still, walking onto the beach, you get a good cross-section view. Under normal conditions, these "back dunes" are the highest. Already they're growing thick with sea oats. Ahead are the secondary and primary dune rows, but they're only now beginning to re-form. Note the beach amaranthus growing here. Coming up almost at the surf's edge, it's a remarkable plant. Far tougher than the better-known marsh grass and sea oats, it's the unsung hero of the dune fields. Wind-driven sand piles against it, it grows higher, and more sand piles up until sea oats can take root.

On the beach today are sanderlings, the most common of the numerous sandpipers here, some ringbilled gulls, and a lone willet. The farther north we walk, the farther off the beaten path we go. There's a turtle program here, too, but we're getting toward the northern limits of the loggerheads' nesting range. Still, an appreciable number of nests are guarded and hatched out every year. Sand crabs are the big danger (elsewhere, it's raccoons). In the far distance is the black rock of the jetty. Completed in 1980 to aid in party boat and com-

mercial fishing, it's changing the face of this beach dramatically. We look first, though, at the debris at our feet. If you pass this way, especially after a storm, you'll find a variety of beachcomber's delights—corals, spider crabs, cockles, razor clams, coraline, sea cucumbers, sponges, penshells, purse crabs, devil's pocketbooks, gooseneck barnacles—all within a few paces.

Next on our right is the unexpected bonus brought about by jetty construction—a large, shallow lagoon filled with shorebirds. Caspian terns, dowitchers, Forster, sandwich, and common terns have already arrived for the winter. Ahead is a second fortuitous formation: least terns and Wilson plovers have chosen the newly formed sand flat to nest on. The nests are staked out as part of a study. Visitors are asked to keep their distance, because the birds chose this place to escape predators like us. The jetty is paved, but be very careful climbing onto it; sand shelves form above the stone. Legs have been broken here. You can walk out to the end, a favorite place for fishermen, or turn left and follow the road back to the beach and the car. For a more inland look at the peninsula (it only seems like an island), drive south.

87.8	**0.0**	**F**rom parking lot, retrace south and continue south to Atalaya parking lot.
89.1	**1.3**	**T**urn left into parking lot.

The Sea Oats Nature Trail

This trail is now closed, but you can turn inland and walk toward and onto the old causeway that once led to Brookgreen. We're past the northern limits of Sea Island cotton, but it's possible that provision crops were grown here during plantation days. During this century, it was peppers and cucumbers. The pines, survivors of ninety years of salt spray, have lost out at last, but other plants have survived. Wax myrtles are common undergrowth; note the waxy leaves. The sheen on their leaves, on the leaves of the live oaks, and on the smilax and pennywort at our feet is a protection against the salt air. The myrtle, however, actually provided wax for the early settlers, obtained by boiling the tiny blue berries. The vines here are particularly thick: They've gained due to the additional sunlight. Grape, yellow jessamine, Virginia creeper, and peppervine twist about with verileafed smilaxes, but most exceptional of all is the poison ivy—watch for it. Notice the pennywort, too. It grows all over the park. The little dark-green umbrellas grow smaller and smaller the closer they are to the ocean. This is particularly noticeable with this plant, but you'll see that all the inland vegetation becomes more stunted closer to the dunes.

Stop, listen for calls, and take a good look. There are still ample birding opportunities here. Eighty bird species are common on the island, and a great many more have been recorded. A much-traveled path carries us out to the beach once more.

Huntington Beach is a combination of three antebellum locales—Allston Island, Theaville, and Magnolia Island—and these were still serving as seaside escapes from malaria when the storm of 1893 struck. The Flagg family was staying here on Magnolia, and though many others died as well, their struggle against the waves was so dramatic and their loss so complete, it was called the Flagg Storm. Genevieve quietly sang a verse from a spiritual of that time—one that has even more meaning for me today:

Six hundred bodies came floating by
And we ain't know what to do.
And then we recognize dem
As the wonderful works of God.

Dr. Ward Flagg, who managed to survive, lived out his life well inland at Brookgreen, dispensing exceptional love and charity to his patients and neighbors.

Atalaya, c. 1938

Open to public.

Interior tours at 11:00 a.m. and 1:30 p.m.

Atalaya means "watchtower," and it's said that Archer Huntington was inspired by a Moorish castle he'd seen in his beloved Spain. There are no blueprints: He kept this idea in his head and conveyed his intentions to the contractor, William Thomson, bit by bit. ("Mr. Huntington, if you tell me much more, I'll find out what you're building.") The contractor used local laborers, who in this Depression era were desperate for work; many were trained on the job. That "dripping" mortar style was called "the Huntington squeeze." The building measured 200 by 200 feet and was built about an existing beach house that was moved just before being enclosed.

We enter the rear of the house by way of the front sun room, where we can pick up a map of the interior. The inner garden still grows thick with palms, for they and the solid old building survived the storm remarkably well. This was meant to be the original entry and is certainly the nicest part of the plan, but a view shielded from the residents. The tower in its center once held a cypress-tank water supply for the complex. The brochure explains most of the house, so I'll just comment on the most obvious omission. A flat-roofed house of solid, fireproof masonry with small, narrow windows and tiny rooms connected by lengthy corridors is a house suited for the Moors in Spain 600 years ago. It makes a very curious beach house for South Carolina, especially one to be occupied in the winter by someone recuperating from tuberculosis. Fires were kept going continually in the many fireplaces, but it's hard to imagine life beyond the edge of the hearth. Actually, it's hard to imagine a comfortable life here, period.

My host, Genevieve, visited as a child, though, and she remembers it that way. When occupied, it was all painted the cream-white now flaking from the brick. Indian blankets, hung from the walls, and furniture that was austere but in keeping with the style, decorated the rooms. No doubt a happy couple, guests, and servants gave a far less forlorn presence to the place. Anna Huntington sculpted the aging horse for her *Don Quixote* in

this studio. There was an oyster-shucking room, and close by, a bear pen. What more could you ask of a Moorish castle?

During the 1930s, dozens of wealthy Northerners moved into the Lowcountry and built or rebuilt antebellum mansions in an attempt to recapture the glory of the Old South. Only one couple chose to emulate the glory of Spain in the days of El Cid. It's an architectural folly, but only in the kindest sense of those words—a building so outrageously romantic that it defies all logical complaint.

89.1	**0.0**	**T**urn right out of Atalaya parking lot, retrace to park entrance gate.
89.2	**0.1**	**T**urn left.
90.2	**1.0**	**A**t park's entrance gates (if you want to continue to Murrells Inlet), turn right onto U.S. 17 North.
91.6	**1.4**	**V**eer right onto U.S. 17 North Business.
94.6	**3.0**	**F**or the next three miles the road is lined with dozens of good seafood restaurants.

7. MURRELLS INLET

Over lunch, Genevieve Peterkin declares with a broad smile that, contrary to rumors, the founder of this inlet was neither a pirate nor a member of the Morrall family. He was just a planter named Murrell who settled here in about 1740. The community of both summer and permanent residents was long noted for its seafood, and today its restaurants carry on that tradition. Several old houses remain, but they're on semi-private lanes, and you're asked to stay clear. One of these certainly bears mentioning, though, for it's the home of Alice Flagg. Sent to school in Charleston, the young girl fell in love with an unsuitable young boat captain and wore his ring about her neck in secret. When she was taken ill with the fever, her nursing father discovered the token and threw it into the marsh. Her despairing brother placed his own ring on her finger, but the dying girl said, "Keep yours, I'll find mine." Many believe her ghost continues the search.

In the center of the community and facing the marsh, the Belin Methodist Church was originally the Episcopal Chapel on Pawleys. Dismantled, it was put in ox carts by my host's grandfathers and others, and brought here. The church was doubled in length, and new columns were added: The old ones were filled with bees and honey.

If you're looking for a good place for dinner, Murrells Inlet is the spot.

———◈———

97.6	**3.0**	**R**eturn on U.S. 17 South Business to U.S. 17 South.
97.6	**0.0**	**C**ross U.S. 17 North, turn left onto U.S. 17 South and return to Charleston on U.S. 17.

We head back down to Charleston on U.S. 17. Just before crossing the river and entering Georgetown, glance back at Waccamaw Neck.

That's where we end this trip. Vásquez de Allyón came here in 1526 to rule and die. A little over four centuries later Franklin Roosevelt came to go fishing and Belle Baruch flew her plane. A lot has happened in between and since. Fortunately, though, the sun is down, and a local spiritual advises us to travel that King's Highway. "Oh, I'm traveling, when you saw me I was on my way." Home.

172.8   **75.2**   North side of Cooper River Bridge.

ADDITIONAL READING

You might enjoy the following books: *The Land Called Chicora*, by Paul Quattlebaum; George Rogers's *History of Georgetown County*; *A Woman Rice Planter*, by Patience Pennington (Pringle); and *Bull's, All Saint's, Waccamaw, and Pawleys Island—A Living Legend*, by Prevost and Wilder. Nancy Rhyne has a good guide to the Grand Strand. *Musings of a Hermit*, by Clarke A. Willcox, is a treasure. For black history, read Charles Joyner's *Down by the Riverside*. Brookgreen Gardens has a good book selection and also a quarterly bulletin for friends and members.

NOTES

NOTES

Tour 7:

The

Savannah

River

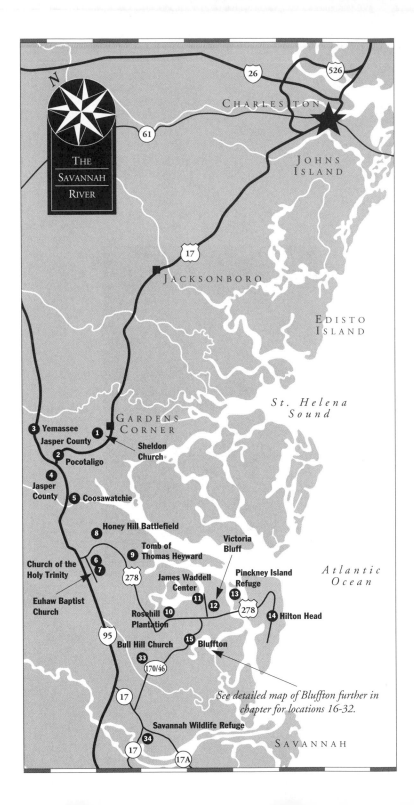

See detailed map of Bluffton further in chapter for locations 16-32.

THE SAVANNAH RIVER

This is a naturalist tour that begins on U.S. 17 approximately fifty-three miles south of Charleston and takes a roundabout path to the Savannah River. In the little pineland village of GRAHAMVILLE we visit two small but handsome churches. Then we drive twenty miles toward the coast to see ROSEHILL, a great Gothic Revival plantation house. (It's being repaired now but hopefully will be open again soon.) Nearby is the JAMES WADDELL, JR., MARICULTURE RESEARCH AND DEVELOPMENT CENTER, which offers an intriguing look at the very latest developments in shrimp and fish farming. And close to that is the VICTORIA BLUFF GAME MANAGEMENT AREA TRAIL that circles through a distinctive "Florida flatwoods." A short drive brings us to marsh-surrounded PINCKNEY ISLAND—great for birding, hiking, or just getting away. We head inland once more, but not far, to the summer retreat of BLUFFTON. Much of it survived the Civil War and even the twentieth century—a true village. Eight miles beyond is the small antebellum BULL HILL METHODIST CHURCH, and then we reach the Savannah River Wildlife Refuge. Here the unusual four-mile SAVANNAH NATIONAL (LAUREL HILL) WILDLIFE REFUGE DRIVE allows us to circle about slave-built rice fields and shows off the best duck marshes in the state. You drive about an hour and a half south of Charleston before this day trip begins, so if you want to fit it all in, leave early and take a picnic lunch.

Church of the Holy Trinity, c. 1855
Building open daily.

Euhaw Baptist Church, c. 1907
Grounds open daily.

Rosehill Plantation, c. 1860
Currently closed.

James M. Waddell, Jr.,
Mariculture Research and Development Center
Modern facility for the study of seafood farming.
Tours available, but you must call in advance.
Telephone: (803) 837-7175.

Victoria Bluff Game Management Area Trail
Nature trail through unique Florida wetlands. A two-hour walk over often boggy firelines, but some rare plants to be seen.
Open daily.

Pinckney Island National Wildlife Refuge
This large island is surrounded by salt marsh, with fourteen miles of nature trails and excellent birding.
Open 6 a.m. to 8 p.m.

Bluffton
Antebellum summer retreat, little touched by the twentieth century. Interesting old houses to be viewed from the street, and two distinctive churches.
Open daily. Self-guided tour.

Bull Hill Methodist Church, c. 1821
Grounds open daily.
Savannah National (Laurel Hill) Wildlife Refuge Drive
A highlight of this tour, a four-mile drive along the route of ancient rice-field dikes is especially beautiful at sunset. Great birding, especially ducks and geese, and several points of historical interest.
Open 7 a.m. until 1/2 hour after dark. Self-guided tours.
NOTE: Watch for posted closing time as you enter. Gates close automatically, so make sure that you are out by the posted time. It's a wonderful spot, but you don't want to spend the night here.

0.0	**0.0**	**B**egin on U.S. 17 South at the south side of the Ashley River bridge.
53.0	**53.0**	**O**n right is Sheldon Church Road S-7-21 (see Tour 4). Continue on U.S. 17 South.

1. SHELDON CHURCH AND SHERMAN'S MARCH
Sherman marched through this area and did a thorough job of destroying it. Just off to our right is the Sheldon Church he burned. Between here and the Savannah River, only a handful of buildings were left standing. The army was a large one, so he broke it into four advancing forces that could supply themselves by following parallel but slightly meandering routes between Savannah and Columbia. Riding out from these were small parties of "bummers" who came and went, bringing in necessary foods and spreading the path of destruction far wider than the actual route of the march. The tactics have been much discussed, and it appears that Sherman knew exactly what he was doing. Charleston was bypassed because there were too many rivers and marshlands for him to cross.

58.9	**5.9**	**A**rrive at Pocotaligo Community.

2. POCOTALIGO
This small rural community was once the chief town of the Yemassee Indians. The Yemassee War began here in 1715, when the most ambitious of our Indian traders, Thomas Nairne, and about ninety other settlers were taken by surprise and killed. During the Revolution the British built Fort Balfour on the opposite side of the Pocotaligo River and surrendered it to Colonel William Harden. Three hundred citizens welcomed George Washington when he toured. The Civil War brought destruction and decline.

59.2	**0.3**	**A**t stop sign, continue straight on U.S. 17 South.

3. YEMASSEE

Off to our right on U.S. 21 is Yemassee, which was founded as a railroad stop. NBC newscaster Frank Blair is from this unlikely spot, and even more unlikely, Frank Lloyd Wright built his only southern plantation house nearby.

| 59.4 | 0.2 | Cross Pocotaligo River and enter Jasper County. |

4. JASPER COUNTY

Formed in 1912, when it separated from Hampton to the north (the vote was 283 to 24), Jasper is our youngest county. In 1877, Yankee railroad directors started the first of the state's shooting preserves here. There were hard feelings at the time, but the outsiders brought "understanding and money." By 1912, much of the land was owned by these hunting clubs, and much still is today.

The county is named for Sergeant William Jasper, who is best known for saving the flag at the battle of Fort Moultrie. Jasper was recruited from the backwoods around Augusta, and here along the Jasper County section of the Savannah River he and a companion (according to Parson Weems, they were in civilian clothes and unarmed) rescued a dozen American prisoners. Wounded in the battle for Savannah, he is thought to have been brought to nearby Purysburg where he died and was buried in an unmarked grave.

| 60.9 | 1.5 | U.S. 17 South and I-95 combine; continue south. |
| 64.8 | 3.9 | Cross Coosawhatchie River. |

5. COOSAWHATCHIE

This small rural community also began as an Indian village. A colonial settlement grew up around a bridge, and in 1788 the little community became the county seat of Beaufort. Unionist James Petigru practiced law here until 1819 and was still alive when the Civil War came. "Everybody in South Carolina has seceded except Petigru," was the popular saying. "South Carolina is too small to be a nation and too large to be an insane asylum," is one version of his reply. This village of a dozen shops and houses never grew appreciably. Prisoners confined to the jail here died of malaria before they could be brought to trial, and those citizens free to walk the streets were often no better off. In 1840, the county seat was finally moved to the nearby but healthier Gillisonville. Robert E. Lee chose Coosawhatchie for his headquarters during the first months of the war and directed his coastal defenses from this strategic position beside the newly constructed railroad from Savannah to Charleston. You'll notice that as we head toward Ridgeland, we travel in a straight line, for the road follows not an old

Indian trail but the tracks of this rail line, one that would be fought and skirmished over for most of the war. Coosawhatchie was in Sherman's path and little survived.

———— ◈ ————

72.7	**7.9**	Veer right onto cloverleaf Exit 21 of I-95.
73.0	**0.3**	At stop sign, turn left onto U.S. 278 East.
73.5	**0.5**	At stop sign, turn right onto S-27-13.
73.8	**0.3**	Go straight through stop sign and turn left into the parking area of Church of the Holy Trinity.

Grahamville

This little village has just about been swallowed up by adjoining Ridgeland, a situation unthinkable to the earliest inhabitants. At the time of the Revolution, Ridgeland could only boast a tavern—George Allison's Punch House—but as a railroad depot it grew at the expense of the older summer retreat. But then, Grahamville had grown at the expense of the earlier but unhealthy Euhaw community, which is just down the road. The population peaked when Grahamville became a refuge for those permanently forced from the Sea Islands by Union troops, and then the town was overrun. One little antebellum church survives.

6. CHURCH OF THE HOLY TRINITY, c. 1855

Open to public.

In 1829, William Heyward donated this crossroad site for the construction of an Episcopal chapel, and twenty-six years later another wealthy planter, James Balan, funded the construction of this Gothic Revival building. It's unusual for the substantial buttressed bell tower to be off to one side and for the windows and doors to have rounded arches instead of the familiar Gothic points. Union troops carried off the Bible, but it was returned in 1928 and is on display in the vestibule. The chaste white plaster walls and simple altar are surprising and pleasing changes from the dark and ornate interiors of most Gothic construction.

———— ◈ ————

73.8	**0.0**	From church parking area, turn left and continue on S-27-13.
73.9	**0.1**	Turn left into Euhaw Baptist Church parking lot.

7. EUHAW BAPTIST CHURCH, C. 1907

Not open to public.

Euhaw Baptist Church

Though this building dates only from this century, this Baptist congregation is far older. First organized in nearby Euhaw in 1751, it was one of the four churches directed by the Charles Town Baptist Association. It was the mother church for the tiny Beaufort congregation. The Union burned the already abandoned Euhaw building, and it would be half a century before this structure took its place. With towers on each side of the entry, the taller one having an open belfry, the building is a pleasing Victorian complement to its Gothic Episcopal neighbor.

73.9	**0.0**	**T**urn right from Euhaw Baptist Church parking lot onto S-27-13.
74.0	**0.1**	**A**t stop sign, turn right onto S-27-29.
74.3	**0.3**	**J**unction U.S. 278 East, continue straight.
75.8	**1.5**	**O**n left, historical marker for Battle of Honey Hill.

8. HONEY HILL BATTLEFIELD, c. 1864

Not open to public.

On November 30, 1864, five thousand Union troops under General J. G. Foster attempted to sever the railroad connection to Savannah, and thus cause its evacuation. They were stopped here by Colonel Charles Colcock, who set fire to a field to delay the enemy and hastily gathered one thousand defenders. The Confederates lost about fifty men, the Union about a thousand. It was the last such Rebel victory.

75.8	**0.0**	**C**ontinue on U.S. 278 East.
78.4	**2.6**	**T**urn right and continue on U.S. 278 East.
78.5	**0.1**	**O**n left, historical marker for Thomas Heyward, Jr.

9. TOMB OF THOMAS HEYWARD, JR., c. 1809

Not open to public.

Beaufort claims this patriot as her native son, but he's buried at the end of this oak avenue. Thomas Heyward started practicing law in 1771, served on several Revolutionary War councils, and was a delegate to the Continental Congress. He signed the Declaration of Independence when he was only thirty. In the years following, he served as a judge and was a founder of the Agricultural Society of South Carolina. The gravesite is on private property.

78.5	**0.0**	Continue on U.S. 278 East.
90.4	**11.9**	Turn right onto cloverleaf and continue on U.S. 278 East in the direction of Hilton Head Island.
94.0	**3.6**	Turn left into entrance of Rosehill Plantation.

10. ROSEHILL PLANTATION, c. 1860

Not open to public at present. Check with guard at entry.

Though there's no definite proof, it seems likely that well-known Charleston architect E. B. White designed this great Gothic Revival house. The owner, Dr. John Kirk, had studied medicine at the University of Pennsylvania and then returned here to practice and grow wealthy as a planter. Begun in 1860, the mansion was never completed and was referred to after the war as "Kirk's Folly." It sat unfinished, slowly deteriorating, until purchased in 1946 and lavishly restored. Steep-roofed and asymmetrical, the building represents a radical departure from the more conventional Greek Revival plantation homes of that era. It was probably the finest example of early Victorian architecture in South Carolina. Unfortunately, fire gutted Rosehill several years ago. It is hoped that the exterior can be restored and that sometime in the future visitors will at least be allowed to admire it from the outside.

94.0	**0.0**	Cross U.S. 278 West. Turn left onto U.S. 278 East.
97.9	**3.9**	Turn left following signs for Coastal Zone Education Center and Waddell Development Center (S-7-744).
100.1	**2.2**	Turn left onto entrance road of Waddell Mariculture Research and Development Center.

| 100.4 | 0.3 | Main office of Waddell Mariculture Research and Development Center. |

11. JAMES M. WADDELL, JR., MARICULTURE RESEARCH AND DEVELOPMENT CENTER

The Fort Johnson Resources Center just south of Charleston is the headquarters for the state's mariculture experiments, but much of the actual work is done here at the Waddell Center. The tour begins with a quick introductory lecture. Twenty experiments are under way involving about a dozen potential crops—shrimp, spot-tail bass, striped bass, carp, clams, oysters, scallops, and more. The center is self-contained in the sense that it is capable, if necessary, of growing its own foods and maintaining its own brood stock. Still, there's continual interaction between it and Fort Johnson, the Dennis Center at Bonneau, and other mariculture centers throughout the world. Density is a major area of study now: Once it is known that an animal can be grown, then how many can be grown per square meter? Bi-culture is another promising line of investigation—growing two crops in the same pond. As in nature, oysters and shrimp are doing exceptionally well together. Lecture done, the actual sightseeing begins.

First, there's a large aquarium so you can have a good look at the subjects. Local white shrimp are present here, but the Pacific white shrimp are being used in the experiment. Our local shrimp are too territorial and cannibalistic for the experiment; the import has been domesticated for at least a century in Central America. There are also tiger shrimp. This dark, striped relative from the Orient grows to tremendous size, but can't stand our cool winters. The few that accidentally escaped gave local shrimpers and cast-netters a shock. In the freshwater tank are striped bass and striped hybrids. The latter only grow up to ten pounds, but they're hardier and have the potential to farm more successfully. The lapia, a carp, also in this tank, feeds on algae and grows to a market size in a single year. This drab white fish is a source of protein for the Third World, but the taste is too bland for our own markets. The prettier pink one that we see here has been bred for Western consumers. In the last tank are tiny spot-tail bass, a fish that's being farmed for both Cajun cooking (blackened redfish) and for local sports fishermen.

The guide leads the way through a warehouse of raceways and increasingly larger fiberglass vats, explaining thoroughly each stage of development in this "nursery" portion of the center. (There are spot-tail bass in here no bigger than BBs.) Outside there are even larger tanks where adult striped bass are being watched: Breeders want a sterile fish that can be marketed in a single year. And to one side is a large building where temperature and light are  artificially controlled to convince tremendous spot-tail bass that their spawning season arrives at least twice as fast as it does in the real world.

Twenty-four large ponds are in the very rear. Ranging in size from one-quarter to one and one-quarter acres, they've been lined with black plastic because the soil here is too porous to hold the water being pumped in from the Colleton River. The ponds are aerated, heated, cooled, and filtered by a number of devices; the Center acts as a consumer report for such aquaculture aids. Larger versions of ponds like these, some converted from old rice fields and others carved out of the highland, are already producing shrimp on a commercial scale and hopefully will grow other seafoods as well. As we stand admiring the tanks, an osprey coasts by overhead: He hasn't heard the old maxim, "There's no such thing as a free lunch." This is a fun place to visit but still a risky way to make a living.

100.4	**0.0**	Retrace to main gate.
100.7	**0.3**	Turn right onto S-7-744.
102.9	**2.2**	Cross U.S. 278 West and turn left onto U.S. 278 East.
103.3	**0.4**	At second crossover (at Colleton River Plantation development), turn left, and then turn left onto U.S. 278 West.
103.3	**100 ft.**	Turn right onto dirt road marked with diamond-shaped sign for Victoria Bluff Game Management Area Trail.
104.0	**0.7**	Park; on left, a small sign on a pine tree marks start of trail.

12. VICTORIA BLUFF GAME MANAGEMENT AREA TRAIL

This twelve-hundred-acre property was at first destined to be the site of an industrial development. Strong objections from environmentalists, however, led to the eventual ownership by the South Carolina Marine Resources Department. Two hundred acres went for the Waddell Center and the remainder was turned over to the Carolina Heritage Trust to administer. It's open for archery hunting for a split two-week season during November and December, so you'll want to avoid that, but the rest of the year the trail is  open. Use a good bug spray and watch out for snakes if they're in season. The property has been cut by fire lines, and it's one of these that's been turned into a nature walk, which twists and turns its way through pine and saw palmetto flatwoods rarely found this far north. A small sign points to the beginning of the trail, but the rest of the way is poorly marked, so be careful.

Note the cabbage palmetto at the start. The stems are smooth and the strands ragged, but it is often mistaken for the little saw palmetto (with sawlike stem) that's predominant here. We start to our right. This is an evergreen woods; only the wildflowers, fungus, and mushrooms like the pink russela add a little color. The opening on our left is a depression left by a lime sink. We'll walk through one later. The predominant pine here is slash. Its cones aren't as large or its needles as long as those of the longleaf—a distinction pointed out in the previous century by Bluffton naturalist Dr. J. H. Mellinchamp when he discovered the species. Don't be confused by the ribbons on the trees; they're left by deer hunters.

Bear to your left and cross over an Indian midden that's been pushed up in an effort to keep three-wheel vehicles off the trail. There are many such shell piles scattered through the woods. Here's the familiar wax myrtle; we follow the fire line, veering left past a large live oak. There are more shells and the path dips into a depression thick with royal and cinnamon ferns and red bay. Loblolly pines are to the left and red maple and tupelo to the right. Black root, native indigo, and blueberry are growing here along with pond pine. Look for rusty lyonia—rust-colored on the underside of the leaf—in this typical Florida landscape: This is the only place in the state where it grows. We cross an open, flat area, take the left fork of the trail and enter a wet area. There's a big live oak on our left and an old fence. We turn left once more and pass a large metal water-monitoring device. A hard left turn carries us into a low bay. The rare pond spice is growing here with panic grass, bracken fern, and St. Andrew's cross. You're almost home; turn left on the road and it takes you back to the car.

———— ◈ ————

104.0	0.0	Retrace back to U.S. 278.
104.7	0.7	At end of dirt road, turn right onto U.S. 278 West.
104.8	0.1	Turn left onto crossover and turn left onto U.S. 278 East.
107.5	2.7	Cross first bridge and turn left into Pinckney Island Wildlife Refuge.
108.6	1.1	On right, historical marker.
109.0	0.4	Parking lot.

13. PINCKNEY ISLAND NATIONAL WILDLIFE REFUGE

The intent of Pinckney Island management seems to be to reduce automobile traffic to a bare minimum which, considering the steady stream of traffic that passes to and from adjoining Hilton Head, isn't such a bad idea. Park your car just inside the refuge entry on your left. There's a bulletin board showing a map of the island, and a small brochure is available. From here, you're welcome to walk or bicycle the fourteen miles of nature trails during daylight hours.

The Refuge, established in 1975, is actually made up of five small islands surrounded by several thousand acres of marsh. We have access to the largest of these, Pinckney Island. Approximately four miles long, but sometimes no wider than the road, it was the Sea Island cotton plantation of Charles Cotesworth Pinckney. He was a signer of the United States Constitution and ran for president in 1804, but he's best remembered for saying, "Millions for defense, but not one cent for tribute." Actually, if Ambassador Pinckney said anything, it was "No, no, not a sixpence."

The original inhabitants preceded him by as much as twelve thousand years and left behind numerous shell middens, some fairly large. The brochure urges an appreciation of the marsh, which crowds in on every side, but the concentrations of snowy egrets and white ibis are more dramatic fare. The island, cultivated for 150 years, is now being allowed to grow up in wax myrtle and pine, and stuck away inside this growth are five small ponds which harbor a variety of wildlife. Don't be confused by the pond names—snowy and cattle egrets, and Louisiana, night, and little blue herons have found nesting spots in ponds named Osprey and Ibis.

This is a beautiful spot and no doubt a welcome retreat for the inhabitants of nearby resorts, but unfortunately, if you're driving down from Charleston there's barely time to take more than a quick look.

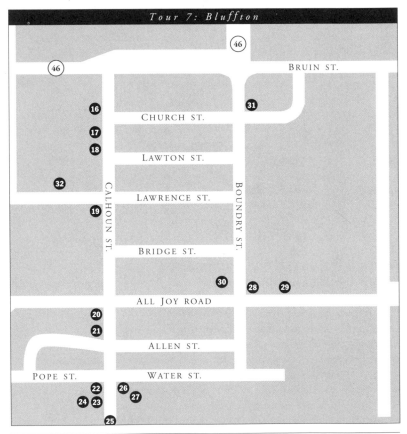

109.5	**0.5**	**R**etrace to U.S. 278. *(If you would like to see Hilton Head Island, cross U.S. 278 West and turn left on U.S. 278 East. Return to this spot to continue tour.)*

14. HILTON HEAD

There are several places of interest on Hilton Head, among them an old fort on the north end and a small Indian shell ring on the south. However, the traffic is heavy and there are guarded gates to get by. In the mid-1950s, I crossed here on the ferry *Pocahontas*; I remember only one car on the island and dozens of the now fabled little marsh tacky ponies. But that's another ferry that's come and gone.

❖

109.5	**0.0**	**A**t stop sign, turn right onto U.S. 278 West.
114.0	**4.5**	**T**urn left onto S.C. 46.
115.6	**1.6**	**A**t stop sign, turn right onto S.C. 46 / Bruin Street.
115.6	**1 block**	**T**urn left onto Calhoun Street.

15. BLUFFTON

This little summer retreat is situated on the banks of "that river which the French call the May." The French made no other contribution to civilizing the area, however, and the Spanish plotted to keep it in the hands of their Indian allies. After the failure of the Yemassee revolt in 1715, the Lords Proprietor divided up these "Indian Lands," and Sir John Colleton drew the surrounding Devil's Elbow Barony. His grandson, also Sir John, built plantations at Victoria Bluff and Foot Point. By the time the British destroyed these places in 1779, Colleton had already divided his barony into six tracts, sold them, and died. The site of Bluffton had gone to Benjamin Walls.

Since the Beaufort County records were all destroyed by Sherman's troops, it's difficult to say exactly who came when. The records were in the process of being moved from Gillisonville to Columbia, where they would have been burned anyway. It appears, though, that the Pope and Kirk families were seeking refuge from malaria here as early as 1800. Other cotton and rice planters from Hilton Head and elsewhere followed, and in the 1830s the streets as we see them were laid out. Though the place was known at first as May River and then as Kirk's Bluff, the name of Bluffton was settled on at a town meeting. The new name was a compromise between the Kirk and Pope families, and an obvious choice since the town has several miles of high bluffs facing into a favorable southeast breeze. The newly named town continued to grow and would soon have both Episcopal and Methodist churches, a private school, a Masonic lodge, and several stores.

Politics was serious business in the otherwise relaxed community, and in 1844 the "Bluffton Movement" for secession began beneath one of these giant oaks. Robert Barnwell Rhett, the *enfant terrible* who would grow up to be "the Father of Secession," was its promoter, but the rhetoric faded when secession actually

arrived. The residents of Hilton Head were evacuated to Bluffton in November 1861, but Bluffton itself was evacuated soon after, and homes with furnishings still in place were abandoned to the Federal troops who occasionally passed through. Confederate pickets were still stationed here to offer token resistance, and in June 1863, one thousand Union troops in three vessels were sent to destroy the community. Though Southern troops took up positions nearby, they could do nothing to stop the enemy from burning two-thirds of the town. Only thirteen homes, eight of which remain, and the two churches were left standing.

While it still had its summer visitors, in the years following the Civil War Bluffton grew back as a commercial center with at least seven large general stores on Calhoun Street. The riverboat was the main link with the outside world until the completion of the Savannah River Bridge in 1926. Businesses then declined, for customers now drove away for their supplies, but popularity as a summer village increased: Savannah residents could commute. Real prosperity didn't return, however, until the development of Hilton Head and other resort communities. Rich or poor, Bluffton has remained remarkably unchanged.

Bluffton is a true village and we can take a tour. The Bluffton Historical Society has published *No. II, A Longer Short History of Bluffton, S.C., and Its Environs* (referred to here as the *Longer History*), which is available at the bank and "The Store." Buy a copy; it covers far more ground and years than are covered here.

Let me say before going a step further that I lived here between the ages of six and eleven (1950–1955), and to make things worse, I've talked over old times with my "Aunt" Anne Bridges who was also living here then. Trust us; Bluffton is a magical place.

115.7	**1st block**	**F**ifth building on right is Planters Mercantile.

16. PLANTERS MERCANTILE, c. 1890
Woodworking Shop

The Patz brothers, Abram and Moses, built this building. Dry goods, groceries, furniture, buggies, coffins and fixtures, and much, much more could be bought here and at a half-dozen similar stores on this street. It's a woodworker's shop now, but when I was a boy we still slid pennies across this counter in exchange for licorice and hard candies.

115.7	**Same block**	**N**ext door on right is Patz House.

17. PATZ BROTHERS RESIDENCE, c. 1890s
Not open to public.

The Victorian house next to the Mercantile was built by the Patz brothers as their residence. Notice the two doors; it's a duplex. The *Longer History* says that the wives of the two brothers feuded and didn't speak to each other for years. Abram accidentally drank carbolic acid when he went to the Mercantile one night looking for an antacid medicine. After that his brother sold out. The residence is a good example of Folk Victorian architecture.

115.7	**Same block**	Next door on right is Carson House.

18. CARSON HOUSE, post–Civil War
Not open to public.
The next house on the right, low to the ground with a veranda, was built by J. J. Carson. At the battle of Chancellorsville, Carson rescued the mortally wounded "Stonewall" Jackson and rushed him through enemy lines. Carson also organized the first Baptist church here in 1902.

115.8	**1 block**	Continue on Calhoun Street. On right at corner of Lawrence and Calhoun streets is the Peoples Store.

19. THE PEOPLES STORE, c. 1904
Gift Shop
Next on your right is "The Store." Jesse Peoples started it. He had five children by his first wife and ten by his second. I think that at least six sons were named after the twelve disciples, and Matthew and Luke ran the store until the early 1950s. The story goes that the hardware stock had been sold down to one of everything, and then the doors locked for good. An itinerant barber came around once a week to scalp us in the shed room on the left. The Store is a gift shop now.

115.9	**1 block**	On far right corner of the intersection of Calhoun Street and Bridge Street is the Fripp-Lowden House.

20. THE FRIPP-LOWDEN HOUSE, c. 1909
Not open to public.
The little house on the corner of Calhoun and Bridge streets was occupied by schoolteacher Sallie Fripp. In this garden she bred the camellia that bears her name. When I was here, the Fripp family store just across the street was still occasionally opened by her son-in-law, who played the violin beautifully and worked as the town plumber. Sad to report, the *Longer History* says that the store was demolished when struck by an out-of-control automobile in 1984.

115.9	**Same block**	On right next door is Seven Oaks at corner of Calhoun and Allen streets.

21. SEVEN OAKS, pre–Civil War
Not open to public.
Colonel Middleton Stuart was the first known owner of Seven Oaks, but the family didn't return after the Civil War. In the 1920s, the old summer house was operated very successfully as a boardinghouse.

| 115.9 | Next block | Second house on right of Calhoun Street is Lockwood House. |

22. THE LOCKWOOD HOUSE, c. 1850s

Not open to public.

This simple summer cottage facing on the churchyard was built for William Allen. Colonel Allen had a net worth of $100,000 in 1860 but was bankrupt in 1866. His daughter bought the house at a forced sale for $10.

| 116.0 | Next block | Next on right of Calhoun Street is the Church of the Cross. |

23. THE CHURCH OF THE CROSS, c. 1857

Grounds open to public.

The church was probably designed by well-known Charleston architect E. B. White, but the tower and vestibule of his plan were omitted with not unpleasing results. Carpenter Gothic is the style, one that would be a favorite Episcopal construction for the rest of the century. This one, however, is unusually large, cruciform, and noted for its rose-colored lancet windows.

Armed with her great ear trumpet, "Miss Susie" defended the front pew against all comers, new and old, and we children were expected to memorize a Bible verse every week. "God is love" and "Jesus wept" were passable and well-worn responses. Our betters told us that the church was fired on by the Union and saved by the Rebels, but the Yankee report says it was intentionally spared. No tombstones or memorials are in sight—just an ancient marble-based sundial that promises, "I count only sunny hours."

| 116.0 | 0.0 | Behind church is Huger-Gordon House. |

24. THE HUGER-GORDON HOUSE, c. 1795

Not open to public.

If you stand to the left of the church, you can catch a glimpse of the Huger-Gordon House. Judged by the brickwork, some portions have been dated back to 1795. That makes it the oldest house in town, as well as the only waterfront home to survive the Union invasion. Minié balls lodged in the door frame give evidence of its narrow escape.

| 116.0 | 50 ft. | At end of Calhoun Street is Steamboat Landing. |

25. STEAMBOAT LANDING

Here at the end of Calhoun Street is where the steamboat docked, an occasion of great celebration in its day. In *Bluffton Boy*, Andrew Peoples describes how the whistle of the Beaufort boat brought out the excited multitudes, and he, forgetting that he was in charge of his little sister Mildred, rushed to join them. The unattended baby carriage went careening down this bluff, to be stopped at the last moment.

| 116.0 | Same block | Across street from church is Squire Pope House. |

26. THE SQUIRE POPE HOUSE, c. 1850s

Not open to public.

Actually, this is only the carriage house and another small building combined to make a home for the impoverished widow of one of the wealthiest of the Hilton Head planters. All we have to judge the original Pope summer house by are these outbuildings and the garden, which still survives.

116.0	0.0	Behind Squire Pope House is Dr. Jakey's office site.

27. DR. JAKEY'S OFFICE SITE

My Aunt Anne tells of a young man going to have his tooth pulled and finding Dr. Jakey stirring a pot of grits over an open fire. The good dentist would pull on the tooth awhile and stir awhile, and pull, and stir, until the grits were done and the tooth came out at the same time. That was a half century before my time, but I keep thinking of the long-abandoned dentist's office being here just beyond the Squire Pope House. (Aunt Anne says that it was a half mile upstream.) Anyway, I'm certain of this: There was a four-hole outhouse for the patients—four holes cut in the shape of a club, a diamond, a heart, and a spade. And when the office had collapsed, it left a grandly mechanical dentist's chair exposed to the weather and encircled by vines.

116.0	0.0	Continue on Calhoun Street.
116.1	2 blocks	Turn right onto Bridge Street / S-7-13.
116.3	1 block	Cross Boundry Street / S-7-66. On left is the Fripp House.

28. THE FRIPP HOUSE, c. 1830s

Bed-and-breakfast.

This distinctive two-story frame house was built by a Pope, not a Fripp. An unusual combination of raised cottage faced with Federalist portico, the great rambling house sits on particularly high brick pillars, which perhaps helped it catch the breeze. The Sams family bought it from the Popes and sold it to the Fripps, who held onto it for thirty-four years.

116.3	Same block	Next door on left is the Card House.

29. THE CARD HOUSE, c. uncertain

Not open to public.

The Card House

Next on your left is an equally rambling structure of unknown origin. Legend calls it the oldest house in town, but it doesn't show up in the records until 1847. The name "Card House" is said to come from a high-stakes poker game played here. William Eddings Baynard won a thousand-acre Hilton Head plantation from John Stoney. Miss Hattie Colquitt, a later owner, suggested instead that it was named so because it looked like a house children would build with a pack of playing cards. It does, and we should mention Miss Hattie in any case, for she was the author of the unrivaled *Savannah Cookbook*. "A hand full of rice" was called for in one recipe, "a case of champagne" in another. "In mid summer, a thick okra soup, generously supplemented with rice and corn bread—preceded with a long mint julep and followed by a slice of iced watermelon—were happiness in the old days." So said Miss Hattie.

116.5	**One block**	Cross bridge, turn around, retrace Bridge Street one block. Turn right onto Boundry Street / S-7-66. On left is the Heyward House.

30. THE HEYWARD HOUSE, c. 1840s

Not open to public.

Carolina Farmhouse or Summer Cottage is the style. Built by wealthy May River planter John Cole, it remains pretty much unchanged. In the back you can spot a small clay-floored kitchen and a one-room slave house.

116.6	**4 blocks**	Cross Church Street / S-7-299. On right is the Campbell Chapel.

31. THE CAMPBELL CHAPEL, c. 1853

Not open to public.

The *Longer History* says it was built by the Methodists, which is probably so, but my Aunt Anne says Miss Heyward (the resident of the last house) told her it was a Camolite church at one time, and the name seems to bear that out. Reverend Campbell started this splinter group of the Presbyterians in Cainridge, Kentucky, and it spread into South Carolina before the Civil War. With their emotional services and many revivals, the Camolite congregations enjoyed a short-lived but enthusiastic stay in the state and then faded away or changed their names. Probably Methodist and Camolite both, this little building was empty by 1874 and was given to the African Methodist Episcopalians (AME) who held services there for another century. The simple Greek Revival design was a popular one of the day, but here the siding is board and batten rather than the traditional horizontal type.

116.6	**0.0**	Continue on Boundry Street.
116.7	**1 block**	At stop sign, turn left onto S.C. 46 / Bruin Street.
116.8	**1 block**	Turn left onto Calhoun Street.
117.0	**3 blocks**	Turn right onto Lawrence Street / S-7-377.
117.0	**1/2 block**	On right is the John Seabrook House.

32. THE JOHN A. SEABROOK HOUSE, c. 1840s

Not open to public.

Probably built by Edisto planter Seabrook in the 1850s, this house fell into Yankee hands in 1876, when the postmaster bought it. A typical raised cottage, it is well preserved and unchanged—something that could be said for this whole unchanging little village. Except that, in 1953, a two-wagon medicine show came this way and set up on the far side of Calhoun Street. It was run out of town on the fourth night. Soon after, a family living a block over on Boundry Street got a television set. We were all invited in to look at the set—which wasn't actually turned on—and to see the collapsible TV tables that they ate on. The rest is history, or at least what passes for it.

117.0	0.0	Turn around.
117.1	1/2 block	At stop sign, turn left onto Calhoun Street.
117.3	3 blocks	At stop sign, turn left onto Bruin Street / S.C. 46.
123.4	6.1	Turn right onto S-7-34 (at a country store).
124.6	1.2	At stop sign, turn right onto S.C. 170 East.
126.1	1.5	Turn left into St. Luke's parking area.

33. BULL HILL METHODIST CHURCH (ST. LUKE'S), c. 1821

Grounds open to public.

John Bull gave a four-acre site for the construction of an Episcopal church in 1786. The first Bull Hill church was gone by 1821, though, and the present one was built nearby. The Civil War ended services, and in 1875, it was sold to the Methodists who still attend here. A neat little Greek Revival–style meetinghouse, it's surrounded by some interesting graves, among them that of Dr. J. H. Mellinchamp. This famous botanist did much of his work at nearby Palmetto Point Plantation, but was always on the lookout for interesting specimens as he drove his buggy about the countryside tending to the medical needs of both masters and slaves. Fifty cents was his charge to set a broken arm. Between the pages of his prescription and accounts books, he pressed flowers and weeds to be carried home for inspection.

———— ◈ ————

126.1	0.0	Turn around and retrace S.C. 170 West.
128.8	2.7	Turn right onto S.C. 170 West / S.C. 46.
130.6	1.8	Cross New River Bridge.
131.0	0.4	Continue straight on S.C. 170 West / S.C. 46.
131.1	0.1	Continue on S.C. 170 West. (Do not take alternate to left.)
134.2	3.1	At stop sign, turn left onto S.C. 170 West.

134.9	**0.7**	**A**t stop sign, cross over north-bound lane and turn left onto U.S. 17 South.
136.1	**1.2**	**B**ear right onto U.S. 17 South. (Do not take U.S. 17 South A.)
138.6	**2.5**	**T**urn left into Savannah National Wildlife Refuge Drive.

34. SAVANNAH NATIONAL (LAUREL HILL) WILDLIFE REFUGE DRIVE

The Savannah Wildlife Refuge consists of over twenty-five thousand acres, about half of which is freshwater marshlands. Two thousand eight hundred acres of this is diked, and visitors may hike all of these dikes and associated pathways during daylight hours. But four miles are set aside for automobile touring. The Laurel Hill Wildlife Drive makes a meandering circuit about the impoundments of four early rice plantations and offers the visitor a simultane-ous look at the past and present of our wetlands.

October and April are the recommended months for viewing wildlife and just getting out of doors. These are good months for birders—260 species have been recorded here—but if you especially want to see the ducks, come in December and January. This is considered the best spot in the state for watch-ing the canvasbacks, ringnecks, widgeon, and the larger swans, brant, and geese that come through.

Roughly one-third of the twenty-eight-hundred-acre impoundment is kept constantly flooded for diving ducks. Another third is drained and flooded again after duck foods have been grown. And the tide is allowed to ebb and flow through the remainder, giving habitat for wading and shore birds. They're also experimenting again with growing corn and other farm crops. I made this trip in early September with my father, who worked out of the Savannah Refuge as a wildlife biologist between 1948 and 1955, and who was associated with this headquarters for the decade preceding that. He likes to look at ducks, but he's equally happy just looking at duck foods. (He can identify five varieties of smartweeds, and I can't even spot one.) As on all our trips together, he's the naturalist, but on this one he added bits of refuge lore as well.

The Tour and a Bit of History

We start the tour at the entrance sign on the left of Highway 17. You can pick up a brochure and a map there. Developed by expanding South Carolina planters, rice cultivation came relatively late to the Savannah River region. By the time of the Civil War, though, it was rivaling even the incredible output of the Georgetown fields. Still, it was a frontier of sorts, and the homes were usually modest, like the one that stood on this knoll at Laurel Hill. Sherman's troops burned the houses on neighboring Argyle Island and many others on the

Savannah River, but mysteriously left this little neighborhood intact. (Incidentally, Union Creek and Union Landing on the northern border of the Refuge were known by those names long before Sherman's arrival.) Nevertheless, the dwellings of the owners and slaves, and the mills and barns, are all gone today.

The low foundation just to your right was a three-story brick mill that was removed when the highway was widened in the 1950s. Only such hints of occupation remain, and you're asked to allow them to remain. Vandalism is a serious problem, made even worse by the innocent removal of "souvenir" bricks, one at a time.

Your brochure points out the smokestacks of the industries along the far bank of the river, a constant reminder that environmental protection is a very real issue here. Water and air are constantly monitored for the protection of wildlife, and people as well. As you drive, look at both sides of the dike. That's tidal on your right, but the water's fresh or brackish, with a low salt content. Wild rice, no relation to the domestic variety, is showing its yellow-green seeds above a sea of cattail and cut-grass. The water to our left is impounded and drained now for the "summer draw down." Each pond, as we said, is managed differently. Good duck foods are growing here—smartweed and giant foxtail (easy to spot, for it looks like a fox's tail). Just before reaching the space-age object ahead, take a look at the old wooden structure on your right. Though it served as a bridge, it was actually a water-control structure built in the early days of the Refuge. Flash boards were placed in or taken out of the slots so that large amounts of water could be moved. It was not just a spillway: If a hurricane or a freshet threatened to cover the dikes, water was allowed in so that the pressure on both sides of the embankments would be equalized.

Grape, mulberry, chinaberry, and morning glory crowd the roadway here along with the prettiest of marsh plants, the cardinal flower. To your left, the strange nose-cone antenna of the VOR TAC station sends out radio signals as a navigational aid to pilots.

Once there were two millstones at this site, but vandals took one. The little path here leads down to the gravestone of the slave Miser, "who was a driver on this plantation for 30 years . . . the noblest work of God." Such stones are rare, for most slave graves were marked only by curious collections of everyday belongings and seashells, which often deteriorated or, like the gravestone, were carried away.

On the dike once more and to your right is tropical cattail. The spike is taller and lighter than the common cattail we've seen up until now. On the left, another good duck food, the giant cut-grass, is going to seed. And on the dike itself, ragweed and pokeberry. Note that no trees are growing here. Now, as in antebellum days, trees were discouraged because their roots would cut through the earth and cause leaks. These dikes and canals have been enlarged and rearranged since 1928, but the rice-field trunk (a structure used for water control) we come to hasn't really changed in two hundred years. You raise the inside gate and the outside gate lets the field drain. You raise the outside gate and the inside gate lets it flood. Theoretically, they could work unattended, but the trunk minder's job was still an important one. He kept out trash and alligators

that could block the gates and made sure that the level of the flow was correct to the fraction of an inch.

Look at the creek bottom to the right of the trunk. Those roots and stumps are the remains of giant cypresses that once forested these wetlands before the rice growers cut them down. Beyond these are the pilings of an old bulkhead. That meant a soft spot in the land which, when it couldn't be diked, was detoured around, as in this case. On the pond side, panic grass and wild millet are growing. The bright orange of trumpet creeper is higher on the dike. We enter a small island thick with yaupon and canopied with live oaks.

We've entered Recess Plantation. The brick cistern to our left is thought to have provided drinking water for the slaves quartered on this knoll. Wells were usually dug, but in this case, it must have been necessary to connect guttering to the roof edges of the cabins. Please don't touch the bricks. A short nature walk starts here if you're tempted to leave the car. Once off the island, impoundments are on both sides (Ponds 6 and 5b on the brochure map), and then ahead is a broad freshwater canal built by the Army Corps of Engineers. They attempted to deepen the main Savannah River channel by blocking off the Back River channel that flows by the Refuge. This brought salt water too far inland, so it was necessary to find a new source of fresh water, most of which is now being brought in from the northern end of this canal. Not a brand-new problem, incidentally. While the hurricanes of the 1890s put most South Carolina rice planters out of business, here much of the blame was put on the 1890s construction of the Savannah jetties. They interrupted the tidal flow needed to flood the fields.

Besides an obligatory great blue heron and egrets, we've seen little wildlife until now, but here in the diversion canal is an eight-foot alligator and five more just as big lurk right around the bend. A white ibis feeds on the bank between the two sets of their protruding eyes. Ahead of us on the dike, a flock of cattle egrets is feeding on grasshoppers, and on the left, gallinules walk on the pigweed. An osprey drifts overhead.

Note the floodgates here: Modern concrete screwgates with handles removed—probably to prevent the fishermen from cracking them open. There are fishermen here and more ahead. They like to fish around the water structures where a little current might be working.

We've started back toward U.S. 17 (far side of Pond 5b). The dike is now a broad earthen structure; the originals were made mostly of peat. The soft peat soil peculiar to this area caused problems for rice planters, and refuge managers as well. This section of the embankment burned down completely when a fire in the adjoining drained field got out of control. A white waterlily grows here, which is good, but so do phragmites, a giant reed newcomer which, if unchecked, can take over.

Cypress are beginning to grow again in the wilderness to our right. The grasses here—sawgrass and giant cut-grass—are aptly named: Both are sharp enough to cut. We pass another modern water-flow structure, and then there's elderberry on the roadside. Its blue berries are still used in winemaking. Next, we see the Chinese tallow known locally as popcorn or Christmas berry. It was imported in hope of making wax.

The next field (Pond 5a) is drained, and we can get a good, clear view of the large face ditch and the much smaller quarter ditches that entered. The uniform draining and flooding of the land was essential in the old days and is helpful even today. In the main canal you can see the giant stumps of a vanished cypress forest.

The next field (Pond 10) is flooded. Wood duck nest boxes have been placed here among the waterlily and cattails to encourage this non-migratory waterfowl. Ahead on the small island, tupelo and cypress are coming in. Red maple and sweetgum are thick, and popcorn berry, now greenish-white, hangs thick beside the road. The marsh mallow is blooming late, and there's red-eyed hylessis. We're back to Highway 17. Day is done and Charleston beckons.

❖

138.6	0.0	At exit gate from Refuge, turn right onto U.S. 17 North.
142.6	4.0	Continued on U.S. 17 North.
146.1	3.5	Turn right onto I-95 North cloverleaf.
174.0	27.9	Veer right at Exit 33 onto U.S. 17 North and continue on this route to Charleston.
235.2	61.2	Arrive at south side of Ashley River Bridge.

ADDITIONAL READING

The Moving Finger of Jasper by Grace Fox Perry is the best and only history of the county. A small pamphlet, "Sergeant Jasper," was published by Pauline Webel and the Ridgeland library has it. "Historic Resources of the Low Country," prepared by the Lowcountry Council of Governments, might be back in print; I depended heavily on my copy, both here and in Beaufort. Pat Young, tour director of the Savannah Refuge, gave me some helpful tips, among them to go ahead and read my ten-year-old copy of James Clifton's *Life and Labor on Argyle Island*. Andrew Peoples's *Bluffton Boy* is funny but hard to find. Charles Pinckney's plantation notes were published by the South Carolina Historical Society. And don't forget *No. II, A Longer Short History of Bluffton, S.C., and Its Environs*. It was a collective effort, but we had an entertaining meeting with its editors and researchers, Ben and Betsy Caldwell—so both their conversation and their book found their way into the Bluffton entry.

TOUR 8:

FOUR HOLE

SWAMP TO

JACKSONBORO

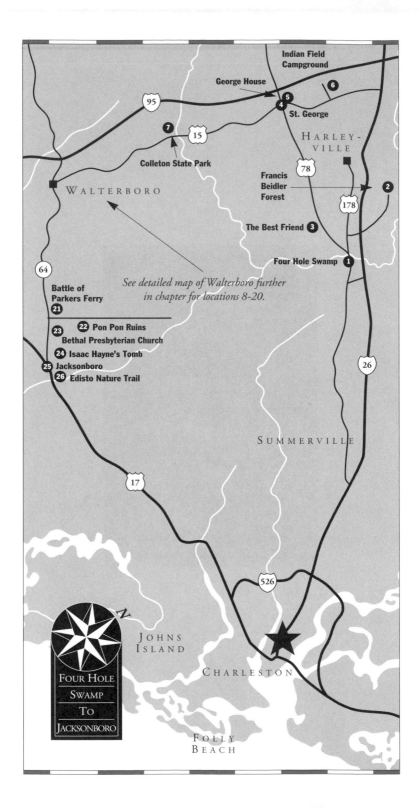

Indian Field
Campground

George House

⑤
④
St. George

⑥

95

⑦

15

Colleton State Park

H A R L E Y -
V I L L E

78

Francis
Beidler
Forest

178

②

W A L T E R B O R O

The Best Friend ❸

64

Four Hole Swamp ❶

Battle of
Parkers Ferry
㉑

*See detailed map of Walterboro further
in chapter for locations 8-20.*

㉓ ㉒ Pon Pon Ruins
Bethal Presbyterian Church

㉔ Isaac Hayne's Tomb

㉕ Jacksonboro

㉖ Edisto Nature Trail

26

S U M M E R V I L L E

17

526

N

J O H N S
I S L A N D

FOUR HOLE
SWAMP
TO
JACKSONBORO

C H A R L E S T O N

F O L L Y
B E A C H

FOUR HOLE SWAMP TO JACKSONBORO

This is a five-star trip for naturalists with a wonderful blend for historians as well. First, we travel about forty-five minutes north of Charleston to FRANCIS BEIDLER FOREST, the largest remaining virgin cypress and tupelo swamp in the world. Then we pass along historic railroad tracks and through the little station town of ST. GEORGE to reach INDIAN FIELD, the earliest Methodist campground and tabernacle in the country. Next, there's COLLETON STATE PARK, where we can picnic beside the Edisto River. Then, it's on to WALTERBORO, an antebellum pineland village grown larger, but still containing lovely homes and public buildings. Heading back to Charleston we pass the PON PON CHAPEL ruin, the ancient BETHEL PRESBYTERIAN BURIAL GROUND, and the tomb of a Revolutionary War martyr, ISAAC HAYNE. We end the day at the EDISTO NATURE TRAIL—an unusual nature walk that carries us back in time at least two centuries. To do this tour in a day, start early and take a picnic lunch.

Francis Beidler Forest in Four Hole Swamp

Untouched swamp forest of gigantic bald cypress and tupelo gum. Self-guided tour along boardwalk. Visitors center, natural history exhibits, restrooms.

Open 9 a.m. to 5 p.m., Tuesday through Sunday.
Call ahead for canoe trips and other activities.
Admission charged.
Telephone: (803) 462-2150

St. George

A small rural community.
Open daily.

Indian Field Campground, c. 1848

Unique early church architecture.
Open daily.

Colleton State Park

Nature trail, swimming, picnic area, canoe landing.
Open daily.

Walterboro

Open daily—self-guided tour.

Parkers Ferry Battle Site

Open daily.

Pon Pon Chapel of Ease, c. 1753

Open daily.

Bethel Presbyterian Church Burial Ground

Open daily.

Tomb of Colonel Isaac Hayne

Open daily.

Jacksonboro

Open daily.

Edisto Nature Trail

Open daily.

0.0	**0.0**	**L**eave Charleston on I-26 West and start mileage at intersection of U.S. 17.
33.0	**33.0**	**E**xit right at Exit 187, Ridgeville–St. George Exit.
33.3	**0.3**	**A**t exit stop sign, turn left onto S.C. 27 / Ridgeville Road.
34.4	**1.1**	**A**t first stop sign, turn right onto U.S. 78 West.
36.9	**2.5**	**S**econd bridge crosses a section of Four Hole Swamp which, downstream, becomes Francis Beidler Forest.

1. FOUR HOLE SWAMP

It's difficult to get a sense of the land driving down well-manicured Interstate 26, but once we exit we can get a closer view. Small fields intersperse large tracts of pine and gum forest. We're traveling through one of the few Lowcountry areas that was never divided into plantations. Farmers worked the land, or it simply remained wilderness. In fact, a small tribe of Indians still lives nearby. This section isn't virgin cypress forest, but it once was.

This bridge site on U.S. 78 was fought over several times during the Revolution. To early travelers, the bridge was a necessity because the sixty-mile-wide swamp was a considerable barrier. One explanation for the Four Hole name is that the low area could only be crossed in four places. The "holes" were passages. Another theory is that it was named for lakes that remained even during the driest times. Yet another is that the swamp was once fed by a four-holed spring that shot water out and drew it back in a strange bubbling fashion.

Technically, Four Hole is a swamp-stream, an arm of the Edisto River just off to our left, and black water is flowing through it at a perceptible rate. The swamp's basin, usually no wider than a mile and a half, is thought to have been carved out by the wind and tide of the receding Atlantic Ocean, but a ridge of limestone close by the Edisto River keeps the drainage partly blocked, and at times, the water here can rise as high as three and a half feet.

———— ◈ ————

37.0	**0.1**	**F**ork right onto U.S. 178 West / East Main Street.
37.7	**0.7**	**T**urn right onto Beidler Forest Road / S-18-28.
41.8	**4.1**	**B**ear straight onto dirt Mims Road when S-18-28 curves sharply to left.

| 42.8 | 1.0 | Turn right through Francis Beidler Forest entrance gates onto Sanctuary Road. |
| 43.7 | 0.9 | Arrive at Francis Beidler Forest parking lot. |

2. FRANCIS BEIDLER FOREST

The entrance to the forest begins between two fields and then runs through a second-growth forest, all of which seems typical of much of the state, but just ahead is a unique experience. Francis Beidler Forest is the largest remaining virgin stand of bald cypress and tupelo gum trees in the world—a treasure owned and operated by the National Audubon Society with help from the Nature Conservancy. Once, these great swamp forests ran through-out the coastal plain, but in the early years of settlement they were clear-cut and burned to make inland rice fields. After the Civil War, those areas that escaped this punishment were lumbered heavily. Francis Beidler, for whom the preserve is named, was one of these early lumbermen. He bought this section in the 1890s and, being one of the few conservationists of his day, simply held onto the land without cutting the trees. His family continued to preserve the forest, and when the estate was liquidated, their cooperation and gifts made possible the construction of the visitors' facilities.

That's where we begin our visit. The parking spaces are the narrowest possible slots in the woods, and the visitors center is equally unobtrusive. Inside we find a staff member happy to answer questions, and a slide pro-gram and displays to help interpret the swamp habitation and inhabitants. Man has not been completely ignored, incidentally, for there's a copper liquor still that was removed from the area and a shingling horse set up, as well as a display of Indian artifacts that suggest at least six thousand years of passage through the area.

Though copies can be purchased, a helpful handbook is lent to the visi-tor. This will be our guide to the one and three-quarters miles of boardwalk that circles through the uncut cypress and tupelo stand. The Audubon Society and the Nature Conservancy have been able to buy about seven miles of the sixty-mile swamp, a fifty-eight-hundred-acre holding that they're gradually expanding; we'll be seeing only a tiny but typical section of the area. Note that the numbers on the handrail correspond to the numbers in the printed guide.

Four Hole Swamp

Hurricane Hugo passed this way, but only one great cypress fell. Unfortunately, the damage was more extensive here on the edge of the swamp. Half the boardwalk has been replaced, but trees and debris were left as they fell. The canopy is more open, allowing some uncharacteristic under-growth, but the staff expects this to vanish as nature heals her own.

My father is along on this trip; he's an old friend of the Nature Conservancy and the Four Hole Swamp. One of the Audubon Society personnel comes along as well, so it's a well-informed excursion. We start on high ground, but looking ahead we can see a descent and a rapid shift in vegetation. The  amount of time water stands in a particular place determines what will grow there, a fact that becomes more and more evident. We start out among loblolly pines, named for the loblollies or low spots where the first settlers found them growing. Pond pines grow here as well. More susceptible to fire, they can't thrive as the loblollies do on the often burnt uplands. We pass quickly downhill into the hardwood flats, and the guidebook tells us to note the lichens and fungus that appear as colorful spots among the decaying browns of the forest stumps and branches. It speaks next of lizards and salamanders and later of a large variety of wildlife. On this hot July morning, however, the swamp is dry in most places. There's scat on the walk and a variety of tracks in the mud. We come upon wrens, cardinals, and even a deer. The small pond (Goodson Lake) at the boardwalk is crowded with alligators, turtles, and an anhinga, but we don't spot the impressive pileated woodpeckers, prothonotary warblers, or any of the more retiring residents.

While the wildlife can vary according to season and mood, the vegetation is rooted in one spot, and that in this case is too dramatic to be overlooked by even the most casual observer. As we drop down the three-foot incline that brings us to the swamp bottom, we notice the vegetation thinning until finally there are only three tree species left, and these for the most part are above our heads. That's water ash on the bottom (understory), tupelo next (midstory), and cypress above (overstory). On the coast, it is salt that dictates what survives, but here it is simply water, and as long as man doesn't interfere, the best-adapted plant life is obviously the great bald cypress. Towering as high as 120 feet, each is supported at the bottom by a swelling butt (twenty-one feet for one of these) and a root system that spreads out a hundred feet wide. Tangling together, these roots pop up as strange knees. Most of the knees are small, knobby wooden stalagmites that come above the water level to "breathe" and then stop, but in places, they too grow monstrous. One knee is as big as a person and because of its distinctly human shape is named "the Madonna." The purpose of these growths is unknown. They may, in fact, help the trees breathe, but there's no proof of this and the tree will continue to live even if the knees are cut off (they are at Cypress Gardens). It seems certain that they do stabilize the tree. The deeper the water, the more knees and the thicker the butt, and even in the softest spots these giants don't blow over. Lightning and old age are the main enemies now that man is no longer a threat. Indeed, the principal feeling of the swamp is one of ancient growth and gradual decay.

In the driest of times fire may pass through, but for the most part the fungus and molds are left to work away at the fallen but slowly rotting trees.

In these spots we see red maples or sweetgum sprouting well beyond their upland bounds. It's not all cypress after all: The tupelos, though kneeless, are almost as grand. If this area had been logged, tupelo would be the dominant species because it reseeds much better than the cypress. A tiny green fly orchid may not be quite so majestic, but it has found a foothold, and we're in luck for it only blooms during the summer.

We pass along "creek edge," visit the "lake," and gradually make our way in a circle up toward higher ground. There's evidence of intrusion: Shinglers have taken a log here. Our guide, a basket maker in his spare time, points out the vine of supplejack used by weavers. The conversation turns to what cypress is worth: We all happen to be fans of good wood. Cypress was and continues today to be prized for interior paneling and exterior siding. Now, real knot-free "black" cypress can't be bought. It takes three to five hundred years to grow trees like the ones we've just passed, and one elsewhere in the forest has been dated to a thousand years. Unfortunately, none of us can wait around quite that long. We spot a doe that's come searching for a drink of water, and then it's up the hill and out.

The boardwalk offers a unique glimpse of an uninterrupted natural cycle. These great cypress stands were once one of the most common sights in the Lowcountry, but, sadly, have now almost vanished. If you want to see even more, and time and weather permit, canoe trips can be arranged. Call ahead for information concerning this and other educational activities. The Audubon Society wants to preserve the Francis Beidler Forest, but it's only too happy to share this National Register wilderness with the public.

———— ◆ ————

43.7	**0.0**	From parking area, retrace to entrance gates of Francis Beidler Forest.
44.6	**0.9**	Turn left onto dirt Mims Road.
45.6	**1.0**	At stop sign, go straight onto Beidler Forest Road / S-18-28.
49.7	**4.1**	At stop sign, turn left onto U.S. 178 East.
50.4	**0.7**	At stop sign, turn right onto U.S. 78 West.
54.0	**3.6**	Look to left at railroad tracks that run parallel to U.S. 78.

3. THE BEST FRIEND OF CHARLESTON

Once we've passed through the crossroads of Dorchester, the highway is paralleled on the left by the Norfolk-Southern Railroad tracks, and much of the well-manicured woods on the right is kept by this company as a shooting preserve. This was originally the South Carolina Railroad Company's Charleston to Hamburg line. Completed in 1833, its 136-mile course made it the longest railroad in the world. The purpose was to rescue Charleston from the competition of Savannah by syphoning off cotton being grown inland of Augusta. Needless to say, Georgia wasn't interested in sharing her new-found wealth. The railroad didn't show much profit, but it was a great convenience to the inland planters of Carolina, who for the most part welcomed its coming.

"The Best Friend of Charleston" was the first American-made locomotive for public service. It was probably the first to blow up, too, which it did when the fireman sat on the annoying steam-release valve soon after service began. Passenger service was not all that could be desired, but it was soon putting towns like Summerville, St. George, and Branchville on the map. (Incidentally, though we take rock-covered railroad grades like this modern one for granted, the first through here was on piling, an almost continuous bridge.)

We won't visit it on this trip, but Branchville has a railroad museum that is currently closed. Located fifteen miles beyond St. George, Branchville is the community that formed when the railroad line between Charleston and Hamburg branched off to Columbia. It's the oldest such station in the world, and the depot, built in 1877, houses a museum containing all manner of railroad memorabilia, including a small model of the "Best Friend of Charleston." A room is set up like a turn-of-the-century railway office, and there were also a restaurant and a gift shop. Unfortunately, this is all closed except during one week in the fall—"Railroad Daze."

| 63.9 | 9.9 | In downtown St. George, turn right at stoplight onto Parker Avenue / U.S. 15 North. |

4. ST. GEORGE

St. George was named for its first settler, James George. Though the town was first called George's Turnout and then George's Station, the "Saint" was added because it had originally been part of St. George's Dorchester Parish. In those early days, it prospered as a depot and water stop, but incorporation didn't come until 1874. By then there was a revival of cotton farming and a large lumber mill made good use of the railroad. The great Victorian houses date from this period, and there's a courthouse built when Dorchester was separated from Colleton County in the 1890s. The main street, U.S. 15 or Parler Avenue, wasn't paved until 1930, so until then they raced horses here on the Fourth of July.

| 64.2 | 0.3 | Four blocks on left is 609 Parker Street, at corner of Minus Street. |

5. 609 PARKER STREET
The George House, c. 1851
Not open to public.

This is the only antebellum home remaining here. Recently restored, it is occupied by a direct descendant of James George.

In 1847, Bishop William Capers founded a Methodist church in St. George, a log building close to the railroad. James George donated the land for the church and went to Charleston and bought a Bible for it and another for the Baptist church. In those early days, the Baptists were "few and poor," but they've gotten ahead in recent years. There was a time, though, in the not-so-distant past, when you couldn't go five miles around here without hitting a Methodist church or finding a child who was named after a Methodist preacher. Well, that may be an exaggeration, but there's no denying that the state's first bishop, Francis Asbury, and his circuit riders found a willing audience here, which brings us to our next stop.

64.2	0.0	Continue on U.S. 15 North.
66.8	2.6	Turn left onto Indian Field Circle / S-18-73.
67.3	0.5	Turn right on Asbury Drive to circle Indian Field campground.

6. INDIAN FIELD CAMPGROUND, c. 1848
Open to public.

Early Methodist circuit riders preached beneath crude brush "arbors" and then in "pole churches." Indian Field, however, contains a tabernacle, the oldest such structure in the United States. Here the place of worship expanded to become a tremendous open-sided shelter for those gathered at week-long "camp meetings." The first of these meetings is thought to have originated in the upper part of South Carolina in about 1800. Two-day business sessions had been held before then, and it was noticed that when the thinly settled population could be brought together and preached to by several ministers, the extended exposure to God's word had a good effect. Preaching could go on night and day. "People slept on the ground sheltered by tents of some common cloth; others . . . were shelters covered with pine bark."

The idea must have spread quickly, for Bishop Asbury himself preached at Indian Fields in 1801. The spot may have shifted a few hundred yards since then, but by 1848, the meeting place had taken on its present form. The tabernacle is basically unchanged. Modern shingles have replaced those of wood, however, and the gable ends were clapboard not so long ago. The floor has always been dirt. The benches are a modern luxury. At one time the worshipers brought their own seats or stood—men to one side of the aisle, women to the other, and slaves to the rear.

Forming a circle about the tabernacle are ninety-nine equally rustic cabins or "tents." (The good shepherd had saved the ninety-nine sheep but still searched for the hundredth that was lost.) With dirt floors, and ventilation strips in place of windows, the narrow buildings are similar, barnlike constructions. Studs and clapboard siding show on the interior—sleeping is done in a second-story loft. It is doubtful they are as old as the tabernacle, but some still contain axe-hewn beams and poles, and the design is repeated even if the building is torn down completely and replaced.

The increase of creature comforts is something of a joke with the old-time campers. Wooden pallets and old springs have taken the place of piles of straw on the floor. Cooking is now done on "cook furnaces"—homemade barbecue grills with chimneys—instead of open fires or Dutch ovens. There are outhouses across the road from each cabin. Light bulbs are a luxury—some cabins have as many as four—and this year, for the first time, campers will be allowed to plug in the refrigerators that have previously just held ice.

The empty campground, of course, can't do justice to a full one. In 1878, "meeting week" was set the week of the first Sunday in October, and this practice continues today. Visitors of any denomination are invited to worship, sing, and enjoy the fellowship.

67.7	**0.4**	**C**omplete circle of Indian Field campground, return to cabin 9; go straight onto S-18-73.
68.2	**0.5**	**A**t stop sign, turn right onto U.S. 15 South, return to St. George.

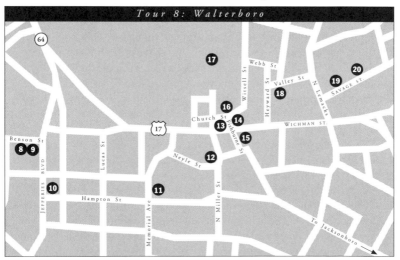

Tour 8: Walterboro

71.2	**3.0**	At intersection of U.S. 15 and U.S. 78 in St. George, continue straight on U.S. 15 South.
79.5	**8.3**	Right of U.S. 15 South, sand pits and Canady Steam Plant towers.

As we reach the river basin of the Edisto, there are sand mining operations. Ahead you'll see the Canady Steam Generator looming above the trees, and in its shadow is a small state park.

80.0	**0.5**	Cross Edisto River.
80.3	**0.3**	Turn right into entrance of Colleton State Park.

7. COLLETON STATE PARK

The park has a nature trail running through a thick grove of loblollies and dogwood. Picnickers, swimmers, and campers are accommodated, and the park is midway along the Edisto Canoe Trail—a newly organized project of the state parks system.

❖

80.3	**0.0**	After visiting state park, return to U.S. 15, turn right onto U.S. 15 South.
84.6	**4.3**	On right, Island Creek Meeting House historic marker.
90.4	**5.8**	Arrive at Walterboro City limits. U.S. 15 becomes North Jefferies Blvd.
91.7	**1.3**	Turn right onto Benson Street. Park on street.

Walterboro's History

Up until 1783, Paul and Jacob Walter had spent their summers in nearby Jacksonborough, but gradually malaria had reduced Paul's family to a single child, and now his wife appeared to be dying as well. Traveling inland for eighteen miles, the two brothers found a high, sandy hill beside a deep, hickory-filled valley. They built two-room log cabins and moved their families here. The place proved safe and others followed.

Local historian Beulah Glover found this 1800 source that gives a rare glimpse of "democratic" frontier summer camping.

> *In order to guarantee social union luxury was discouraged. The houses were of logs, merely barked and lined with clap board . . . no frame house, no iron in the building, wooden hinges, shingle roofs . . . chimeneys [sic] were made of logs well covered with clay, tables of pine yet how comfortable did we make these houses; a little taste and a contented heart made them as neat and pleasant as a splendid mansion.*

The same writer goes on to describe roads and paths cut between the homes, with nightly fires burning on the tops of tree stumps serving as street lamps. Supplies were brought the sixteen miles from the Pon Pon or Jacksonborough area, and a beef was killed and shared each week. In addition, there was a single store whose second story served as a meeting house for traveling preachers and as a community center and ballroom the rest of the week. It was an idyllic situation, the writer said, and added an unusual architectural note on the cabins.

> *This little community lived in great unanimity. The refreshing scent of the pine . . . so thick a wood preserved a constant shade and a healthy fragrance. Having no glazed windows a wide bush shed surrounded the house, kept us cool and rendered it unnecessary to close the wooden shutters during the rain.*

After the first frost this community dissolved, and its members returned to their plantation homes, but in 1817 the county seat was placed here, and by 1830, changes had occurred. The town still centered about the valley, which was considered its true heart, but the summer population had swollen to nine hundred. There was a courthouse, a jail, three churches, a market, and a male and female academy. Greek Revival mansions, or at least substantial raised cottages, replaced log cabins, but then the turmoil of the nationwide nullification debate disturbed the tranquil village.

8. 109 BENSON STREET
The Chamber of Commerce

The staff here is happy to answer any questions, and tour pamphlets to guide you through the community are kept in the entry hall. The pamphlets give a brief history of the town and list forty-six sites of interest that are marked on the map. Following is a much-shortened tour.

91.7	**0.0**	To left of chamber of commerce facing Jefferies Blvd. is Old Colleton County Jail.

9. CORNER OF JEFFERIES BLVD. AND BENSON STREET
The Old Colleton County Jail, c. 1856

Public offices.

Charleston's leading architects Lee and Jones designed this miniature castle with parapet—a Gothic Revival facade no doubt considered appropriate for a jail. A modern renovation has rearranged the interior, so you can appreciate it just as well from the street.

91.7	**0.0**	Turn around and return to Jefferies Blvd. At stop sign, turn right.
91.8	**2 blocks**	Turn left onto Hampton Street; on left is Colleton County Court House.

10. CORNER OF JEFFERIES BLVD. AND HAMPTON STREET
Colleton County Court House, c. 1822
Public offices.

Approach the courthouse from Hampton Street in order to appreciate the portico designed by South Carolina's first and best-known architect, Robert Mills. The original building is only the center part, which bears a strong resemblance to Mills's Fireproof Building in Charleston. In 1822, this was the extreme eastern edge of a town centered on Old Hickory Valley. The Confederate Monument, found in all the older county seats, is appropriately placed by the steps.

Antebellum Homes

Traveling along Hampton Street we pass a variety of distinctive antebellum and Victorian homes. By the mid-1890s, the town had the biggest railroad depot on the Savannah to Charleston line. Sawmills and farming brought a renewed prosperity. The business district shifted to its present location a block over to our left. You might want to visit there, too, for it's been spruced up and revitalized with particular care.

We cross Memorial Avenue, earlier known as Railroad Avenue, where some of the finer and fashionable homes were built.

91.8	**0.0**	**C**ontinue on Hampton Street.
92.1	**3 blocks**	**A**s you cross Memorial Avenue, look to left to see Walterboro Water Tower.

11. WALTERBORO WATER TOWER, c. 1915
Not open to public.

This 133-foot landmark is constructed of concrete and holds 100,000 gallons of water. The small slits are windows.

92.2	**1 block**	**T**urn left onto North Miller Street.
92.3	**1 block**	**O**n left at corner of North Miller and Neyle streets is the Methodist Church.

12. CORNER OF MILLER AND NEYLE STREETS
St. John's Independent Methodist Church, c. 1897
Not open to public.

This simple meetinghouse structure also served another congregation and is sometimes called the Old First Baptist Church.

Hickory Valley

We've reached the original Hickory Valley settlement area. Early residents measured out from the Little Library here three-quarters of a mile in every direction to design the town, so this was both literally and symbolically the center of the community. In 1879, however, a tornado passed through, destroying the church and many of the early residences, and uprooted the trees that had shaded the citizens for almost a century.

92.4	**1 block**	**A**t stop sign, turn right onto Wichman Street / U.S. 17A.

| 92.5 | 1 block | Turn left onto Fishburne Street and park. On left is Walterboro Library. |

Walterboro Library

13. CORNER OF WICHMAN AND FISHBURNE STREETS
Walterboro Library Society Building, c. 1820
Not open to public.
The Little Library on our left survived the tornado, but actually it has been moved since then from the spot on our right now occupied by St. Jude's Church.

| 92.5 | 0.0 | To right facing Fishburne Street is St. Jude's Episcopal Church. |

14. FISHBURNE STREET
St. Jude's Episcopal Church, c. 1881
Open to public.
The Episcopalians built this Carpenter Gothic church to replace the one destroyed by the cyclone. It's equally pretty on the inside.

| 92.5 | 0.0 | Look to right across Wichman Street to St. Peter's AME Church, which faces Fishburne Street. |

15. FISHBURNE STREET
St. Peter's AME Church, c. 1900
Not open to public.
This striking Gothic Revival building was constructed only a few years after its Episcopal neighbor.

| 92.5 | 0.0 | Look behind Library Society Building to 205 Church Street. |

16. 205 CHURCH STREET
The Lucas House, c. early 1800s
Not open to public.
The large columned home built by Richard Bedon was one of the few in the immediate neighborhood to survive the cyclone. Bedon had donated the land for the library.

92.5	0.0	Continue on Fishburne Street.
92.5	1 block	At stop sign, turn right onto Church Street.
92.6	1 block	Turn left onto Witsell Street / S-15-240.
92.6	1/2 block	On left is Hickory Valley.

17. THE REAL HICKORY VALLEY
This deep, tree-filled ravine to the left was the Hickory Valley around which the Walters and others first settled.

92.6	1/2 block	Turn right onto Webb Street / S-15-291.
92.7	1 block	Turn right onto Heyward Street / S-15-290.
92.8	1 block	Turn left onto Valley Street / S-15-289. On right is the Klein House.

18. 104 VALLEY STREET
The Klein House, c. 1844
Not open to public.

This Greek Revival house originally had double piazzas, now replaced with great columns. Either version is a far cry from the "democratic" log structures that served for the first summer camping. The commercial district shifted as well, for the town's first drugstore was on this lot.

92.8	0.0	Continue on Valley Street / S-15-289.
92.9	1 block	At stop sign, turn right onto North Lemacks Street / S-15-152.
92.9	1 block	Turn left onto Savage Street / S-15-79. On left is Glover-McCloud House.

19. 109 SAVAGE STREET
The Glover-McCloud House, c. 1824
Not open to public.

This great house surrounded by a camellia garden was called "Mounds" because the owner buried two white horses on either side of the entry.

| 93.0 | 1/2 block | Next door on left is Perry-Smoak-Lubs House. |

20. 125 SAVAGE STREET
The Perry-Smoak-Lubs House, c. 1814
Not open to public.

The next house, also garden-surrounded, is an 1814 raised cottage. Architecturally, this was the transition between cabin and mansion. Building high off the ground put the residents above the mosquitoes.

| 93.2 | 1 block | At stop sign, turn right onto U.S. 17A /South Wichman Street. |

As we travel U.S. 17A /South Wichman Street, we'll pass several more antebellum raised cottages and some larger Victorian homes.

| 94.0 | 13 blocks | Turn left onto Lucas Street. |
| 94.2 | 2 blocks | At second stop sign, turn left onto Hampton Street. |

The Road to Jacksonboro

The tale is told of a famed prankster who dragged a dead fox through the church on Saturday night, then loosed his dogs to run wild through the congregation the following morning. A far more serious "joke" got him run out of town soon after, but we're leaving of our own free will. The road we're on now leads to Jacksonboro, so we're traveling back in time. There are several sights with historical markers on the roadside, but sometimes you have to look closely for them.

95.1	**0.9**	**A**rrive at junction with S.C. 64. Continue straight on S.C. 64 East.
106.5	**11.4**	**T**urn left onto dirt road S-15-705 at historic marker for Battle of Parkers Ferry.

21. BATTLE OF PARKERS FERRY

The battle wasn't actually fought here, and there's nothing to see, but shortly after the death of Colonel Hayne (next marker), Francis Marion was sent into this area to aid Colonel Harden. The British had confiscated the rice in the area and were landing at the nearby ferry. With 400 men, Marion waited at the causeway and ambushed a force of 540 Hessians, British, and Tories. Beaten badly, the enemy withdrew to Dorchester and then to Charleston. There had been at least a half dozen other skirmishes and battles in the area, but this one, coming shortly after Colonel Hayne's execution and just before the Yorktown surrender, is noted as an important psychological victory for the Americans.

107.3	**0.8**	**A**rrive at stop sign at intersection of S-15-40. Continue straight on dirt road S-15-705.
107.4	**0.1**	**T**urn right into churchyard at ruins of Pon Pon Chapel.

Pon Pon Chapel of Ease

22. PON PON CHAPEL OF EASE RUINS, c. 1753

Open to public.

In 1725, this parish was provided with an Anglican chapel of ease, but the present ruin dates from 1753. It burned sometime between 1796 and 1806, and is still known as "the Burnt Church." The building, with its distinctly marked water table, arched windows, and unusual Jacobean gables, must have been considered grand for a mere chapel, but not much remains. There are a dozen old gravestones, some dating from the late eighteenth century, which offer the briefest of records for the passing years. "A tender and Affecationate Mother, Endowed with the ornament of meek and quiet spirit" was placed here in antebellum times. Close by is a veteran gassed in World War I.

107.4	**0.0**	**T**urn left out of churchyard onto dirt road S-15-705.
108.3	**0.9**	**A**t second stop sign, turn left onto S.C. 64 East.
109.0	**0.7**	**O**n left is historical marker for Bethel Presbyterian Church site.

23. BETHEL PRESBYTERIAN CHURCH

Also known as the Pon Pon Church, this was one of the early Presbyterian churches founded by Reverend Archibald Stobo. Built in 1728, the building served until the congregation moved to Walterboro and was already abandoned when it burned in 1886. Several dozen gravestones from the eighteenth and nineteenth centuries survive. Captain Dent, who commanded "Old Ironsides," gets special mention, but there are others of interest. A Mr. Bowman was well remembered: "Firm and generous friend, A keen sportsman and true Patriot lies here. His friends mourn their lost. These woods that so often Echoed, The Crack of his Rifle, (still) Hear his cheerful cry." That stone is broken off and on the ground.

109.0	**0.0**	**C**ontinue on S.C. 64 East.
109.8	**0.8**	**T**urn left onto dirt road beside Isaac Hayne's historical marker.
110.8	**1.0**	**A**rrive at Isaac Hayne's grave site.

24. COLONEL ISAAC HAYNE'S TOMB

During the Revolutionary War, Colonel Hayne was taken prisoner at the fall of Charleston and, after promising not to fight the English, was paroled. When ordered to fight against his comrades, however, he refused, broke parole, and rejoined them. Captured, he was hanged by the British. A more detailed account is given at the site, but his inscription reads in part: "In life a soldier of his Country, In death a martyr to her sacred cause. His memory an undying inspiration to his fellow countrymen, His monument the freedom of his Native Land." Crepe myrtle, holly, and live oaks cover the knoll, which is also the homesite of the Hayne and Parks families.

110.8	**0.0**	**R**etrace on dirt road to S.C. 64.
111.8	**1.0**	**A**t stop sign, turn left onto S.C. 64 East.
113.2	**1.4**	**A**t stop sign, turn left onto U.S. 17 North. (NOTE: U.S. 17 is a four-lane road and you must

		first cross the southbound lanes.)
113.5	**0.3**	On left is field with pecan trees and the location of Old Jacksonboro.

25. OLD JACKSONBORO'S HISTORY

A historical marker is placed at the next stop, but here the site is only commemorated by weeds and some giant trash containers. Originally, this was the Indian village of Pon Pon (translated as "black water"). The spot was granted to John Jackson and by 1735, a settlement had started. Jackson had a bridge here, and there has always been a bridge or at least a ferry since, for it was the main route down the seaboard. A town plan of 1780 shows 113 lots, and the community boasted a free school, race track, tavern, Masonic lodge, and Episcopal and Presbyterian churches close by. Two years later when Charleston fell to the British, Jacksonboro became South Carolina's capital for a season. Then it served as county seat until 1822. The particularly deadly malaria that invaded the Lowcountry following the Revolution took a heavy toll here, and finally put an end to the original town. In 1783, the Walters had moved inland to Walterboro and eventually everyone else followed. The newer Jacksonboro we drive through on Highway 17 got its start when the railroad came through in 1859 and was further aided by the phosphate mining of the 1890s.

		Turn left into parking lot of Edisto Nature Trail.
113.6	**0.1**	

Westvaco

The sponsor of this trail is Westvaco Timberlands Division, and it's probably the best example of corporate responsibility to the community we'll come across. Westvaco began in 1888 when it pioneered a process for producing wood pulp. Today, it has fifty plants and fifteen thousand employees and has expanded beyond paper making into a variety of land-use industries. The Southern Woodlands Division, under whose jurisdiction this path falls, looks after half a million acres of woodlands, most of it loblolly pine and most of it here in the Lowcountry. The company is conscious of environmental issues and recognizes that it is dealing with what should be a renewable resource, but for the sake of efficiency, timber is usually harvested in blocks by increasingly mechanical means and replanted with seedlings genetically engineered to produce lumber faster. This, too, will pass. If you don't think so, walk its trail.

26. EDISTO NATURE TRAIL

This excellent self-guided nature trail shows the many uses to which the land has been put over the last three centuries. Actually, there are two trails offered here, a half mile and a mile. Take the longer if you have the time. It leads quickly out of the familiar loblolly forest and is a trip not only through a river swamp bottom but through time itself. Trees and plants are identified along the way and there's a map of the trail available in the mailbox on the site or at a nearby gas station. For your own safety, stay on the path, use the handrails on the bridges, and obey the other safety notes.

Unlike Four Hole Swamp, this is not virgin but third-growth forest you are entering. The brochure has a list of trees and plants to be found here and many are labeled. I made this trip in the middle of the summer with my father. The mosquitoes weren't too bad, but we sprayed for them and around our ankles to keep off the redbugs.

The sound of U.S. 17 traffic is loud as we enter on a wide path that was once "Old Charleston Road." On both sides is an abandoned field now grown up with tremendous loblolly pine. (It's sometimes called "old field pine" since it volunteers so readily in these areas.) The yellow jessamine (a little scarce in the labeled site) is our state flower. The berries of the familiar wax myrtle once made candles for the first settlers.

We have crossed over to a second old road, The King's Highway. Usually laid out along the Indian trails, this was our nation's first intrastate highway— the main connector for the original colonies. Crossing a canal, we drop down into the river-bottom swamp of the Edisto. There is another abandoned field here, but this one has been planted with fast-growing slash pine. This species lost some of its early popularity with timber companies because it did not fare well in ice storms, but here the weather is still warm enough for it to grow. Watch out for the poison ivy—it has three leaves and a hairy vine. The devil's walking stick got its name from those menacing thorns. Tornado damage in 1983 killed this loblolly; though it's beginning to rot, we can still make out the rings. It's fifty-three years old. Note the centermost rings, for they show that the young tree was growing two inches a year and then slowed as it matured and had to compete with the surrounding forest.

The muscadine grape is native to America and similar to the domesticated scuppernong. If it's getting sunlight and is a female vine, it will bear fruit, to be enjoyed—in this case by raccoons. The same Alabama supplejack we saw earlier in the day at Four Hole Swamp was a favorite of furniture and basket makers. The black cherry has tiny bunches of black fruit prized by local wildlife that also feeds on the Southern crabapple. Note that the squirrels are eating the loblolly cones. They cut them while still green and the debris litters the path. American beautyberry or French mulberry is another favorite of wildlife. The switchcane or native bamboo, on the other hand, was recently proved by science to be a nutritious cattle food—a fact long known by the early cattlemen who burned these woods each year to get the new green shoots sprouting. Good for cows, it made a wasteland of woods like these.

A big loblolly has fallen here, and a briar patch of vines is quick to take advantage of the sunlight. The labeled live oak is dead. (The same thing happened to the first labeled cypress in Four Hole Swamp—"surest way to kill a tree," the guide joked.) The American hornbeam was locally called "Ironwood" and used to make implement handles.

A sawmill water hole was dug to provide water for the steam engine, but liquor-still operators often dug identical wells—you'll spot them by the bro-ken jars—and before that, water holes were dug for the half-wild cattle. The dwarf palmetto has been seen all along, but it's labeled here. Unlike the cabbage palmetto, it grows no bigger. Note the rock that is beginning to show on the surface of the path. There's more to come.

A boardwalk leads us out onto an old slave-built dike. Early in the 1700s, inland swamps were cleared of cypress and gum and planted in rice. The fields were usually smaller here than in the marshland because the ground of each field had to be perfectly level so that it could be flooded properly. The canal system is not so elaborate either, but still we see numerous ditches running through what was once all rice fields and is now forest.

Yaupon is marked here, but is struggling because it's so far removed from the coast. The "black drink" of the Indians, it was a local tea for white settlers, who were still drinking it in the 1920s.

These rice fields might have been abandoned even before the Civil War, but in the years after, rice cultivation would eventually end. Phosphate mining began during Reconstruction and continued into this century. The topsoil was scraped away (in this case not too deeply) and the rock was mined to be used for fertilizer. All that remains are the dirt mounds and pebbles in the path.

On the boardwalk here we see the bald cypress with accompanying knees. This was probably the predominant species to begin with, and the site is not unlike what we saw at Four Hole. A pileated woodpecker has been working on the dead tree here. The largest of the remaining woodpeckers, he scrapes away the bark and digs in. The barge canal to the river probably dates from rice-planting days. Flats carried the rice out to the Edisto River where it could be carried to the mill. There's an old building site here, a knoll with a few bricks, and just beyond that the site of a phosphate factory. Some scraps of iron gear and bolts are visible, but nothing else shows that rock was pounded here except some spots of gravel.

The den tree is a dead live oak, a home for raccoon, squirrel, and much else. We cross from the dike to the bed of an old railroad tram. A single, small piece of iron rail is all that remains, which isn't too surprising, for such lines weren't permanent. This one may have served the phosphate mill we just passed, but during the early part of this century, the Lowcountry was crisscrossed by these narrow-gauge tracks. Timber crews followed in their wake, loading the rail cars with logs that could be dumped into rivers like the Edisto and floated to distant mills, or sawed on the bank and sent away by barge or ship.

Sapsuckers have been pecking on the labeled green ash. The spruce pine, an easy victim of fire, is rare and growing rarer still. The yellow poplar is called a tulip tree. It has a tulip-shaped leaf, but the yellow tulip-shaped flower gives it the Latin name tulipifera.

Leaving the tram road, we're once more on the edge of the loblolly hardwood forest where we began. There's a spring marked here, dry on this summer day, and then we pass through the great trees of the long-abandoned field and back into the twentieth century.

We start our day with the virgin forest of Four Hole and end it here with the much-used bottom land on a downstream section of the same Edisto River. There's no giant cypress and less wildlife is seen here. A few squirrels and a startled owl on this day, and the sound of the U.S. 17 traffic and a passing train have intruded. Nevertheless, there's something reassuring in the fecundity of this forest. If not bulldozed and concreted into complete oblivion or poisoned by acid rain, nature has a remarkable ability to restore herself here in the Lowcountry, and with surprising speed can soften and eventually cover over the enterprise of man.

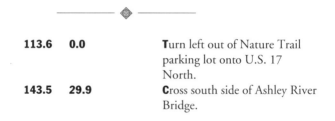

113.6	**0.0**	**T**urn left out of Nature Trail parking lot onto U.S. 17 North.
143.5	**29.9**	**C**ross south side of Ashley River Bridge.

ADDITIONAL READING

Not a great deal has been written about this area's history, but Mrs. Beulah Glover's several good books can be found at the Walterboro public library. At least two enjoyable histories of the Methodist Church are around. Four Hole Swamp is mentioned often in ecology-minded publications.

TOUR 9:

WEST SHORE

OF THE

COOPER RIVER

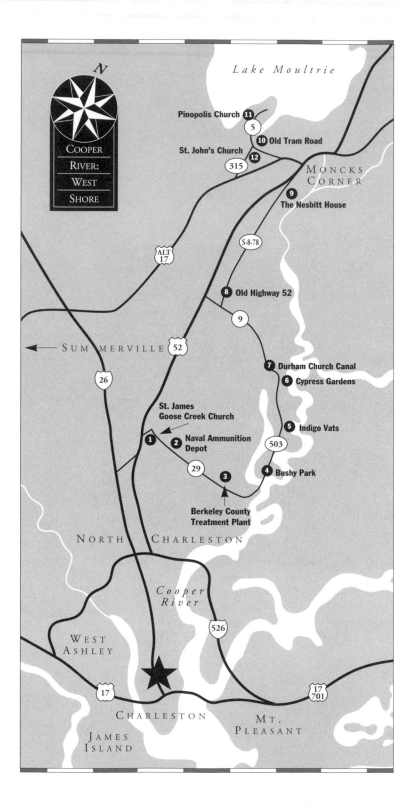

WEST SHORE OF THE COOPER RIVER
Including Goose Creek, Cypress Gardens, and Pinopolis

We start this tour just north of Charleston in the historic Goose Creek area and travel through Moncks Corner. The first stop is ST. JAMES–GOOSE CREEK CHURCH, the second oldest and most baroque of the rural Anglican churches. Then we cross over Back River to visit INDIGO VATS, and head north again through the pine forest of BUSHY PARK, a well-hidden industrial park. Next we visit CYPRESS GARDENS, a spot famous for its boat trips through cypress-filled ponds and the azaleas and camellias on its pathways. Traveling a seldom-used and scenic old Highway 52, we soon reach MONCKS CORNER. Here the chamber of commerce is housed in a 1725 house. Nearby is PINOPOLIS, a pretty little pineland village with pines, crepe myrtle, and some of the original houses dating from the 1840s. We end our day in Pinopolis with visits to PINOPOLIS METHODIST CHURCH and to ST. JOHN'S BAPTIST CHURCH.

St. James–Goose Creek Church, c. 1708
Grounds open daily. Interior shown by appointment.

Naval Ammunition Depot
Not open to public.

Lower Berkeley County Waste Water Facility
Tours available by appointment.
Telephone: (803) 572-4400

Bushy Park
A secluded industrial park hidden in pine forest.

Indigo Vats
Open daily. NOTE: No photographs allowed.

Cypress Gardens, c. 1927
Boat tours through beautiful cypress-crowded reservoir and great lengths of flower-lined paths to wander.
Open daily, 9 a.m. to 5 p.m.
Admission charged.

The Nesbitt House, c. 1725
Houses Moncks Corner Chamber of Commerce.
Open Monday through Friday, 9 a.m. to 5 p.m.

Moncks Corner
Downtown district open daily.

Pinopolis Community
A charming pineland village dating from the 1840s.
Open daily.

Pinopolis Methodist Church, c. 1900
Grounds open daily.

St. John's Baptist Church, c. 1884
Grounds open daily.

A DAY ON THE COOPER RIVER

Now there is nothing gives a man such spirits,
(Leavening his blood as cayenne doth a curry,)
As going at full speed—no matter where its
Direction be, so 'tis but in a hurry.

Dr. John Irving begins his 1842 *A Day on Cooper River* with this quotation from Lord Byron—the good doctor speaking with tongue in cheek of a steamboat that could go up the river and back in a single day. His anecdote-filled account was edited and advanced by Mrs. Louisa Stoney in 1932, and though we're going even farther even faster in these two Cooper River tours, and though some good histories have been written since, I'm inclined to rely on this couple and the other old-timers.

◈

0.0	0.0	Leave Charleston on I-26 West and start clocking mileage at intersection of U.S. 17.
12.4	12.4	Veer right at Exit 208–Goose Creek Exit, onto U.S. 52 West.
14.6	2.2	Veer right at Goose Creek Church historical marker onto Nad Road.
14.7	0.1	At stop sign, turn right onto Goose Creek Road.
15.3	0.6	After crossing railroad tracks and Goose Creek Bridge, turn right at stoplight onto Goose Creek Road/S-8-29.
15.6	0.3	Turn right at St. James–Goose Creek Church sign (difficult to see, watch carefully).
15.6	200 ft.	On left is church.

Goose Creek's History

We start at Goose Creek, a sprawling and decidedly new suburb of Charleston. The original community, however, was almost as ancient as the colony. Governor John Yeamans of Barbados settled here; it was Yeamans's Creek then. He harassed the earlier settlers and then did the infant colony the favor of dying. Rice and indigo were cultivated, and more political turmoil as well—the most powerful planters of the day, the Barbadian Goose Creek men, continually fought to control the colony's government. In 1706, they had the Church of England established as Carolina's official church. Politics, not faith, seems to have been their prime motivation, but the grand mansions have all fallen into ruin while the second-oldest and finest of the rural Anglican churches is still standing and just ahead of us.

The creek was once navigable, but it's crowded with pigweed now, and this particular section is blocked off as a reservoir. Geese were hunted here well into the twentieth century, but the ancient name of Goose Creek may have come from the local pronunciation of the name of a Dutch settler, Goes.

1. ST. JAMES–GOOSE CREEK CHURCH, c. 1708
Grounds open to public.
Started in 1708, this little jerkin-headed building wasn't completed until almost a decade later. It's been called one of the most interesting of early English churches. Historian and church member Sam Stoney called it the most baroque. It's certainly unique, for it's the only one in existence containing the Royal Coat of Arms, and one of only two that has a hatchment still hanging. This Izard family coat of arms was probably left there after a funeral.

Perhaps you can get a look inside. The brightly colored Lion and Unicorn are high above the finely worked pulpit and sounding board and are flanked on both sides by elaborate dadoes, almost as if to suggest that the king's word was above God's. It is said that British soldiers spared the church because of the Royal decoration.

Outside the church the window arches are faced with cherubs, but of particular interest is the pelican feeding her young found on the pediment. This was the symbol of the Society of the Propagation of the Gospel in Foreign Parts, which supplied ministers to this and other Anglican churches. The first here, Samuel Thomas, did not find life easy, and his replacement, Reverend Francis LeJau, was often exasperated by his contrary congregation and meager to non-existent salary. The church was built during his tenure but he died just before its completion; he lies buried beneath the altar.

"Sober, well disposed, and attentive to public worship" was how the congregation was described in 1723, and the church enjoyed a modest success until the Revolution. The Coat of Arms stayed, but it's said that a minister offering a prayer for the king had a prayer book thrown at him. It was about this time that the most colorful of British Revolutionary War officers, Mad Archy Campbell, asked a Charleston belle, Margaret Philips, to go riding with him, and then raced the carriage to St. James where he forced the minister at pistol point to marry him to the protesting woman. Not so, their descendants claimed. She loved him madly and married gladly.

The church never really recovered from the Revolution and has had only limited regular services in the last 150 years. Still, the building has been well looked after, extensively restored in 1840 and again after severe damage by the great earthquake of 1886. That pelican is at least the third—one contractor tried in vain to model the bird from a reluctant Muscovy  duck. Even the Coat of Arms is actually a faithful copy of one destroyed by the quake. It's all held together pretty well, considering. Extensive restoration is going on now, but it may take a while longer to finish up.

15.6	0.0	**R**etrace to Goose Creek Road / S-8-29.
15.7	200 ft.	**T**urn right onto Goose Creek Road.
15.7	50 ft.	**V**eer left and continue on Snake River Road / S-8-208. (Goose Creek Road veers to right.)
16.1	0.4	**A**t stop sign, turn right onto Red Bank Road / S-8-29.
17.5	1.4	**O**n left is entrance to Polaris Missile Facility.

2. NAVAL AMMUNITION DEPOT
Not open to public.
The Polaris Missile Facility is on your left. Missiles stand at the gate. Although the fence is mostly on the right, the Naval Ammunition Depot occupies land on both sides of the road. A century ago, the citizenry here made red tiles and had Methodist camp meetings at the Red Bank Landing. But that was before Dr. Ravenel had invented the first effective semisubmersible submarine, and the concept of "nuclear deterrent" was just a futuristic dream.

| 17.5 | 0.0 | **C**ontinue straight on Red Bank Road / S-8-29. |
| 20.3 | 2.8 | **O**n left is Lower Berkeley County Waste Facility. |

3. BERKELEY COUNTY
WATER AND SEWER TREATMENT PLANT
This treatment plant is the third largest in the tri-county area with its daily capacity of fifteen million gallons. Its average dry-weather flow is seven million gallons daily, which are discharged after aeration, clarification, and disinfection into the Cooper River.

20.3	0.0	**C**ontinue straight on Red Bank Road / S-8-29.
20.8	0.5	**T**urn left onto Bushy Park Road / S-8-503.
21.3	0.5	**O**n right is Back River Reservoir.

4. BUSHY PARK
Once a plantation, Bushy Park is now the home of five large industrial plants. The Back River, famous for its rice growing and brickmaking, is partly impounded to ensure a constant supply of fresh water for these manufactuing processes. But located in the midst of all this is a tiny reminder of old times.

| 21.3 | 0.0 | Continue on Bushy Park Road / S-8-503. |
| 22.4 | 1.1 | Turn right into Miles Corporation visitor parking lot to visit Indigo Vats. Located between the parking lots. |

5. INDIGO VATS

Open to public. No photographs.

There at the gate of the Miles Corporation is a set of indigo vats. Most of these were built of wood, but here's one of brick. Note the two linked sections separated by a sliding door. Not only was the cultivation of indigo a closely guarded secret, but the processing was as well. In about 1744, Eliza Lucas and others had to rediscover it. The stalk and leaves of the plant went into the first vat, where they fermented for about fourteen hours. Then this liquid was drawn into the lower "battery." Here, the solution was thickened by beating it with paddles, then allowed to settle. Finally, the water was drawn off and the lumps of sediment dried out and sold. The "indigo maker" watched this process day and night until it was completed. The end product could produce three shades—copper, blue, and purple—and was valuable enough to bring fortunes to some early planters, and important enough for the English to pay an extra bounty to keep it out of the hands of the French. These vats are owned by the Berkeley Historical Society, but you're parking courtesy of the Miles Corporation and it asks you not to take photographs.

———————— ◈ ————————

22.4	0.0	Turn right out of Miles Corporation parking lot onto Bushy Park Road / S-8-503.
27.9	5.5	At stop sign, turn right onto S.C. 9 East / Cypress Garden Road.
28.0	0.1	Turn right into entrance of Cypress Gardens.
28.3	0.3	Parking lot of Cypress Gardens.

6. CYPRESS GARDENS, c. 1927

Cypress Gardens was heavily damaged by Hugo; restoration continues. Upon entering, the visitor receives a map and brochure that show the route of several miles of paths and list the main points of interest. Cypress Gardens is owned and operated as a park by the City of Charleston. The azaleas of spring are what the Gardens is famous for—and the quiet boat rides that a paddler gives visitors through the black water of the cypress-crowded reservoir. The park service is broadening its appeal: There are plants both wild and introduced to brighten most of the year, and wildlife (squirrels to alligators) abounds. A full-time naturalist is on hand. Rice is being cultivated. The water can get shallow by late summer, but you're encouraged to come any time for the boat ride and the self-guided walking tour about the reserve's perimeter.

This was originally part of Dean Hall plantation. William Carson built a fine home here (which has now been moved and reassembled near Beaufort) and married the daughter of Unionist James Petigru. A Unionist widow when war came, Mrs. Carson carried her younger son off to Italy where she supported herself as a painter. Older son James stayed to fight for the Confederacy and, after a career as a mining engineer, finally retired here to the river. Benjamin Kitteridge bought Dean Hall in 1909 and, inspired by the wild azaleas growing about the old rice reserve, decided to turn it into a more formal garden. Azaleas were his pride and he planted thousands, many of which now tower like trees. Camellias were added, too, and wisteria, tea olives, pines, dogwoods, and magnolias, but the Gardens' hallmark is the cypresses.

Hurricane Hugo damaged the original gift and sandwich shops, but they've been impressively replaced. A new visitors center houses a gift shop and cafeteria (during the spring, a tearoom, as well). And a replica of the old gift shop will soon open as an educational center, with interpretative displays and space for school lectures and community gatherings.

———————— ◈ ————————

28.3	0.0	Retrace to Cypress Gardens entrance gates.
28.6	0.3	At stop sign, turn left onto S.C. 9 West / Cypress Gardens Road.
28.7	0.1	Cross Durham Church Canal.

7. DURHAM CHURCH CANAL
Just as you leave the Gardens, you cross the canal connecting the West branch of the Cooper with the Back River Reservoir. There's an avenue of young magnolias and a turnoff to the wildlife reserve, the Bluff.

———————— ◈ ————————

| 28.7 | 0.0 | Continue on S.C. 9 West / Cypress Garden Road. |
| 32.5 | 3.8 | At stop sign, turn right onto S-8-78 / Old U.S. 52 West. |

8. "OLD HIGHWAY 52" is pretty well deserted now and makes a quiet, green drive. There are several well-known plantations along the way, but they're private property. Ancient Mulberry Castle was the home of Thomas Broughton and served as a refuge and fort during the Yemassee attack. Lewisfield is typical of the fine, well-ventilated houses being built even before the Revolution. Today, it's the home of Senator Rembert Dennis. Gippy, a Classical Revival house built on the eve of the war, can be seen but it's in the middle of a residential area. This pasture land was once for dairy cattle, and Gippy milk is still for sale.

39.9	**7.4**	**T**urn right, onto Dennis Blvd. / S-8-554.
39.9	**20 ft.**	**T**urn right into Nesbitt House parking lot.

9. THE NESBITT HOUSE, c. 1725
Moncks Corner Chamber of Commerce Office

This was the overseer's house at Dean Hall. Dating back to 1725, it has been reassembled and refurbished here where the ground floor now houses the chamber of commerce. Stop in; they're happy to give you information about the area.

Moncks Corner's History

This land from Mulberry Castle north was originally granted in 1672 to Lord Proprietor Peter Colleton and was known as the Fair-lawne Barony. Two of Peter's grandsons, John and Peter, would eventually settle in Carolina and leave honorable descendants, but gradually the great sixteen-thousand-acre holding was broken up. In 1735, Thomas Monck purchased a thousand acres of it, the corner that was bounded by Stony Landing, the Charles Town Road, and the rest of Fairlawn—the corner belonged to Monck. Since this was on a main trade route to the nearby landing, several stores were built there, and a tavern and race track. This community, located somewhere close to where highways 17A and 52 join, seemed to have faded away after the Revolution, but the coming of the railroad and the choice of the new village as county seat in the 1890s brought it back to life. This new Moncks Corner spread out, finally encompassing the old. There's been some debate over the years about the spelling of Monck, and the relatively recent arrival of Trappist monks has added to the confusion. It was Monck with a "c," says historian Orvin, and he quotes as proof this 1744 newspaper article: "Thomas Ellis, alias Stick in the Mud, alias Tom Thump the Devil, convicted of stealing a horse the property of Thomas Monck was sentenced to be hanged."

Bordering on Hell Hole Swamp, an ancient hideout for outlaws, runaway slaves, and unpatriated Indians, the Moncks Corner community had a tradition of lawlessness, or at least willful independence. This reputation was only heightened during Prohibition, when moonshiners boldly plied their trade even more boldly than elsewhere in the Lowcountry, if that was possible. "Not a goiter to the gallon," the 1940 WPA Guide declares of this apparently safe-to-drink distillation. Today the town is better known for its association with recreation provided by Lake Moultrie. Fish camps, outboard motor boats, and the best fried catfish in the world are what they advertise today.

◈

39.9	**0.0**	**F**rom Nesbitt House parking lot, cross to far side of traffic island on Dennis Blvd. / S-8-554 and turn left.
39.9	**6 ft.**	**A**t stop sign, turn right onto S-8-791 / Old 52 Highway.

40.3	0.4	At second stoplight, turn left onto S.C. 6 West / East Main Street.
40.7	0.4	Cross Seaboard Coast Line Railroad.
42.2	1.5	Fork right onto Pinopolis Road / S.C. 5.

Pinopolis

Pinopolis

Drive slowly and look carefully. We enter Pinopolis today on a central paved road lined with crepe myrtles. Before Hurricane Hugo this was literally a forest of pines, but most were lost. Several dirt lanes lead off the main road, but most are dead ends and private driveways, and we'll have to be content with the view from here. By the time of the Civil War, the village boasted twenty or thirty fine houses, and a few of those that remain can be glimpsed through the trees.

| 43.9 | 1.7 | Look right at 1764 Pinopolis Road to see bed of old tram road. |

10. OLD TRAM ROAD

Just inside the village proper, the highway crosses the bed of an old tram road. Power lines run down it today, but you can see the cut made to secure a proper grade. Built in 1892, this ten-mile rail line connected to the main line in Moncks Corner and led off to our left to the visionary "New England City." This real-estate development went bankrupt fourteen years later and its site was flooded by Santee Cooper in 1940.

| 44.0 | 0.1 | On left, Pinopolis Methodist Church. |

11. PINOPOLIS METHODIST CHURCH, c. 1900

Grounds open to public.

Next on your left is the Pinopolis Methodist Church built in 1900. A nice, simple Victorian building with modest gingerbread trim, it's apparently the first built here. The Methodists, however, date back far earlier. The Wesley brothers had visited Mulberry Plantation in 1735. Both Bishop Asbury and William Capers rode a circuit in this area around 1800. And just seven miles away is the Friendship Methodist Church. On the site of early camp meetings, a church was built in 1825, and the present building incorporated one of its floor timbers at its center. The earliest church at this site, however, was a Baptist one.

44.0	**0.0**	**C**ontinue on Pinopolis Road / Main Street / S.C. 5, touring Pinopolis' side streets (approximately 1.7 miles).
45.7	**1.7**	**R**eturn to post office on Pinopolis Road / Main Street / S.C. 5.
45.7	**0.0**	**S**tarting at post office, retrace Pinopolis Road / Main Street / S.C. 5.
46.9	**1.2**	**B**ear straight onto Murray Lane / S-8-315.
47.0	**0.1**	**O**n left is St.John's Baptist Church.

12. ST. JOHN'S BAPTIST CHURCH, c. 1884

Grounds open to public.

Constituted June 15, 1851, with eight members from Goose Creek and Mount Olive churches, the first church was located at today's Methodist church site that we visited earlier. Services in this building started in 1884 and continued until 1926, when members transferred to Moncks Corner. But in 1970, the building was renovated and services were resumed.

47.0	**0.0**	**C**ontinue on Murray Lane / S-8-315.
47.4	**0.4**	**A**t stop sign and caution light, cross S.C. 6 and continue on S-8-315.
50.6	**3.2**	**A**t stop sign, turn right onto U.S. 17A South.
57.1	**6.5**	**A**t stoplight, cross U.S. 176 and continue on U.S. 17A South.
61.0	**3.9**	**T**urn right onto I-26 East to Charleston.
82.7	**21.7**	**E**nd of I-26 at intersection of U.S. 17. Exit 221 in downtown Charleston.

ADDITIONAL READING

For additional reading on the Cooper River area, see the list at the end of Tour 10, East Branch of the Cooper River.

NOTES

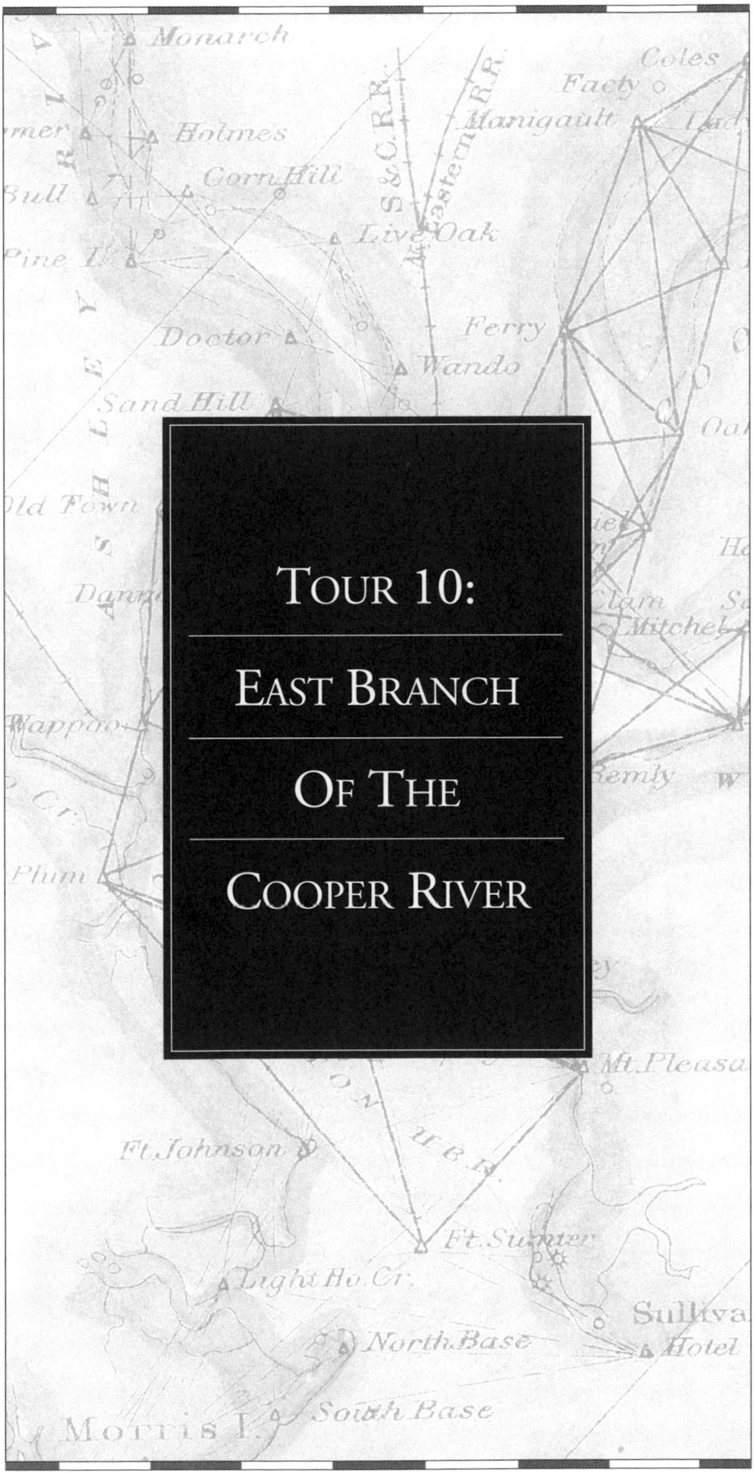

Tour 10:

East Branch Of The Cooper River

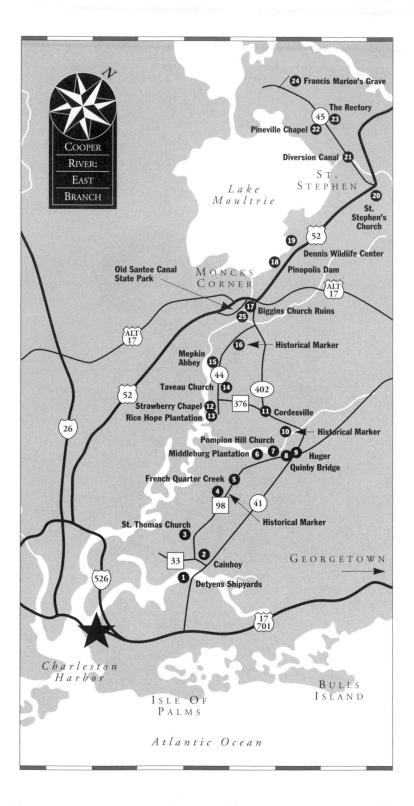

EAST BRANCH OF THE COOPER RIVER
Including the Eastern Shore of the West Branch of the Cooper River

This tour is for people who enjoy riding and viewing the countryside. It offers the best opportunity to see the rubble of Hugo. We travel through the heart of the Francis Marion National Forest, as well as private timberlands where $100 million of timber was lost the night of September 21, 1989. The lumber loss equals one thousand million board feet, or enough to make a board twelve inches wide reach around the world seven times.

At the northernmost part of the tour, we begin to travel through farmland where cotton is making a comeback.

The main stops are MEPKIN ABBEY, LAKE MOULTRIE DAM, and STONY LANDING PLANTATION HOUSE. Along the way, we get a glimpse of the bygone rice culture with its great plantations and churches that once lined the banks of the Cooper River. And there are many wonderful picnic sites on this tour. Start early—there's lots to see!

Detyens Shipyards, Inc., c.1962
Not open to public.

Cainhoy Community
Open daily.

St. Thomas Church, c. 1820
Grounds open daily.

Brabants Plantation
Historical marker.

French Quarter Creek

Middleburg Plantation, c. 1697
Not open to public.

Pompion Hill Church, c. 1763
Not open to public.

Quinby Bridge

Huger Community

Silk Hope Plantation
Historical marker.

Cordesville Community

Strawberry Chapel, c. 1725
Grounds open to public.

Rice Hope Plantation, date uncertain
Open to public.

Taveau Church, c. 1835
Not open to public.

Mepkin Abbey, c.1949
A Catholic monastery set on the grounds of statesman Henry Lauren's plantation.
Open to public 9 a.m. to 4:30 p.m.

Francis Marion
Historical marker.

Biggins Church Ruins, c. 1755
Open daily.
Jefferies Generating Plant and Pinopolis Dam at Lake Moultrie
Check with guard at gatehouse for admission.
Dennis Wildlife Center
Natural history displays and tours of fish hatchery.
Call ahead for guided tour.
Telephone: (803) 825-3387
St. Stephen's Episcopal Church, c. 1768
Grounds open to public.
Pineville Community
A rural community with antebellum chapel.
Open daily.
Francis Marion Grave, c. 1790s
Open daily until dark.
Old Santee Canal State Park (Stony Landing)
Museum, interpretive center, antebellum home, canoe and paddle boat rides on historic canal, and nature trails.
Open 9 a.m. to 4 p.m.

0.0	**0.0**	**S**tart mileage at north side (away from downtown Charleston) of Cooper River Bridge on U.S. 17 North.
7.5	**7.5**	**T**urn left onto S.C. 41.
12.5	**5.0**	**O**n left as you cross Wando River is Detyens Shipyard.

1. DETYENS SHIPYARDS, INC. c. 1962
Not open to public.
Detyens' three hundred employees can accommodate up to a 500-foot, 10,000-ton ship for repairs at one of their many dry docks. Ninety percent of their work is for the United States government.

12.5	**0.0**	**C**ontinue north on S.C. 41.
12.9	**0.4**	**V**eer left onto S-8-33.

2. CAINHOY
This small rural community had a few settlers as early as 1680, but its official existence dates from 1735. Five early buildings remain, but this is a village of narrow dirt lanes and private drives, so if you get off of S-8-33, you see very little. The name, Cainhoy, some suggest, was from an early ferryman of that time being hailed from the far bank—"Cain hoy!" More likely,

it's an Indian name. Francis Marion headquartered here for a while, and soon after, Bishop Asbury would find a welcome at the Capers home. Besides a Methodist meeting ground, there was a Presbyterian church whose graveyard still exists. Bishop William Capers left this description: "Cain Hoy was the most notable place . . . a high reputation for society, hospitality, and all that." The fabled Cainhoy ferry is another that's come and gone.

13.7	**0.8**	**T**urn right onto S-8-98, which parallels the East Branch of the Cooper River.
16.0	**2.3**	**O**n left is St. Thomas Church.

3. ST. THOMAS CHURCH, c. 1820

Grounds open to public.

When St. Thomas parish was laid out in 1706, it was discovered that the settlers of the French Quarter couldn't understand English well enough to follow the service. For this reason, a parish within a parish, St. Denis, was established. The two had long since combined when the original Cainhoy church burned in an 1815 forest fire. Built soon after, this little Greek Revival building, with its high walls and full gables, is an interesting contrast to the earlier churches we've seen elsewhere.

There are several dozen gravestones scattered among the loblollies. Richard Fordham was "master carpenter on board the U.S. Frigate *Randolph* in the Revolution."

This graveyard and church were also the scene of the Cainhoy Massacre. A Negro Republican meeting in 1876 was attended by a group of whites from Charleston. These visitors were fired upon, and at least one man was killed before they could retreat to the ferryboat nearby. Look closely at the little vestry building, for bullets are said to have scarred it. (It has recently been restored, so the scars might be hard to

spot.) Uneasy with the narrow margin of victory, the Democrats soon after gerrymandered the black and Republican voters out of Charleston and into the newly formed Berkeley County. Historian Orvin says it was called derisively "the baby county or black county," a block of the political landscape

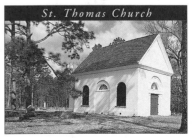

St. Thomas Church

that would be chipped away and rearranged for another twenty years. Affectionately referred to as "the mean one," my great-grandfather was sheriff here for much of that time.

| 16.0 | 0.0 | Continue on S-8-98. |
| 20.2 | 4.2 | On left is Brabants Plantation historical marker. |

4. BRABANTS PLANTATION

Historical marker.

Following the Revolution, this was the home of South Carolina's first Episcopal bishop, Robert Smith. It also happens to be the spot where Mad Archy Campbell drew his last breath. Surely the most colorful of British Revolutionary War officers, Mad Archy Campbell invited a Charleston belle named Margaret Philips to go riding with him, and then raced the carriage to St. James where he held a pistol to the head of the Goose Creek minister, demanding that he marry him to the protesting woman. But the minister declared he would marry Campbell only "with the consent of the young lady and her mother." Here at Videaru's bridge, Campbell was taken captive in 1782. The British actually won the battle, so if he had not bolted, he would have probably been rescued. But Nicholas Venning shot him dead, as a tombstone in Christ Church attests.

| 20.2 | 0.0 | Continue on S-8-98. |
| 20.8 | 0.6 | Cross French Quarter Creek. |

5. FRENCH QUARTER CREEK

We are traveling through the French Quarter. Following the revocation of the Edict of Nantes, Huguenots settled this region almost as heavily as French Santee to the north and, as happened there, they were eventually absorbed into the Anglican congregation.

| 24.5 | 3.7 | Look to the left for the white gates of Middleburg Plantation. |

6. MIDDLEBURG PLANTATION, c. 1697

Not open to public.

Middleburg also is closed to the public except for special tours, but you can catch a glimpse of the house at the end of this long avenue. Simple clapboard, two stories, with narrow veranda, it was built in 1697, which makes the home of Huguenot Benjamin Simons the oldest house in South Carolina.

| 24.5 | 0.0 | Continue on S-8-98. |
| 24.8 | 0.3 | On left is the historical marker for Pompion Hill Church. |

7. POMPION HILL CHURCH, c. 1763

Not open to public.

Pronounced "Pumkin" Hill, this little chapel of ease was built in 1763. As at St. Stephen's, a Villeponeux and an Axson left their marks on a finely crafted little church, but unfortunately, it can't be seen from the road and is closed to the public except for official tours.

24.8	0.0	Continue on S-8-98.
26.6	1.8	Cross Quinby Bridge.

8. QUINBY BRIDGE, c. 1735 or older

Colonel Coates, with five hundred infantry and one hundred cavalry, fought to a draw the combined American forces of Lee, Hampton, Marion, and Sumter. The dead were hastily buried along this roadside, and it's said that heavy rains used to wash out their bones. The ghosts of headless British troops have been heard to clatter by at night.

26.6	0.0	Continue on S-8-98.
26.8	0.2	At stop sign, turn left onto S.C. 41 North.

9. HUGER

Present-day Huger (use the somewhat French pronunciation "Hewgee" or "Ugee") doesn't show much sign of its ancient age, but this community dates back at least to 1735.

26.9	0.1	Veer left onto S.C. 402 West.
28.0	1.1	On left, Silk Hope historical marker.

10. SILK HOPE PLANTATION

Historical marker.

At this plantation in 1690, colonial governor Sir Nathaniel Johnson was reportedly raising a multitude of silkworms and had planted 24,000 mulberry trees. He's best known for repelling a Spanish and French invasion of the colony in 1706 and passing the Anglican Church Act in that year.

28.0	0.0	Continue on S.C. 402 West.
34.4	6.4	At Cordesville, turn left onto S-8-376.

11. CORDESVILLE
Little remains to remind us that Cordesville was one of the principal summering spots of the Cooper River planters.

38.3	**3.9**	**A**t stop sign, turn left onto S-8-44.
38.8	**0.5**	**T**urn right onto Strawberry Chapel Road.
39.0	**0.2**	**O**n right is Strawberry Chapel.

12. STRAWBERRY CHAPEL, c. 1725

Grounds open to public.

This chapel is all that remains of the would-be town of Childsbury. A victim of a nobleman's tyranny, James Child fled to the New World and hoped to regain his fortune at this ferry landing. There's no trace of Bay Street or College Square, but a school did operate here until 1754, and the town had a market day and race track. It's speculated that the site was abandoned after the Revolution because, like so many others, it was unhealthy. Whatever the reason, by 1815 it ceased to exist except for this chapel.

The site for the chapel was left by Childs in his will, and in 1725 the modest little jerkin-headed building was constructed as a Chapel of Ease. As the name implies, a chapel was meant to provide an easier traveling distance for parishioners who could be served by a shuttling priest. It would possess only "the parochial rights of baptizing and burying, and have neither Rectory nor Endowment." This chapel would eventually replace the ill-fated Biggin Church that it was meant to supplement. Strawberry is kept locked today, but fifty years ago, Dr. Johnson reported that before the war the simple interior had been decorated with "Glory to God in the Highest" spelt out in longleaf pine cone scales and that this was still in place above the altar.

The graveyard is storybook famous since Catherine Chicken, granddaughter of founder Childs, was boarded in the town with the schoolmaster. As punishment for wandering away, the homesick little girl was tied to one of the tombstones and abandoned for the night. Found unconscious by a faithful retainer, the released child pleaded for the life of her tormenter, so he was only "seized by rough hands, stripped of his tie, wig, and his long-skirted black coat, and tied, face tailward on a mule" and ridden out of town. The terror of the night left one side of Miss Chicken's face drawn for

life, but she married well and presided as mistress over nearby Middleburg.

The Ball family, familiar to students of Cooper River history, has a large family plot here, the names inscribed within. The "son of Posthumous Nicholas of Bossis" rests here. And Reverend Dwight, who spent his life recommending the faith of the Church of England, departed here in 1748. Of special interest as well, however, is the large open Harleston vault to the right of the building. The thin fern growing above its entry is spider brake or "Huguenot fern," so named because it was discovered growing in Charleston's Huguenot cemetery in 1868. Like so many other Huguenots, this wayfarer has ended tucked away among the Anglicans.

39.0	0.0	U-turn and retrace to stop sign.
39.2	0.2	At stop sign, turn right onto Comingtee Road / S-8-44.
39.5	0.3	Turn right onto Rice Hope Drive / S-8-1054.
39.7	0.2	Turn left and continue on Rice Hope Drive / S-8-1054.
39.7	50 ft.	On right, gates to Rice Hope Plantation.

13. RICE HOPE PLANTATION, date uncertain

Bed-and-breakfast. Call ahead.

Surrounded by extensive gardens, a 1920s mansion faces a broad expanse of the Cooper River. The topics of interest are early rice planting and a Revolutionary War battle, but historian Stoney says Rice Hope was best remembered for its hospitality.

39.7	0.0	From Rice Hope Plantation, turn left onto Rice Hope Drive / S-8-1054.
39.7	50 ft.	Turn right and continue on Rice Hope Drive.
39.9	0.2	Turn left onto Comingtee Road / S-8-44.
41.0	1.1	On right is Taveau Church.

14. TAVEAU CHURCH, C. 1835

Not open to public.

Coming from Edisto Island, Martha Carolina Swinton was a Presbyterian and felt strongly that her Anglican neighbors should have a chance to hear the true word. The second wife of John Ball, she bore him eleven children, outlived him, and as Miss Stoney writes, "had the temerity to marry a Taveau." This small frame church was given to the blacks soon after her death and then came under the jurisdiction of the Methodists. It's a little the worse for wear now. Hurricane Hugo took off the steeple, but the Berkeley Historical Society has fenced it off and plans to restore the little Federal-style mission in the near future.

41.0	**0.0**	Continue on S-8-44.
41.6	**0.6**	Turn left into Mepkin Abbey gates.

15. MEPKIN ABBEY, c. 1949

This Cistercian Trappist monastery at Mepkin was founded in 1949. Hurricane Hugo bent but failed to break its oaks, magnolias, and dogwoods. It's still a beautiful, quiet spot, and the only Catholic place of worship mentioned in these tours, so definitely try to visit. Drive by the painted brick gatehouse and stop at the new wooden one that's just up from the main buildings. A brother will be happy to talk with you and then you can walk across the monastery grounds and enter the balcony of the chapel. Once silent, the monks now speak occasionally and can be seen carrying out their mixed duties of prayer and work—duties that begin many hours before daylight. The Mepkin brochure reads, "A road and a journey toward truth and peace and beauty and faith—living out in fellowship with those who share a vision, and tempered by a proved and rather demanding discipline." Visitors are made to feel welcome and accommodations are available for short retreats. Once bread was baked here, but now chickens are raised and eggs sold at bargain prices.

In Italy, almost fifteen hundred years ago, St. Benedict founded the first true monastic order and gave it direction with his "Holy Rule" which stressed communal living, humility, and obedience. In 1098, the Cistercian order was founded in France. Called "White Monks" because they wear a white habit beneath a black scapular, its members felt it necessary to return to a stricter interpretation of St. Benedict's teaching. Though primarily contemplative, these men, beginning under the leadership of St. Bernard, made great advances in agricultural techniques and contributed to the development and spread of Gothic architecture throughout Europe. The Renaissance and then the Reformation took their toll, however, and those remaining broke into many small independent congregations, the best known of which are "strict observance," or Trappist, like this one.

Mepkin Plantation Grounds, c. 1762

Open to public.

Mepkin Plantation is the 1762 home of South Carolina merchant, planter, and statesman Henry Laurens. The property was purchased in 1936 by Henry and Clare Boothe Luce, best known as the publishers of *Time* and *Life* magazines. They gave the majority of the land to the Trappists. Mr. Luce and other family members are buried here beside the great oak avenue in the terraced garden overlooking the Cooper River.

42.4	**0.8**	Proceed straight to reach the Luce graveyard parking area. Walk to the high bluff overlooking the Cooper River. Along the edge of the woods to your right, 60 feet from the Cooper River bluff, is the path leading to the Laurens burial plot. WATCH YOUR STEP.

Grave of Henry Laurens

The son of Huguenot immigrants, Henry Laurens was sent to England to study business and returned to Charleston, where he amassed a fortune. In 1750, he married Eleanor Ball, and in 1776, retired to devote himself to planting and politics. Active in Revolutionary War politics, he eventually became a member of the Continental Congress and was its president when the Articles of Confederation were signed, which is why he is sometimes considered our first president. He was remembered by his less than reverent neighbors, however, as "Tower Henry." Going to Holland in 1779 to negotiate a loan for the rebelling Americans, he was captured and thrown into the Tower of London. He remained there two years until exchanged for Lord Cornwallis.

Laurens is also remembered as the first person in South Carolina to be cremated. His young daughter had been declared dead, but revived before she could be buried. Laurens lived in dread that the same thing would happen to him, and left strict instructions for his own disposal: "That his body be wrapped in twelve yards of tow cloth and burned until it was entirely consumed." Several of his more eccentric neighbors seem to have been adversely influenced by this final act and numerous legends surround it—but the truth is rather ordinary. His ashes are buried beneath this 1792 grave marker.

Also in this plot is his son, John Laurens. On Washington's staff, he led the decisive charge at Yorktown and was one of the two commissioners who settled the terms of surrender there. Returning to South Carolina, he was killed by the British in a skirmish south of Charleston.

| 42.4 | 0.0 | Return to Mepkin Abbey gates and turn left onto S-8-44. |
| 46.1 | 3.7 | On right at intersection of Hard Pinch Road / S-8-359 is Francis Marion historical marker (difficult to see). |

16. FRANCIS MARION

Historical marker.

Parson Weems suggested this as the birthplace of Francis Marion, but he also said Marion was born "no bigger than a Maine lobster, and stayed that size until he was 12," so his account is highly suspect. Family tradition says so, too, though, and an ancient black retainer of the family was certain. "Enty, he born at Cordes." (He was born at Cordes Plantation, wasn't he?) In infancy he was moved to Winyah Bay and grew up there.

46.1	0.0	Continue on S-8-44.
48.1	2.0	At stop sign, turn left onto S.C. 402 West and immediately cross Wadboo Creek.
49.5	1.4	On left are the Biggins Church Ruins.

17. BIGGINS CHURCH RUINS, c. 1755

Open to public.

A large portion of at least two walls remains, and an ancient, flower-crowded burial ground surrounds it. St. John's Parish was one of the original nine established by the Church Act of 1706. "A pleasant and healthful part of the country, where the planters were generally good, sober and teachable people." Sir John Colleton donated the site. Thomas Broughton "adorned the interior" of the first church, which burned accidentally in 1755 and was replaced the following year by this one. Close by Biggin Creek, which is now erased by the Tail Race Canal, the building was strategically located at the intersection of three roads. As was often the case, it was of strategic importance to military forces as well. In 1781, Lieutenant Colonel Coates garrisoned his troops here and burned the building when he withdrew. The church was rebuilt on these walls soon after and Reverend Dalcho reports it prospering in 1820. The interior was vandalized in the next war, however, and the abandoned building burned completely in an 1890 forest fire. Much of the walls was carried away, but the remains are being looked after by the Berkeley Historical Society, which recently repaired window arches and quoins, and replaced the errant doorsills.

An interesting and beautiful old graveyard surrounds the site. Sir John Colleton was laid to rest here, but only after he willed a watch to his unhappy wife "so that she may take notice how time passes and earnestly entreat her to make better use of the time than she has in the past." Dr. Johnson says that old "Turpentine John" Palmer and his brother Joseph were imprisoned in a low-arched vault (now a ruin) during the Revolution because John's son was with Marion. The cuts inside the brick were their attempt to cut a way out, and once released they were so weak it took them two days and nights to walk the ten miles home. And Johnson tells of an 1812 stone that reads, "and as I am, soon will you be, Prepare for death and follow me." A St. Stephen's wag scratched under the epitaph, "To follow you I n'er consent, until I find which way you went." Not all are so strange or flippant. The Moultrie family and many others rest in ordinary peace beneath these oaks and dogwoods.

❖

49.5	0.0	Continue on S.C. 402 West.
49.7	0.2	Turn left and continue on S.C. 402 West.
49.9	0.2	At stoplight, turn right onto U.S. 52 West.

| 51.6 | 1.7 | Turn left at Jefferies Generating Plant sign onto Power House Road / S-8-20. |
| 52.9 | 1.3 | Pinopolis Dam on Cooper River that forms Lake Moultrie. |

18. JEFFERIES GENERATING PLANT AND PINOPOLIS DAM, c. late 1930s

Open to public on limited basis. Ask guard at gate.

You're looking at the Pinopolis Dam and the Jefferies Hydroelectric Plant. Constructed in just thirty-one months, it didn't actually dam a river, so the one-and-one-half-mile-long concrete structure is set into twenty-six miles of flanking earthen dike. The steps lead to an overlook that gives a good view of the lake and the original generating plant. The overlook is blocked off now but may be opened again at some time in the future, so check with the guard at the gatehouse about access.

If you've reached the top of the steps, that's the powerhouse to the left. The large Art Deco structure's soft, rounded lines say a lot about the optimistic outlook for an industrial future. (The Lowcountry was short on optimism and cash, and the only other industrial Art Deco building that's even close to our tour path is the Coca-Cola Bottling Company in distant Ridgeland.) Five turbine generators are housed here; beyond is the navigational lock that still raises boats the seventy-five feet up from the Tail Race Canal. The collection of steel power poles on your left is the hydroelectric switchyard where the generated power is changed into different voltages and sent on its way.

The plant that we first drove by generates electricity with steam generated by burning coal and oil. It was built in 1953 when it was discovered that the hydroelectric plant could not keep up with increasing demand. Today only a small percentage of the Santee Cooper power comes from the original generators. There are a nuclear plant and two other conventional power plants elsewhere.

The WPA and the Lakes

By 1793, it had been determined that there was a considerable drop in elevation between the Santee and Cooper rivers, but it wasn't until 1934 that the Santee Cooper Authority made this ambitious attempt to generate electrical power by diverting the water from one river to the other. The nation was in the midst of the Great Depression and much of this section of the Lowcountry was poverty-stricken and desolate. With the sponsorship of Franklin Roosevelt and strong local political support led by Senator Richard Jefferies, two hundred thousand acres were eventually cleared and turned into the man-made lakes, Francis and Moultrie. These would be the reservoirs for two hydroelectric plants.

Nine hundred families, mostly black, had to be relocated and six thousand graves as well. Several large plantation houses and churches were saved, but many were lost, along with a tremendous river-bottom forest. Even today, there remains some bitterness over this forced eviction, but as a result of the project, rural areas of the state finally did receive electricity, and the lives of many people were made healthier and more comfortable. The enlarging Navy Yard had a source of power which, with the approach of World War II, became even more important as construction went on. Other industries located near the source of cheap power, and these brought jobs. And as an added bonus, one that would eventually provide as much revenue as the generators themselves, the lakes would become a mecca for fishermen and vacationers. On the minus side, the diverted water would carry silt into Charleston harbor. Now, water first diverted by the 1793 canal and again by this 1941 project has been re-rediverted to where it flowed for ages—the Santee River.

———————— ◈ ————————

52.9	**0.0**	**R**etrace S-8-20 to U.S. 52.
54.2	**1.3**	**A**t stop sign, turn left onto U.S. 52 West.
58.5	**4.3**	**T**urn left onto Black Oak Road/S-8-42.
59.2	**0.7**	**T**urn left into Dennis Wildlife Center.

19. DENNIS WILDLIFE CENTER

This administrative building with adjoining facilities is the center for wildlife research and management in the surrounding lakes and woodlands. In the lobby of the main building you'll find an interesting natural history display—225 clutches of bird's eggs collected by antebellum naturalist William Elliott, wing identifications, and mounted local fish. And outside in the nearby holding pens, you might see deer and other small animals temporarily confined. The main business of the center, though, is striped bass.

Each river system of the East Coast has its own population of striped bass. Living part of their life in salt water, they, like salmon, lay their eggs in fresh water. It was a surprise, then, when fishermen and biologists discovered that the striped bass (often called rockfish) of the Santee and Cooper rivers had adapted themselves to the newly created Lake Moultrie and Lake Marion and were flourishing there. By the early 1950s, this fishing had become nationally known. In 1961, a fish hatchery was opened on the Tail Race Canal, and its work is continued by this one at the Dennis Center.

The hatchery is the largest producer of striped bass larvae in the world—up to 100 million a year. The stocking of the lakes with fingerling bass and an 18-inch minimum size limit on fish taken was begun in 1984, for—as was the case with electrical power—demand exceeded supply. (In 1988, 2.5 million fish were released here.) In addition, the center is also experimenting with a hybrid striped bass, catfish, and other local and exotic species. Blue catfish, introduced from Arkansas in 1964, reach a healthy size. My father and I watched a couple of thirty-pounders being unloaded at a fish camp on the far

side of Lake Moultrie, but the record fish are coming out of the adjoining Cooper River—86 pounds, 4 ounces the largest so far.

Visitors are welcome at the Dennis Center. April through May, the center is open seven days a week because this is spawning time, and trips to the hatchery can be arranged. June through October is also a good time, and the fingerlings are harvested in October. November through March, you're warned the water is muddy so there's not much to see. No matter what time of year, it's best to call ahead because occasionally the staff is called away to duties elsewhere.

> *And there was mooted many a day,*
> *The question on which each gourmet*
> *Throughout the Parish had his say,*
> *Which is the best,*
> *Santee or Cooper River bream?*
> *Alas, the evening star grew dim*
> *ere any guest agreed with him,*
> *or he with guest.*

That's the question posed by Snowden in "A Carolina Bourbon," and if you can't get an answer here, then there probably isn't one.

———— ◈ ————

59.2	0.0	From Dennis Wildlife Center, turn right onto Black Oak Road / S-8-42 and retrace to U.S. 52.
59.9	0.7	At stop sign, turn left onto U.S. 52 West / Main Street.
67.0	7.1	In St. Stephen's, at second stoplight, turn right onto S.C. 45 East / Church Street.
67.4	0.4	Just after curve turn right onto Mendal Rivers Road / S-8-122.
67.4	250 ft.	Turn left into St. Stephen's Church yard.

20. ST. STEPHEN'S EPISCOPAL CHURCH, c. 1768

Grounds open to public.

"The church is one of the handsomest country churches in So.Ca. and would be no mean ornament to Charleston," wrote Dalcho in 1820. That was certainly the intent of the vestry and builders, F. Villepontoux and A. Howard, for they had wrangled hard and long to get the best in materials and labor. The design was meant to emulate Charleston's St. Michael's, at least in the high-coved ceiling, which is why the exterior boasts the high gambrel roof and distinctively curved gable ends. (This ancient Jacobean detail also appears at the Pon Pon and Georgetown churches and in the rebuilt Middleton Plantation.) You can't get inside unless it's Sunday morning, but note the careful brickwork of the exterior and the signatures of contractors and masons about the doorways.

Like many other Anglican churches, this one fell on hard times immediately

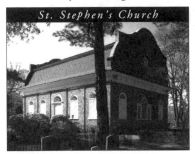

St. Stephen's Church

after the Revolution. In his reminiscence, parish resident Sam Dubose wrote, "In 1786, I was baptized by a Presbyterian minister . . . who lived more than 50 miles off and whose presence among us was accidental and I never saw a minister until I was 12." Dubose put the blame on a lack of morals among some of the new Episcopal priests. But it was because a series of freshets on the Santee wiped out crops and fevers swept through the area that the congregation moved inland and reformed in the little chapel of the Pineville community. Involved in a lawsuit, this independent little group did not officially join the diocese until 1843, and then it fell on even harder times. Despite the lack of churchgoers in the area, however, St. Stephen's was restored three times in the next 150 years. Now it has opened its doors once more.

The graveyard is one of the prettiest around and crowded with stones. No matter what the status of the church, this "public burying grounds" was kept in use. It wasn't uncommon, Sam Dubose says, to be buried on the homestead, but when the adjoining countryside was flooded in 1941, many of these family plots were relocated here. Dubose adds that in those early days, a layer of boards had to be placed in the grave to keep the wolves from digging them up. This was called "English Santee" then, but you would hardly guess that from the French names inscribed. "The family of the Gaillards lie here interred," wrote Reverend Dalcho. Another comment for this resting place: "A mighty army am the Porchers."

There are several ghost stories associated with the building, one concerning Dave Peigler, the unofficial mayor of the outlaw community of Scuffletown. Horse thief and Tory, he raided the homes of patriots who were away fighting until one of these, Captain Theus, happened not to be away. Peigler was about to be hanged here when he escaped, but he was brought back, and his hanging was proceeding when the British arrived—moments too late. It's said the ghost of Peigler wanders the churchyard, "a rope around its neck, a bottle of rum in one hand and a pistol in the other."

Porcher wrote of the three roads that once joined at this church: "Strange that they should unite for all lead to the grave."

———— ◈ ————

| 67.4 | 0.0 | From churchyard, turn left onto Mendel Rivers Road / S-8-122. |
| 67.5 | 0.1 | At stop sign, turn left onto S.C. 45 West / Church Street. |

68.0	0.5	At stoplight, turn left onto U.S. 52 East / S.C. 45 West.
68.0	1 block	Turn right onto S.C. 45 West.
70.0	2.0	Cross new diversion canal, Lake Moultrie to Santee River.

21. DIVERSION CANAL, LAKE MOULTRIE TO SANTEE RIVER

Because diverted water carried silt into Charleston harbor, the water first diverted by the 1793 canal and again by the 1941 WPA project has been recently rediverted to the Santee River.

---------- ◈ ----------

| 74.3 | 4.3 | In Pineville, turn left onto S-8-204. |

Pineville

Little remains of this summer haven that began in 1794 and eventually blossomed to include at least sixty substantial houses, public library, school, church, tavern, and race track. A superstitious faith was placed in the "good" air of Pineville, and anyone who breathed it was warned to remain in the vicinity for the rest of the season. Porcher says the planters visited their plantations in the morning, hunted sometimes, and returned to lodge at the post office. Then came siesta and afternoon tea before visiting could begin. "Every excuse was used to have a dancing party which closed at frost with the Jockey Club Ball." Just two miles from the Santee Swamp the site didn't remain safe, and in the 1830s, epidemics of fatal fever sent much of the population elsewhere. Then, in the final days of the Civil War, almost all the houses were burned. (Estimates range from seven to eighty.) The chapel, a few abandoned stores, and the rectory survived.

| 74.3 | 400 ft. | Turn left into Pineville Chapel parking lot. |

22. THE PINEVILLE CHAPEL, c. 1810

Not open to public.

Note the fish weathervane of this 1810 Episcopal church. In Greek, the word for "fish" is an anagram of "Jesus Christ, Son of God, Savior," so it's said this, not the cross, was the first symbol of the church. "More zeal and less voice" is Porcher's description of the service. "Old Capt. Palmer, the patriarch of the village certainly possesed no musical talents but he had zeal and fancied he had accomplished the 100th psalm."

---------- ◈ ----------

74.3	0.0	From Pineville Chapel parking lot, turn right onto S-8-204.
74.4	400 ft.	At stop sign, turn left onto S.C. 45 West.
74.7	0.3	On right, white house with green trim is The Rectory.

23. THE RECTORY, c. 1810

Not open to public.

The rectory was spared by Civil War conflagrations, and so were the 1830 post office and 1826 library now tacked onto the rear.

❖

74.7	**0.0**	Continue on S.C. 45 West.
77.9	**3.2**	Turn right at brick gate onto dirt road to Francis Marion's grave.
78.9	**1.0**	Grave parking lot.

24. FRANCIS MARION'S GRAVE, c. 1790s

Open to public. Maintained by State Park Service.

Hero of the American Revolution, Marion was a master of guerrilla warfare and, with his small band of men and boys, provided the Americans with victories when they were getting none elsewhere. After the fall of Yorktown he was elected to the Jacksonboro Assembly, where he urged reconciliation with Tory neighbors—even as he and his troops continued to fight the British. Late in life, Marion married a widow with a hot temper. It was said that he threw his hat through the window before entering the house and if it didn't come sailing out, then this veteran of shipwreck, Indian War, and hero of the Revolution, knew it was safe to enter. At his death, however, his wife was inconsolable, so it's nice to see them lying now peacefully side by side.

❖

78.9	**0.0**	Retrace to S.C. 45 West.
79.9	**1.0**	At stop sign, turn left onto S.C. 45 East.
90.0	**10.1**	In St. Stephen's, turn right onto U.S. 52 East.
103.7	**13.7**	Cross Tail Race Canal, which connects Lake Moultrie and west branch of Cooper River.
104.1	**0.4**	At second road after the bridge, turn left onto Rembrant Dennis Blvd. / P-0801.
105.1	**1.0**	Turn left onto entrance road to Old Santee Canal State Park and Stony Landing House.
105.8	**0.7**	Old Santee Canal State Park entrance gate.

25. OLD SANTEE CANAL STATE PARK (STONY LANDING)

Historic Stony Landing has been rejuvenated and incorporated into The Old Santee Canal State Park. A variety of experiences are offered to the visitor, for the 250 acres is rich in natural beauty, accessible by several miles of trails and boardwalks and by canoes as well. In addition, the antebellum Stony Landing house, once the Dennis family home, has been restored and is open to the public. The Berkeley County Museum, a project of the local historical society, will help explain the history of the area. Boat docks on the Tail Race Canal, picnic areas, natural amphitheater, submarine model, newly opened interpretive center—the park has much to offer. The centerpiece is the old section of the Santee Canal which ends here, edged on both sides by the steep bluffs of Biggin Creek.

Stony Landing and the Santee Canal

Stony Landing, first called Stone Landing, was used by the earliest Indian traders. They could follow the famous Cherokee Trail to this point and then carry their skins on to Charleston by water. The trail became the Congaree Road; planters used it to bring their rice and other produce to town. Flats and even schooners took the place of canoes on the Cooper. Stores were built here and, before and after the Civil War, building stone was cut and cement made on the stony site. Biggin Creek, at first impassable beyond this point, had been cleared out by early planters. Following the Revolution a far more ambitious project was launched. The Santee Canal was begun in 1793 and completed in 1800. Four feet deep, twenty feet wide, and twenty-two miles long, its purpose was to route back-country produce into Charleston harbor. The earliest such undertaking in the United States, the construction was a great struggle—far greater than it should have been, argued F. A. Porcher, the canal's historian. He claimed that the vanity of the Swedish engineer and perhaps the personal interest of a board member caused them to ignore easier routes and pushed the price of construction up to a then staggering $800,000. At that price it would never show a profit, but the ditching and building of locks did provide much-needed revenue for planters who had lost the bounty paid on indigo and been hit by a series of bad freshets: They rented out their slaves to the corporation. Once completed, the canal would also provide a very useful service to the inland settlers. Plagued by a lack of water necessary to raise and lower the canal boats and flats through the locks, and having to compete with the South Carolina railroad, the waterway officially closed in 1850.

Stony Landing

Even as the canal was being built, it was discovered that inland cotton could be grown and ginned and bring a handsome profit, so this would be the major cargo during the next half century. Seven hundred and twenty boats, each paying a $22 toll, delivered seventy thousand bales to Charleston in 1830. But historian Porcher reports that in

1831 he personally witnessed the strangest shipment to pass this way. "A gentleman from the upper country of high social position, but of a decidedly sportive tendency," passed by on a canal boat loaded down with fighting gamecocks. "He had heard the Governor of Havana was a lover of the cockpit and with this venture he was going to try his fortune in that city." You're not likely to come upon such a sight, but the canal itself is impressive enough and is now open to canoe and paddleboat traffic.

A full-scale model of the *Little David*, the first semisubmersible submarine, here marks the vessel's birthplace. In 1863, the Union ironclad *New Ironsides* had a stranglehold on Charleston Harbor, so Dr. St. Julian Ravenel built this little torpedo boat in secret here at his Stony Landing home. In a true case of David against Goliath, the little cigar-shaped ship with only its conning tower above water slipped up on the giant *Ironsides*. A Union officer who spotted her at the last moment was killed with a shotgun by the *David*'s captain, and then the torpedo struck. The wave resulting from the explosion flooded the engine room of the submersible, and all her crew abandoned ship except the pilot, who could not swim. Then, seeing that the craft hadn't sunk, the engineer climbed back aboard and took her back to Charleston. The *Ironsides* required only a trip to the dry dock, but Rear Admiral Dupont of the blockading fleet was duly impressed and rated his enemy's attack "successful."

We started these two tours of the Cooper River with one bit of verse, so we'll end them with another. This one is not from Dr. Irving and his *Day on Cooper River*—it's about him.

> *Through pleasant fields, on river banks we stray,*
> *Where beauteous Cooper winds his placid way,*
> *Now classic grown, since Irving's spreading fame,*
> *Has given it, for aye, a place and a name.*

───────────◆───────────

105.8	**0.0**	To return to Charleston, from entrance gates, retrace to Rembrant Dennis Blvd. / P-0801.
106.5	**0.7**	At stop sign, turn left onto Rembrant Dennis Blvd. / P-0801.
107.4	**0.9**	At stoplight, continue straight onto U.S. 52 East.
123.2	**15.8**	Turn right onto U.S. 78 West.
125.2	**2.0**	Turn left onto I-26 East.
140.8	**15.6**	End of I-26 at intersection of U.S. 17. Exit 221 in downtown Charleston.

ADDITIONAL READING

A good guide to the area is J. Russell Cross's *Historic Ramblin's Through Berkeley County*. Dr. John Irving and Louisa Cheves Stoney's *A Day on Cooper River*, the *Memoirs* of Frederick Adolphus Porcher and his *History of the Santee Canal*, Dubose's *Reminiscence of St. Stephen's*, Maxwell Orvin's histories of Berkeley County and the town of Moncks Corner—all are excellent. This is a well-documented section of the Lowcountry and there are many more titles, such as family histories of the Balls, Ravenels, and other Cooper River people. Waring's *St. James Church* and Misenhelter's *St. Stephen's Episcopal Church* cover those churches well. I enjoyed Walter Edgar's *History of Santee Cooper*. Elias Bull's *Historic Preservation Inventory of Berkeley County* was a great help. The Berkeley Historical Society is well organized and from time to time produces brochures and pamphlets on various subjects. Trappist monk Thomas Merton, a resident of Mepkin's mother house, Gethsemane Abbey in Kentucky, wrote the popular spiritual biography *Seven Story Mountain.*

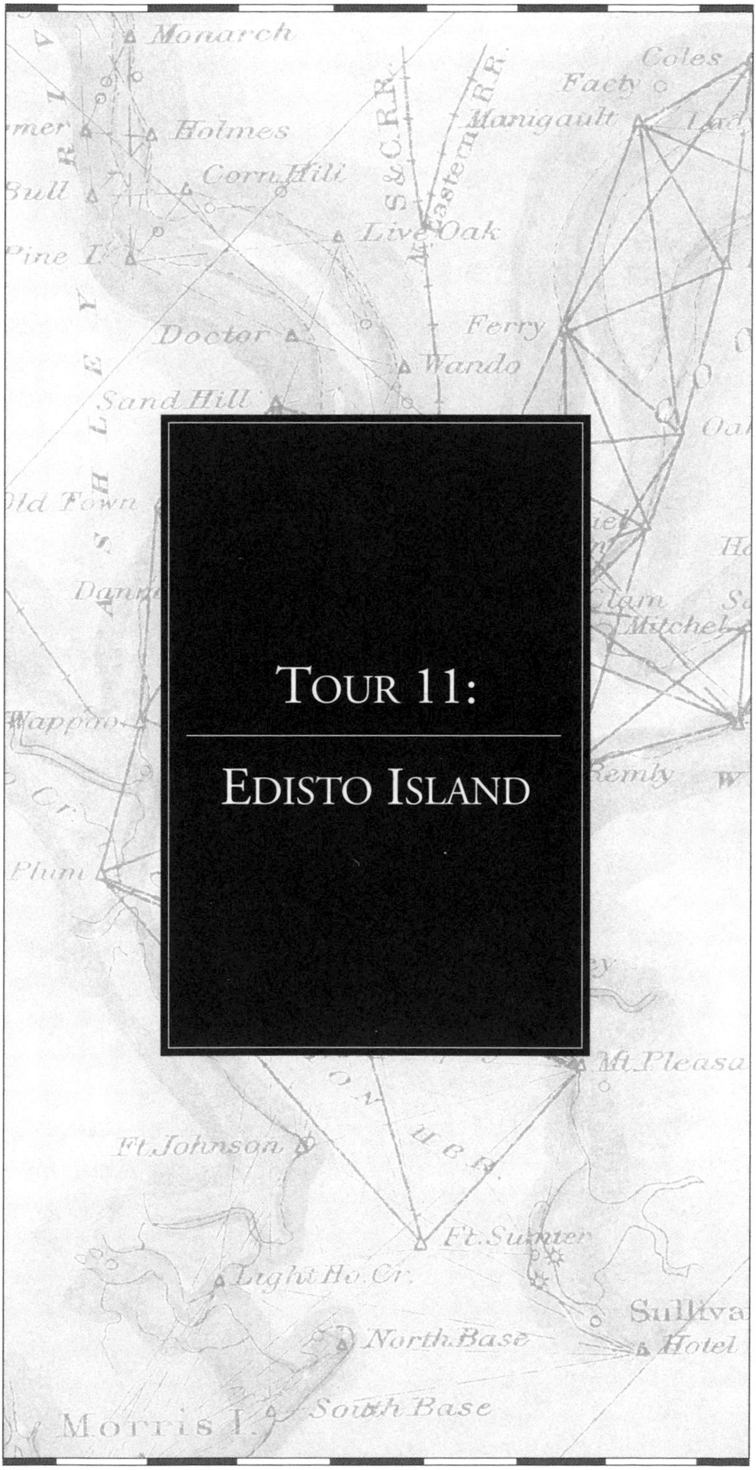

Tour 11:

Edisto Island

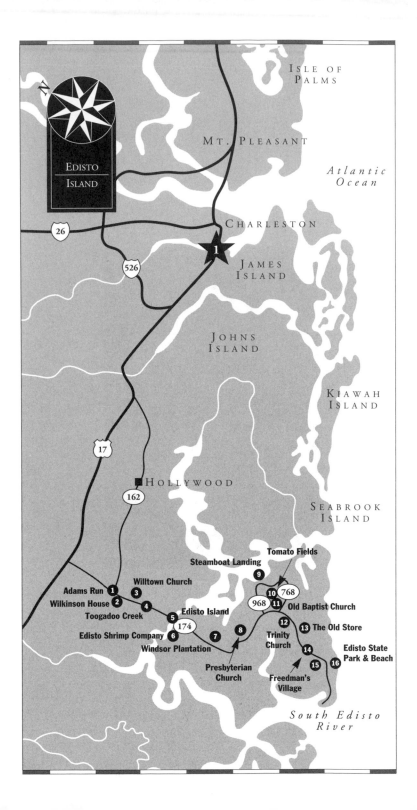

EDISTO ISLAND

On this day trip, we head south on U.S. 17 for about half an hour and then turn toward the coast. We pass through the village of ADAMS RUN, whose pretty little WILLTOWN CHURCH immigrated with the population. Then it's on to the Sea Island "principality" of EDISTO ISLAND. Here we drive through a landscape not yet changed by developers to visit two distinctive old churches. Next, we walk the EDISTO STATE PARK NATURE TRAIL that winds through a coastal forest and ends at a four-thousand-year-old Indian midden. Last, we beach comb on EDISTO STATE PARK BEACH, a spot famous for its Pleistocene fossils. Here's a trip you can fit into one leisurely day, but if you're not up to the walk, you might want to skip the lengthy nature trail in favor of the beach.

Adams Run
A small rural community dating from 1839.
Open daily.

Willtown Church (Christ Episcopal Church), c. 1835
Open daily.

Edisto Island
Open daily.

Windsor Plantation, c. 1857
Private residence on Edisto Island.
Not open to public.

Edisto Presbyterian Church, c. 1830
Grounds open daily.

Steamboat Landing
Public boat landing with a good view of the river.

Tomato Fields
Private; not open to public.

The Old Baptist Church, c. 1818
Not open to public.

Trinity Episcopal Church, c. 1880
Grounds open daily.

The Old Store, Freedman's Village
Open to public.

Edisto State Park Nature Trail and Indian Mound
A two-hour walk through a maritime forest ends at a four-thousand-year-old Indian mound.
Open daily.

Edisto State Park Beach
A popular state park beach noted for excellent beach combing, especially the collecting of fossils.
Open daily, 6 a.m. to 10 p.m. (hours vary in winter).

0.0	**0.0**	**T**ake U.S. 17 South from Charleston. Start mileage from south side of Ashley River Bridge (far side away from downtown Charleston). NOTE: *For information about these first 23.4 miles, see Tour 4, Beaufort and the Sea Islands.*
23.4	**23.4**	**T**urn left onto S.C. 174 South.
25.9	**2.5**	**T**urn right, continuing on S.C. 174 South.

1. ADAMS RUN

This little summer retreat started in about 1839 when the Wilkinsons of nearby Summit Plantation began to lease lots for $15 a year to planters from the Pon Pon and Edisto River area. It was called Wilkinsonville then, but mysteriously changed to Adamsville, then to Adams Run. (There was no Adams family on record.) At some point, lots were sold and substantial houses built, and in 1852, a legislative act declared the citizens of Adams Run, temporary and otherwise, "a body politic."

26.0	**0.1**	**O**n right, Wilkinson House.

2. WILKINSON HOUSE, c. 1838

Not open to public.

The large house on the right as you enter was built by the town's founder, William Wilkinson, in 1838, but was sold for taxes after the Civil War. During the conflict this was a center for Confederate defenses; in the years after, a small center for agriculture-related commerce. It's the "Village" described in Ambrose Gonzolas's 1922 Gullah account *Black Border*—a distinction now grown dubious. The main coastal road came this way, but the community was bypassed by U.S. 17 in the late 1930s. Today it appears even sleeper than in Gonzolas's time.

26.1	**0.1**	**C**ontinue on S.C. 174 South. On left, Willtown Church (Christ Episcopal Church).

3. WILLTOWN CHURCH (CHRIST EPISCOPAL CHURCH), c. 1835

The reason you find the Willtown Church here in Adams Run is that the congregation deserted nearby Willtown before the Civil War. In 1879, they disassembled the building and brought it along. Described originally as being of "singular beauty and completeness," it's hard to say exactly how

close this comes to the brick-columned
structure of Willtown. It still seems of
"singular beauty and completeness,"
especially in this setting of oaks, dogwoods, and azaleas.

Willtown Church

Willtown
Willtown, on the nearby South Edisto
River, ranked second only to Charles
Town in the early days of the colony.
Records are few, but it was substantial enough to survive the Yemassee
War, and the men of the Presbyterian congregation put down the Stono
slave rebellion in 1739. By the beginning of the nineteenth century, howev-
er, the town was being abandoned as a place of business and retreat. All
that remains is the rectory that accompanied this church, and that's on
private property.

| 26.1 | 0.0 | From Christ Church, continue south on S.C. 174. |
| 28.4 | 2.3 | Cross Toogadoo Creek. |

4. TOOGADOO CREEK AND THE OTHER PLACES
In discussing this little corner of the world, Dr. Johnson mentions the
Clementia Springs of the Clement family. Their famous sulphur water was
taken for medical purposes. And he tells of Revolutionary War patriot
Mellinchamp who received seventeen saber wounds and was left for dead by
the British. He crawled away and was nursed back to health by a squatter
woman. When William Gilmore Simms used the incident in a novel, he just
changed "squatter" to "aristocratic" so it would make better reading.

   We soon cross the headwaters of the Toogadoo River, on the banks of
which once lived Francis Wilkinson Pickens, governor of South Carolina. He
was also ambassador to Russia—the apple of his eye, Lucy Holcombe, would
only marry him if he became an ambassador. She had been bitterly disappoint-
ed in love, for her first fiancé had dashed off with Narciso López in 1853 to
liberate Cuba, where he was quickly stood up against a wall and shot. The
Toogadoo was also the home of the Queen of Bohemia, Ada Clare (born Ada
Agnes Jane McElhenney). Growing tired of provincial Carolina, she went to
New York and moved with the Greenwich Village literary set. She wrote in
defense of women's rights, had a child out of wedlock, and spent the years of
the Civil War writing for newspapers, first in San Francisco (where she knew
Mark Twain), and finally in Hawaii. Returning to America, she found success
as an actress in a touring company, then was bitten by a mad dog in New York
and died.

   She didn't tarry long on the Toogadoo and neither do we; we're on our
way to Edisto. There are soybean fields along the way. Oaks crowd against the

highway. Large vistas of open marshland begin. This is the mythical community of Nelly—"You is Nelly to Edisto." So if you're going to read the history, read it quickly.

28.4	0.0	Continue south on S.C. 174.
30.8	2.4	Cross Dawhoo River Bridge.

5. EDISTO ISLAND

In the years preceding the Civil War, this little community was so wealthy, isolated, and ready for independence that it was called "the royal principality of Edisto." By then it already had a couple of centuries of recorded history under its belt. When the Spanish first spoke of the "Orista," or Edisto, they had the Port Royal inhabitants in mind, but by 1670 these Indians had been pushed to this island. That's where the English found them, and in 1674 the Earl of Shaftesbury (Lord Ashley Cooper) at least made an offer to buy it from the tribe. He renamed it Locke Island after his philosopher, secretary, and physician, John Locke. (Besides writing Carolina's first constitution, Locke helped install the gold tube that continually drained the Earl's liver. You see, he had a cyst on it that is usually found only in sheep.) Anyway, Shaftesbury's dream was to set up a feudal estate here complete with serfs, but it's likely he never meant to come and was only trying to confuse his many enemies. Paul Grimball, secretary to the governor, was living on the island, however, so it was his house that the Spanish burned when they came around to restate their claim in 1686. The tabby ruins are still there.

Hardy Welsh and Scotch immigrants came soon after. It seems likely they traded with the Indians and raised cattle. It's known they attempted to grow rice, but soon switched to indigo. By 1714, there was population enough to request a road and causeway. In 1720, Paul Hamilton, tired of being harassed by pirates on the front of the island, moved back and built the first true mansion on a more protected inland site. This substantial "château" didn't burn for another two hundred years. During the Revolution the islanders formed a company of patriots. According to most sources, Edisto wasn't a battleground, but in her *Historic Houses*, Harriette Leiding says that privateer Tories and Mediterranean Sea sailors in long "refugee boats" paddled up from Savannah  and raided the island for cattle and whatever else they could carry off. The real scourge came after that war, though. Sea Island cotton quickly replaced indigo and brought great wealth, but the deadly fever of the time took a particularly heavy toll here. In 1808, David Ramsey's history reports that over three-fourths of the inhabitants died during these bad years, and some of the old family names disappeared altogether.

The days of island royalty, however, had already begun. The tiny white population, outnumbered by slaves ten to one, had virtually all available acres under cultivation. Boys were sent to Yale and Princeton, and even girls were educated. Within two years, William Seabrook built the mansion that would set the princely style for those to come. There was little place for hunting or thoroughbred horses on the small island, so fishing and fast sailboats took their place. Religion was better practiced than on the mainland; dancing parties fewer.

In 1825, Lafayette made his fabled visit, and the following year Robert Mills's Statistics reported that such royal treatment as he received was not just reserved for French noblemen. The hospitality of the island was indeed legendary. No tavern was ever attempted, for none was needed. The threat of sickness lessened because summers were spent at Eddingville Beach. (Mills correctly diagnosed the source of the problem as several small, undrained swamps on the island.) But then, Eddingville had its own dangers, for there in "the Sands" duels were fought. A jocular remark concerning a bathing costume, a neighbor's domestic quarrel—no excuse was too petty to set up these deadly encounters. Chivalry flourished. Knights and their lady loves, who were in ordinary life simply planters and their wives, competed to see who had the finest house and garden and entertained in the grandest style. "No," says Mikell, "these country functions were conceived in love and carried out with big hearted hospitality." They argued passionately for separation. "Gentlemen, if South Carolina does not secede from the Union Edisto Island will," declared Colonel Jenkins in 1860.

This scene of romantic spectacle soon ended. The island was quickly evacuated, and in 1862, Union soldiers and sailors and freed slaves were living in the mansions. At war's end, Sherman confiscated Edisto and settled ten thousand more freedmen there. But this emergency order was overturned and in 1866, the white population returned to find its homes vandalized but still standing. The blacks now worked on shares, a salary, or a combination of both, but not surprisingly they were no longer enthusiastic about giving the cotton the handwork it needed—fertilizing with marsh mud, marsh straw, and manure, and constant hoeing. By 1900, the boll weevil had appeared, and in 1920 Sea Island cotton was given up for good. Truck crops replaced cotton because the completion of the Dawhoo Bridge made it easy to get these crops to market. Unneeded black labor began to migrate away. At the same time visitors began to arrive.

A Sumter-based resort group opened up the beach, but growth was slow. There was no electricity, nor were there any other conveniences, so the island remained uninhabited enough for rumrunners to run their "cedar pencil" business on the beach's lee shore. In the late 1930s, however, the state park was started, and Edisto was discovered by mainlanders. In a thick stand of palmettos and high dunes, Civilian Conservation Corps workers built park buildings and the road was paved, but the hurricane of 1940 destroyed most of this. Both private and public sectors started over. Five surviving park cabins were moved inland to a safer spot, and the beach was refurbished with sand pumped from a back lagoon. Today park visitors continue to increase and the beach continues to wash away. And as on many other Sea Islands, resorts are quickly taking the place of plantations.

Dawhoo Bridge, Whooping Island, and Little Edisto

You're crossing the Dawhoo River, which is also the Intracoastal Waterway. The narrow iron drawbridge seems a quaint holdover from far earlier days, but for this island it's still the latest advancement. Until 1920 you crossed here by ferry. This is Whooping Island on the far side: You stood here and "whooped" for the ferryman. Beyond the next marsh expanse, Little Edisto Island begins.

32.3	**1.5**	**O**n right, Edisto Shrimp Co.

6. EDISTO SHRIMP COMPANY

Not open to public.

Some farming continues on these islands, but to your right, highland tomato fields have been turned into saltwater ponds and shrimp are raised at Edisto Shrimp Co.

32.3	**0.0**	**C**ontinue on S.C. 174 South.
34.0	**1.7**	**J**ust after crossing the second bridge (Russell Creek Bridge), pull off road to the right and look back across creek downstream to Windsor.

7. WINDSOR PLANTATION, c. 1857

Not open to public.

To the left and across Russell Creek is Windsor Plantation. The cleared fields around it were so low they had to be diked to protect the cotton from spring tides. As you look back after crossing Russell Creek, the house that you see was a wedding gift to E. Mikell Bailey. Built high on piers to catch the breeze and stay above the storm tides, it's typical of many such Sea Island homes, but not of the Federalist and Greek Revival mansions on Edisto proper. Take a good look anyway, for these other homes are well off the road, and unless there's a special church or historical society tour, this is probably the only one you'll see clearly. Descendant Swinton Whaley kept the last patch of seed cotton going here, in hopes that the boll weevil would someday be conquered and he'd be ready with the seed.

34.0	**0.0**	**C**ontinue on S.C. 174 South.
37.3	**3.3**	**T**urn left into parking area of Presbyterian Church on Edisto Island.

8. PRESBYTERIAN CHURCH ON EDISTO ISLAND, c. 1830

Grounds open to public.

This Presbyterian church has the distinction of being "the oldest existing in its original location and of unbroken continuity in South Carolina." Church membership, however, did not grow appreciably until 1821, when William States Lee began a memorable pastorate that would last half a century. In 1830, the current building was made possible by cotton wealth and renewed religious enthusiasm. Six years later, famed planter William Seabrook left the church $5,000. A cove ceiling was added to the interior and this large belltower and portico replaced the original modest entry. The planters living on the inland portion of the island entered through the "burrough door" on the left. The others entered through the "seaside door" on the right.

Reverend Lee was responsible for bringing a large number of blacks into the church, something the Presbyterians usually could not accomplish. But during the Civil War these freed slaves took over the building, and in 1866 Lee led a small white membership into a Sunday service and reclaimed the building "in the name of God and by authority of the U.S. Government."

The church has to be appreciated from the outside since it's usually locked, but the graveyard is open to those willing to show it quiet respect. And it offers insight into the island's personality and personalities. The tombs are often ornate, some even monumental. Dr. Johnson records that the prominent wreath-encircled column once had a stone flame at its top. It was erected by a mother for her son, cost $5,000 (the same as the portico and steeple of the church), and came from Italy. Even those not so grand are inscribed with telling bits of verse or statement. Certain that he would lose a duel to a notorious outsider, one islander arrived with a mattress to bear his own body away. Instead, he won and paid for his opponent's stone—which warns, "Prepare to meet thy God." "Perished in the wreck of the steamboat *Pulaski*, which was lost by the explosion of her boilers," says another. "Left us in the full assurance of a seat in that Grand Lodge above," is inscribed for an entombed Mason. Far to the left are

Edisto Presbyterian Church

three stones giving names and only the date "Christmas 1865." They were Union missionaries drowned while crossing St. Pierre Creek after a Christmas Eve gathering. Their friends put them over there, as far from the secessionists as possible. A suicide denied burial was placed here anyway, and a substantial fence erected to guarantee he stayed. The tiny vestry building standing in the midst of this stone garden was a place where living islanders could raise their voices in argument without profaning the church.

37.3	**0.0**	Continue on S.C. 174 South.
37.9	**0.6**	Turn left onto Steamboat Road / S-10-968.
39.5	**1.6**	Dirt road dead-ends at Steamboat Landing parking lot.

9. STEAMBOAT LANDING

There are numerous narrow, oak-shrouded lanes you can drive down; this one leads to Steamboat Landing. Water always connected the island with Charleston, and most of the planters had their own craft. On the eve of the Civil War, a young Mikell was carried off by the slave-rowed canoe *Nellie Fier* or *Nullifier*, depending. In the 1820s, however, patriarch William Seabrook had begun a regular steamboat service to Edisto. That paddlewheeler, *The William Seabrook*, would end as a small but notorious blockade runner, and his wharf would end up as today's public boat landing. It's a short, pretty drive and offers a nice view of the North Edisto.

39.5	**0.0**	Retrace Steamboat Road / S-10-968.
40.3	**0.8**	Turn left onto Jenkins Hill Road.
41.9	**1.6**	Veer right onto S-10-768 / Oak Island Road (unmarked).

10. TOMATO FIELDS

At this intersection you see tomato fields on both sides of the road. The island's main cash crop, staked tomatoes are grown on black plastic with underground drip irrigation beside each plant. Like all farmers, Edisto farmers have experienced harsh times with cheap prices. Hopefully, this farm will still be in business by the time you pass this way.

43.8	**1.9**	At stop sign, on left is the Old Baptist Church.

11. THE OLD BAPTIST CHURCH, c. 1818

Not open to public.

From the road you can appreciate this old Baptist church. The story is told that Hephzabah J. Townsend began her life under the most perilous of circumstances. She was born in the midst of the Revolution; her mother died almost immediately and, fearing smallpox would get her as well, two faithful slaves smuggled the infant out of the blockaded city. From such a beginning grew a woman of conscience and resolve. She insisted over her husband's objections on building this church in 1818, and eventually gave it to the Baptist slaves. Immediately after the war, the little Greek Revival meetinghouse was doubled in size and the portico added. The monument at the rear is Mrs. Townsend's. Her children wrote: "Her character was so strongly cast, and her impulses were so generous that she was an object of indifference to no one."

43.8	**0.0**	**T**urn left onto S.C. 174 South.
44.0	**0.2**	**O**n right is Trinity Episcopal Church.

12. TRINITY EPISCOPAL CHURCH, c. 1880
Grounds open to public.

This parish was one of those laid out by the Church Act of 1706, but the first building didn't come until 1774. After the Revolution, however, when other congregations floundered, this one remained active and in 1840 built an impressive new church—perhaps even grander than the Presbyterian. Inspired by St. Michael's of Charleston, it seated two hundred people and had a steeple one hundred feet high. It burned in 1879, and was replaced the following year with this little Gothic building. The hurricane of 1893 did severe damage, but a former slave craftsman put it back together and added the remarkable interior woodwork. Though it's usually locked, you can appreciate the Tiffany glass from the outside. The stones of the surrounding graveyard are far older than the present church, and though not so grand or eloquent as those of the one already visited, they are certainly a clear reminder of the incredible mortality, especially among the young, on the island.

Trinity Episcopal Church

44.0	**0.0**	**C**ontinue on S.C. 174 South.
44.6	**0.6**	**O**n left, The Old Store.

13. THE OLD STORE, date unknown
Gift shop.

Originally the bridge passed over Store Creek to the left of the store, so it faced the road the other way. That wasn't its first move though, for it was brought from Eddingville Beach and reassembled here. It and the nearby home of Willie Bailey are on the National Register. The store is now a gift shop specializing in fine handmade items, and beside it where the old post office stood is a new restaurant. One ethnologist suggests this was about where the Lord Proprietor's explorer Sanford went in 1666 to be royally entertained at the main village of the Edisto Indians. (The tribe was driven here not long before by the man-eating Westoes.) The English entered a "large house of Circular form," observed "fair forest" and "diverse fields of maize," and watched a ball game played with "bowle and six foot staves." The remnants of this tribe sided with the settlers in the Yemassee War, and a few may have remained on the north end of the island well into the eighteenth century.

44.6	0.0	Continue on S.C. 174 South, crossing Store Creek.
46.5	1.9	Freedman community.

14. FREEDMAN'S VILLAGE

Most of the island's plantations were kept intact at the Civil War's end, but here one was broken up and sold to the newly freed slaves. The creek was always a ready source of food, and the new owners worked as tenants or planted their own small patches in cotton until the boll weevil arrived. When they felt the plantation stores were getting the better of them, "midnight gin houses" made sure some of the cash went into their own pockets at the end of the year. Religion was very important—besides the ones we've seen, many smaller churches flourished on the island. Some of the old stories and spirituals have been recorded, which is good, because even if Freedman's Village and the other small communities survive, it seems inevitable that resort development will erode much of this island's Gullah culture.

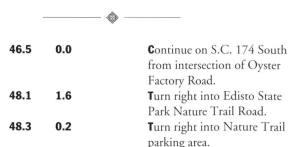

46.5	0.0	Continue on S.C. 174 South from intersection of Oyster Factory Road.
48.1	1.6	Turn right into Edisto State Park Nature Trail Road.
48.3	0.2	Turn right into Nature Trail parking area.

15. EDISTO STATE PARK NATURE TRAIL AND INDIAN MOUND

The beginning of the nature trail is marked by a small bulletin shed that shows the path and may contain brochures with maps. The park naturalist takes an early morning walk through here once a week during the summer. The brochure says some stamina and time are required and warns of poison ivy and cactus. The trail to the mound is over four miles and takes at least two hours. My sister Becky and I made the trip at midday in mid-August and found enough mosquitoes to keep us miserable even with bug spray. I went back the first week in October and made the trip again with the naturalist and about twenty visitors. No bugs. It went like this.

On this day, our leader is Dianne Belle, who is usually here only in the summer and spends most of her time in the beach area of the park. She's very good with fossils and children, but says she's still learning plants and animals. She claims the woodpeckers laugh at her and stay out of sight. I know the feeling. Part of this account is hers, part mine, but I'll take credit for the mistakes.

None of these trees appear ancient, so this was probably in cotton or even truck crops not too long ago. But as we walk on toward the water, more typical Sea Island forest will emerge—live oak, water oak, gum, and loblolly pine, with palmetto, magnolia, and hickory increasing toward the end. That yucca at the beginning is a rare one—note the blue-green leaves. We'll see the common variety at the mound.

A marker points out a turn in the trail and there's a small struggling Virginia pine. A saw palmetto grows close by. It's shorter than the cabbage palmetto that we'll be seeing and has a sawlike stem. Sweet gum are shedding prickly balls here; the seed pods are inside. Sapsuckers have drilled their distinctive rows of small holes in the bark. Ferns are coming back where this area accidentally burned two years ago. A blown-over oak shows the shallow root system typical of this moist area.

Some of the trees are marked with small signs and you can follow most of this in the brochure. Spanish moss is not a parasite: It is attached to the tree but gets its nourishment from the rain and air. We're told it was once used to stuff mattresses and even baby diapers. A large ropelike grapevine hangs in the trail; raccoons feed on the grapes. The path is thick with pine cones that have been clipped by the squirrels. One dead tree is so full of woodpecker holes our guide calls it a "natural condominium." We see deer tracks and hear bird calls. I'm guessing that wrens are making the "cheerily" sound.

We cross a narrow marsh slough on a boardwalk. It's high tide and periwinkles have climbed to the tops of the marsh stalks. My sister and I saw a yellow-crowned night heron here, and one yellow feather remains. Just over the bridge is coral bean. Said to be poisonous, it grows close to the ground, with a bright red pea in a dark pod. On our left is a waterhole, more grapevines and sassafras, and the "mitten tree." The leaves are different shapes, but we must look up to see them because deer have browsed on the lower branches. We reach the edge of the creek for a moment, then the trail veers away. Thick goldenrod and more deer tracks are here. Bootleggers used this point in the 1930s for unloading. We've reached the mound. Below the sign saying, "Don't use metal detectors or remove artifacts," sweet bay is growing and wild grasses seeding up. We cross over the top of the shell mound and down to its eroding face. There's yucca struggling to hold on here. Its root was once used in soap and medicine, we're told.

Unfortunately, Spanish Mount, as the shell midden is known, has eroded greatly in recent years, but what remains is still interesting. Indians made it, not the Spanish. It's a refuse dump or kitchen midden dated at about 2000

B.C., but it could have been occupied off and on since. (The few pieces of pottery I looked at didn't go back quite that far.) There are several large shell rings nearby on the North Edisto River, and I'd assume that this shell pile  was begun by the same early people. They were eating mostly oysters, but there's one small conch visible, with a few clams, and an unusual number of periwinkle and saltwater mussels mixed in. We see the shell, but overlook the many tiny bone fragments that suggest a much more varied diet, at least at sites studied. Deer and fish may have been just as important and, of course, the hickory nuts and much else growing nearby. Pottery and the concentration of shell suggest the beginnings of a semi-stationary life. Still, it would be at least another 2,500 years before the coastal native Americans reached the stage of development observed by Sanford when he visited the Edisto camp.

The way home is marked by a couple of dramatic incidents—dramatic for a nature trail anyway. We meet horses, dogs, and children. The dogs are Jack Russells and a Dalmatian. On the path are the remnants of a blue jay that has been eaten, its blue feathers scattered. Except for two red-bellied woodpeckers, this is the one bird I can positively identify for the day. Even though we've just been told that the feathers have no real color and the blue will appear gray if held up to the sun, I forget to do it and so does everyone else. The path turns into a road and then into another road that was used once to haul sand for asphalt making. The group members are stretched out some distance along the way, but all seem happy with the morning. There's talk of copperhead snakes and the hunt for fossils on the beach after lunch.

48.3	**0.0**	**T**urn left out of parking area and retrace to S.C. 174 South.
48.5	**0.2**	**T**urn right onto S.C. 174 South.
49.1	**0.6**	**T**urn left into Edisto State Park Beach gate.

16. EDISTO STATE PARK BEACH

With a half-million visitors a year, you wouldn't expect too many surprises from two miles of beach, but actually this one offered some pleasant ones. Unless there's an official tour going on, you won't get to see any of the island's famous plantation houses, but the beach is always open. This was once a thick stand of palms with high dunes, but most have washed away. There is only room for seventy-five campsites, most of which are booked well in advance. For daily visitors, though, there are picnic tables, a store, restrooms, and during the summer, lectures and guided beach walks. The beach takes part in the sea turtle program, so the nests are marked and protected, and some nights groups go out in hopes of watching a turtle lay her eggs.

What the beach is famous for, however, is fossils. Though a few are found on Pawleys Island and Litchfield Beach, Edisto is the best place to look for these relics of the Pleistocene epoch. If you don't know what that is or what a fossil looks like, then the best place to start is across the  street in the gift section of the supermarket or other area stores and restaurants where you can buy *Fossil Vertebrates—Beach and Bank Collecting for Amateurs* by M. C. Thomas. It explains it all and contains an invaluable photographic guide. On this day, the other thirty beachcombers and I are lucky enough to have the park naturalist along. She told us part of the following, but some has been taken from other sources. What follows isn't meant to be a scientific guide to fossils, just suggestions to help you enjoy your beach visit a little more.

Fossils

For at least the last million years the world has been going through a series of ice ages, which means that glaciers have spread and retreated across much of the Northern Hemisphere and the oceans have been rising and falling. (Twelve thousand years ago, the ocean at Edisto started about six miles farther out, and it has been moving inland ever since.) During this period there were many migrations of animals between continents. North America was once separate from South America but connected—at least by ice—to Asia, so there is evidence of all sorts of unexpected occupants— many of them extinct all over the world and others only missing from America now. The glass display case in front of the store shows fossilized parts of tapir, sharks, parrotfish, mastadon, mammoth, horse, and armadillo, all found here. Some of these finds are quite large, and we're warned not to expect anything so dramatic.

The beach here is wide. Along the normal high tide line there is a fairly thick strip of mostly worn shell—oyster, clam, cockle, bulls eyes, and lettered olives (our state shell). Higher up on the beach, there's a second strip where the storms reach; along here are the now empty sea turtle nests still marked by flags.

For successful fossil-hunting, here's what you need to know:

1. For our purposes, a fossil can be defined as the mineral deposit where bone, tooth, cartilage, or shell has been. (We aren't likely to find vegetation, burrows, or imprints here.)

2. The color in fossils comes from the surrounding material—brown if the dead animal was buried in sand, black if the bone was in mud or vegetation. These are the two colors usually found on Edisto, but some shells do turn grayish-white or even golden.

3. The fossil is normally heavier than the original, but if you're uncertain which you have, dry it and burn a corner. Fairly new bone has protein and will still smell when burned.

4. Look for the porous marrow part of the bone. This is an easy way to distinguish fossil from stone, but there are many exceptions: stingray plates, ear bones, ivory, and teeth. Pieces of clam and oyster shell can weather into strange shapes and colors and easily fool you.

5. Look for fossils at the ebbing tide or at low water, preferably after a storm. The bigger items will be thrown higher on the beach and are more quickly buried in the sand. The lighter ones will drift back with the surf.

6. Watch the beach in front of you. In her fossil book, Thomas says don't talk to your companion, and wear a hat. I don't recall our guide wearing a hat, and she was happy to stop and answer everybody's questions. (If you want professional identification and no one's around, contact the Charleston Museum.)

Most of the members of the group had pretty good luck. I found the earbone of a porpoise when we first stepped onto the beach, and later some unidentifiable bone and the shell of a pond turtle. If you count sharks' teeth, some of the children came up with hundreds of items. We walked down to Jeremy Inlet, where the beach had pushed back so quickly it left last year's salt marsh stubble now facing the ocean. The dueling grounds, "the Sands," would have been here or just offshore. Along the way there was much evidence of the seashore retreat Eddingville, whose forty houses, stores, and churches washed away in the hurricane of 1893—brick, chips of china, and broken white and green glass. The morning before, an arrowhead had been picked up, and someone in our group got a piece of pottery. Just inside the inlet on the far side is another mound washing into the sea, so perhaps it is the source. The seashells were pretty battered, but we found a few nice ones. Some crystallized coral and the crystallized skeletons of marine worms that I've always just called "rock," were also collected.

Back at the starting point, we were shown the ankle bone of a bison, a horse's leg, a mammoth tooth, an alligator jaw, and a deer antler, all found very recently, as well as some of the very early punctated Indian pottery that has washed up. There was even a shark's tooth fashioned into an arrowhead. (You can keep this pottery and the fossils if you find any.) What happened to these Indians is a mystery, but an even bigger one is what happened to the horse and mammoth. They were here only ten thousand years ago, but gone when the makers of this pottery arrived. Ancient history. It takes at least five thousand years to form a fossil, and these are dated from ten thousand to one million years ago, with some, like the sharks' teeth, going back much further. On that scale, Lafayette's visit and the duels in the Sands are only a split second ago. We should be able to hear the echo of the shots on a quiet fossil-hunting morning.

❖

49.1	**0.0**	**F**rom Edisto State Park Beach gate, turn right onto S.C. 174 North.
66.8	**17.7**	**T**urn right onto S.C. 164.
69.0	**2.2**	**J**unction with S.C. 162.

EDISTO ISLAND

69.0	**0.0**	Continue straight on S.C. 162.
71.8	**2.8**	Town limit of Hollywood.
78.6	**6.8**	Town limit of Rantowles.
79.9	**1.3**	At yield sign, continue straight onto U.S. 17 North.
91.5	**11.6**	South side of Ashley River Bridge.

ADDITIONAL READING

You can start with Graydon's *Tales of Edisto*. Clara Puckette's *Edisto: A Sea Island Principality* is excellent. Two good oral histories, *Sam Gadsen Tells a Story* and *The Life and Times of Bubberson Brown*, were published by Nick Lindsay. Mikell's *Rumbling of the Chariot Wheels* is in most libraries. A little five-page history of the island is in print. Don't forget *Fossil Vertebrates* by M. C. Thomas. A biography of the Queen of Bohemia is in the works.

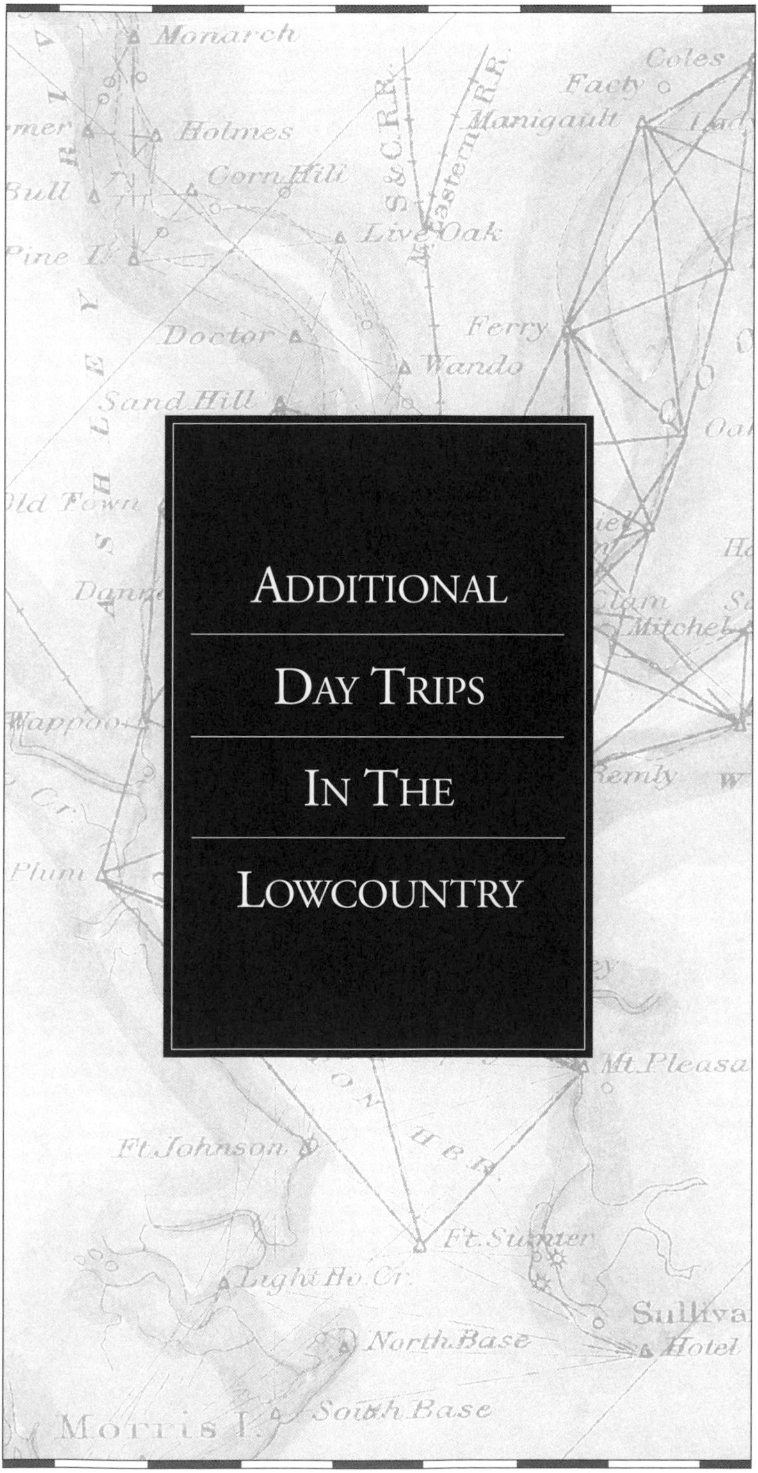

Additional Day Trips In The Lowcountry

SHELL ISLAND TOUR

Visit a barrier island and enjoy shell collecting. This boat trip is available March 25 through June 14, on Friday and/or Saturday, depending on demand, and begins at 9 a.m. The tour lasts approximately four hours. Admission is charged. This is one of the special tours available from Capt. Sandy's Tours, 709 Front Street, Georgetown, S.C. (803) 527-4106.

0.0	0.0	From Charleston, take U.S. 17 North; begin clocking mileage at north (Mount Pleasant) side of Cooper River Bridge.
57.0	57.0	Turn left into Days Inn Georgetown County Visitors Center. Check here for current dock location for Capt. Sandy's tour boat.

❖

SOUTH ISLAND

Wildlife abounds and bird watchers are particularly thrilled by "one of the largest concentrations of waterfowl in the Southeast." To tour South Island, you must register at least a year ahead and cross by ferry. A guide directs a bus tour of a small portion of the twenty thousand acres. Contact the Tom Yawkey Wildlife Center at (803) 546-6814.

0.0	0.0	From Charleston, take U.S. 17 North; begin clocking mileage at north (Mount Pleasant) side of Cooper River Bridge.
40.8	40.8	Santee River Delta.
49.0	8.2	Turn right onto White Hall Avenue / S-22-23.
51.5	2.5	At stop sign, turn right onto South Island Road / S-22-18.
56.2	4.7	Road ends at South Island Ferry. Ferry on call 7 a.m. to 11 p.m.

❖

BULL ISLAND

"Certainly one of the wildest and most beautiful of the barrier islands," was the original description I gave of Bull Island. The island took the brunt of Hurricane Hugo, however, and lost the vast majority of its almost tropical forest. The paths have been cleared, and the island is open to the public again on a restricted basis. I've walked the beach a half-dozen times since the storm.

There's still a beauty there—it's just not the kind that's easily recognizable.

The *Carolina*, bringing the first settlers to this colony in 1670, made landfall here and slipped in behind the island to take on fresh water and to con-verse with the Indians. The years since weren't always idle ones. "Live oakers" cut many of the ribs for our first Navy ships here, and cultivation and livestock herding were intensive. In 1935, however, the island became a part of the Cape Romain National Refuge, and nature was quick to reclaim her own: The island grew thick with oaks, palmettos, and magnolias. The hurricane has left behind mainly palmettos. Eighteen miles of winding roads and trails crisscross the island, passing by and over ponds and savannahs, and out onto a beach famed for its "boneyard" of driftwood stumps. Wildlife is still in evidence—deer, raccoons, fox squirrels, alligators. Bird watching can still be enjoyed; Peterson did work here as well as South Carolina's own Chamberlain and Sprunt, and over 260 species have been reported. The island also has fresh- and saltwater fishing, an "old Spanish fort," and photography opportunities. The biggest drawback is still the bugs. During the summer the mosquitoes can be bad except along the beachfront, and the ticks are the worst in the world. Carry repellant and don't wander too far off the trails.

The trip over from Moore's Landing is an adventure in itself, as the pontoon boat twists and turns through a maze of saltwater channels. Remember that you're there for the whole day and are responsible for bringing your own lunch, film, and bug spray.

0.0	**0.0**	**F**rom Charleston, take U.S. 17 North. Begin clocking mileage at the north side of the Cooper River Bridge (Mount Pleasant side).
14.6	**14.6**	**T**urn right onto Seewee Road / S-10-584.
17.9	**3.3**	**T**urn right onto Bulls Island Road / S-10-1170.
19.4	**1.5**	**A**rrive at Moore's Landing pier parking lot.

BEAR ISLAND

Bear Island Wildlife Management Area, located between the Ashepoo and Edisto rivers, consists of 7,633 acres of varied coastal habitat. Marsh impoundments of 3,747 acres (former rice fields), tidal marshes, maritime-influenced woodlands, and managed agricultural lands provide refuge for game species ranging from bobwhite quail to white-tailed deer. In the fall and winter, the area hosts thousands of waterfowl. Hunting is allowed by special annual draw-ings and permits. Bear Island is also home to numerous non-game and endangered species, including alligators and bald eagles. Late January through March is the recommended season for visitors interested in bird watching and general wildlife observation and photography. Incidentally, this is the cornerstone of the ACE Basin conservation project. On advance notice, Wildlife and Marine Resources Department personnel may give presentations concerning various aspects of wildlife natural history and management techniques. For more information, call (803) 844-8957 or (803) 844-2952.

0.0	**0.0**	From Charleston, take U.S. 17 South; begin clocking mileage from south side of Ashley River Bridge.
37.7	**37.7**	Turn left onto S-15-26.
50.5	**12.8**	Turn left into Bear Island W.M. Area.

❖

PLANTATION EXCURSION

You will enjoy this boat cruise that highlights beautiful plantations and nature's treasures on Lowcountry rivers. This is one of the special tours available March 25 through June 14 from Capt. Sandy's Tours, 709 Front Street, Georgetown, S.C. (803) 527-4106. The tours are Monday through Thursday at 1 p.m., and last for approximately three hours.

0.0	**0.0**	From Charleston, take U.S. 17 North; begin clocking mileage at north (Mount Pleasant) side of Cooper River Bridge.
57.0	**57.0**	Turn left into Days Inn Georgetown County Visitors Center. Check here for current dock location for Capt. Sandy's tour boat.